EDUCATION AFTER OCTOBER 7

Essays about Teaching and Learning in the Jewish Diaspora

EDUCATION AFTER OCTOBER 7

Essays about Teaching
and Learning in the
Jewish Diaspora

Edited by
MATT REINGOLD

ACADEMIC STUDIES PRESS
BOSTON
2025

Print LCCN: 2025030769

Copyright © Academic Studies Press, 2025

ISBN 9798897830695 (Hardback)
ISBN 9798897830701 (Adobe PDF)
ISBN 9798897830718 (ePub)

Book design by Lapiz Digital Services
Cover art by Dana Barlev

Published by Academic Studies Press.
1007 Chestnut Street
Newton, MA 02464, USA
press@academicstudiespress.com
www.academicstudiespress.com

This volume is dedicated in memory of Avidan Gamliel Tordjman, a victim of the Nova massacre on October 7, 2023. Avidan lived with a contagious smile and a heart wide open. He was a soulful connector, a man of kindness, courage, and joy, who uplifted others with his vibrant presence and unwavering generosity. Whether helping a stranger in distress, quietly ensuring the needs of the vulnerable were met, or infusing joy and unity into his family, Avidan was always exactly where he needed to be—loving, giving, and building bridges. He believed in working hard to grow one's soul and never ceased striving to bring goodness into the world. He was a devoted son, a beloved brother, and the proudest uncle, full of dreams for the future and deep care for Am Yisrael.

Contents

Acknowledgements	ix
1. Introduction *Matt Reingold*	1
Section One: Worries and Anxieties: The Voices of Students, Parents, and Children	**21**
2. "A lot of horrible things have happened": Jewish Children's Beliefs about October 7 and Its Aftermath *Sivan Zakai and Lauren Applebaum*	23
3. Trauma Reach and Response: Teacher and Parental Reports of the Impact of October 7 and School Programming on North American Jewish Day School Students *Rona Novick and Jenny Isaacs*	39
4. Collective Trauma, Resilience, and Jewish Education: How German Jews Navigate Life after October 7 *Maor Shani, Jana Gerber, and Marie Herb*	63
Section Two: Pedagogical Innovations: Teaching Anew after October 7	**89**
5. Rethinking Innocence and Building Resilience: Early Childhood Jewish Educators' Responses to October 7 *Meir Muller, Lyndall Miller, and Alana Rifkin Gelnick*	91
6. Teaching Palestinian Perspectives and the Pedagogy of "Historical Empathy" *Benji Davis*	112

7.	Teachers' Identities in Transition: Hebrew Education in Light of October 7 and the Aftermath *Vardit Ringvald and Sharon Schoenfeld*	131

Section Three: Teaching about Home: Israelis Abroad   155

8.	The Impact of the October 7 War on Emissary Teachers—*Shlichim*: A Study of Pedagogical Adaptations, Non-Formal Educational Initiatives, and Community Interactions in North American Jewish Schools in 2024–2025 *Michal Shapira Junger*	157
9.	"Can we talk about it?": Implementing Israel Education during Wartime at Jewish Summer Camps *Tal Vaizman*	178
10.	Testifying to October 7: Israeli Voices and Experiences at North American Jewish Overnight Camps *Matt Reingold*	

Section IV: After October 7: The Future of Jewish Education   219

11.	Meeting the Challenges of the Moment: How to Think about the Purposes of American Jewish Education after October 7 *Jon A. Levisohn*	221
12.	Solidarity, Criticism, and Complexity: Jewish Educators Responding to Difficult Times *Ezra Kopelowitz*	252
13.	Beyond Tinkering: Adjustments to Israel Education in the Aftermath of October 7 *Alex Pomson and Samantha Vinokor-Meinrath*	280
14.	Conclusion *Matt Reingold*	298

Contributors	309

Acknowledgements

Over two years after October 7, 2023, I remain devastated about what happened on that day and in the months since. It is, therefore, devastating to me that a volume such as *Education after October 7* needs to exist in the first place. I am, however, grateful that thoughtful and inspiring educators like those featured in this book exist. Their commitment to helping students during these times offered a life raft in turbulent waters.

I want to express my profound gratitude to the Tordjman family for allowing me to dedicate this volume in Avidan's name.

From the very beginning, Alessandra Anzani and her team at Academic Studies Press have been supportive of this project and committed to helping ensure that it reaches as many readers as possible. Their professionalism and enthusiasm for the work has made my work as an editor so much easier.

The illustration on the cover was made by Dana Barlev. It was important to me to include Israeli art on the cover, and I am grateful that Dana agreed to create this powerful image about teaching and learning after October 7 specifically for this volume.

I am profoundly grateful to The Israel and Golda Koschitzky Centre for Jewish Studies at York University for providing a publication grant that helped subsidize the costs associated with this publication.

Thank you to each of the authors of this volume for trusting me with your work, supporting this project, and responding to my many emails. This book could not exist without each one of you.

To my many friends and family who have offered support, words cannot express the gratitude that I have for you. Thank you to Adam, Amy, Alex, Ari and Stephanie, Ben and Jess, Choni, David E, David T, Eema and Abba, Ilana and Marcos, Mark, Mum, Odelia, Shayna and Teddy, Yoel and Alissa. My life is richer for having you in it.

And most importantly, to my wife Chani and Sloan, Nora, Micah, and Boaz. Each of you completes me in a way that I could never have imagined, and I am so grateful for all that you bring to my life and to the world.

Introduction

Matt Reingold

When the bell rang to mark the end of the school day on Friday October 6, 2023, I had been teaching my twelfth graders about the proposed judicial reforms that had been dividing Israeli society throughout 2023. The proposed legislation was first announced by Prime Minister Benjamin Netanyahu in January 2023 and it was presented as an attempt to return legislative power to the country's elected representatives and not remain concentrated in the hands of the appointed judges who had veto power over all laws passed in parliament. Throughout the first month of the school year, the conversations in my twelfth-grade elective had been shaped by the judicial overhaul. Even though many of the students in my course did not fully understand what the judicial overhaul was or why Netanyahu's ruling coalition wanted to change Israel's justice system, most had seen photos or videos on their social media accounts of the protests and counter protests that had been occurring in Jerusalem and Tel Aviv. Some of my students even shared stories with the class about their own experiences attending the protests during trips to Israel the previous summer. As we learned about how Israel's system of government worked, the nuances of the proposed reforms, and the different reasons to support and oppose them, students' own political leanings began to bleed into the learning, with students articulating visions of whether the government or the courts should be the ultimate arbitrator in determining the law in a country.

And then we never talked about the judicial reforms again for the rest of the year. This is because on October 7, 2023, Israel experienced the worst terror attack in the country's history when Hamas launched over 4000 rockets at the country's southern communities while over 6000 Hamas terrorists breached the Gaza-Israel barrier and began murdering and kidnapping Israeli civilians. On the day of October 7 itself, 1195 people were killed. An additional 251 Israelis and foreign nationals were taken captive back to Gaza where some were used as leverage in negotiations with Israel for the release of detained security prisoners while scores remain in captivity as of January 2025. Following the attack of October 7, Israel declared war on Hamas, with Israeli forces entering the Gaza Strip in order to fulfill two goals: defeat Hamas and rescue the hostages. Coinciding with the outbreak of war in southern Israel, on October 8, Hezbollah began launching rockets at northern Israeli communities from its base in southern Lebanon. Israel's initial response involved targeted bombing before invading Lebanon in October 2024.

In the immediate wake of the October 7 massacre and the subsequent war, teaching and learning in my classes shifted, with students wanting updates about the status of the hostages, the ways that international governments were (or were not) supporting Israel, and the history of Gaza. As the weeks turned to months and curriculum resumed, time was still allocated to discussing the ongoing conflict. This included announcements of significant events like the rescuing of hostages but also discussions about what the best course forward for Israel should be in order to achieve its goals in returning the hostages and defeating Hamas alongside debates about which of the two goals should take precedence over the other. Even after I resumed teaching the original curriculum, it, too, was taught in light (within the framework or under the shadow) of October 7. Teaching and learning were thus dramatically altered.

Education after October 7: Essays about Teaching and Learning in the Jewish Diaspora is not a book about my classrooms and the ways that my teaching and learning about Israel shifted after October 7. Rather, it is a book that is borne out of a reality that teaching and learning about Israel in *every* Jewish educational space in the Jewish diaspora changed after October 7 and a belief that these changes will fundamentally alter the nature of Jewish and Israel education for years to come. Israel educators and administrators around the world needed to rapidly pivot in their instructional planning in order to create spaces in their schools for new content and for providing students with social and emotional support. As one of the fulcrums of North American Jewish identity, Israel plays a prominent role in the lives of North American Jews. For

Jewish learners, the mass devastation that happened on October 7 was more than just another example of violence and terror in the world; rather, it was an attack that was felt deeply and personally by diaspora Jews, leading places of learning to, inexorably, assume new responsibilities for helping students navigate this new reality.

Israeli history is rife with seminal moments—the founding of the state in 1948, the capture of Jerusalem in 1967's Six Day War, the near defeat in 1973's Yom Kippur War, the signing of the Camp David Accords in 1978, the Oslo Accords and Yitzchak Rabin's assassination in the early 1990s, the waves of suicide bombings between 2000 and 2005 during the Second Palestinian Intifada, and 2005's Gaza Disengagement—and all of these are taught in Jewish schools and at Jewish camps by Israel educators. How they are taught and learned has also been studied by researchers. And while some studies have explored how students learn about very contemporary events in Israel (Reingold, 2021a; Reingold and Reznik, 2024; Zakai, 2024b), research into how Israel is taught and learned primarily focuses on how Israel's past is taught in the present (Golden and Kadden, 2024; Hassenfeld, 2016 and 2018; Reingold, 2017 and 2018; Zakai, 2015). This is because, as a field of research, empirical studies of Israel education in practice are a relatively recent phenomenon. For example, prior to October 7, the most recent example of a watershed moment in Israeli society was the 2000–2005 Second Intifada followed by the Disengagement from Gaza. No studies exist that explore how Israel educators of the early 2000s created, modified, and adapted their curricula as the events were unfolding or how students learned about these events as they were transpiring.

Such is not the case with October 7 and it is this research that *Education after October 7* brings together. Within days of October 7, researchers began drafting research agendas, designing and implementing surveys, interviewing educators, parents, and children, and piecing together the disparate ways that schools, synagogues, and camps were pivoting in their planning for the upcoming year. This data is invaluable for understanding how educational choices in the teaching of Israel were made *in* the moment of crisis rather than how the moment of crisis was taught retrospectively as is the case with most empirical studies of Israel education. Rather than studying how students reacted to learning about a period in Israel's history that at the original moment might have been fraught for Israelis but was not so for students in the classroom, the unknowns of the learning after October 7 while the war was still ongoing created a pedagogical challenge. This is because the content was of great relevance to students and was also accompanied by emotional turmoil because of the ongoing conflict. With the story tragically being still written, educators could not offer students the cathartic satisfaction of a conclusion and instead were forced to grapple with how to teach about the present when doing so is fraught with tension for the learners.

This volume is built on two foundational premises. First is that October 7 and the subsequent war is an event unlike any other in Jewish or Israeli history. Second is that, because of the enormity of the event, Jewish education has undergone a seismic shift and has needed to recalibrate itself in response to the moment. Each of the chapters in *Education after October 7* seeks to answer a different question about what happened in educational spaces in the days, weeks, and months after the initial terror attack. These considerations include how to teach about terror when it is ongoing, what is the role of the educator in responding to learners' questions and fears, how are students themselves processing what is happening in Israel, what are the decisions being made by parents on behalf of their children, what is the role of Israelis in diaspora spaces, and what are the new needs that teachers and students have. When read in concert with each other, what emerges is a complex portrait of dynamic educational processes in flux. The chapters reveal that, beyond the need to evolve educationally in response to October 7, multiple strategies—pedagogical, psychological, curricular—are necessary in order to adeptly meet and respond to the moment.

Israel Education and Studying Israel Education

Israel education has undergone a significant evolution over the preceding near-century. Whereas once it was peripheral to Jewish education, it is now a core component of Jewish education (Krasner, 2005, 2006; Zakai, 2022). As a subject matter, its teaching and learning predate the State of Israel (Davis and Alexander, 2023) and it has been referred to by different names over the last century. These subject names include "teaching about Palestine/Zionism," "teaching about Israel," "teaching Israel," "Zionist education," "Israel engagement," and "Israel education." While some of these names clearly point towards particular moments in time—"teaching about Palestine" as a pre-1948 term—or towards specific desired outcomes—"Israel engagement"—the teaching and learning about Israel is a common denominator of all of them, even if the purpose of the teaching may be different. Unless otherwise indicated, this volume will use the term "Israel education" to refer to the teaching and learning of Israel as it is the most-used term in the twenty-first century (Zakai, 2024a), but it is important to acknowledge that, much like "mathematics" or "science," "Israel education" is a broad catch-all term. This is because, like other subjects, Israel is taught to learners of all ages and at all stages of life. Israel is also taught in different sites, including early childhood education centers, elementary, middle, and high schools, university lecture halls, and synagogues. Israel is also taught at experiential sites like camps or museums, and on travel programs that bring Jews to Israel to encounter the country first hand. Equally, as a country with a rich history, a strong political and civic activity, diverse religious and ethnic populations, and a range of cultural practices, what is taught about Israel can also vary as educators of different disciplines, including history, literature, religious studies, and politics, can employ Israel in their teaching.

As a subject for scholarship, academic works about Israel education have primarily been concerned with either the desired outcomes of Israel education or empirical investigations into the teaching and learning of Israel as a subject matter. With regards to the former, while there is agreement that "Israel education should engage learners with Israel in all its multiple complexities, voices, and narratives" (Davis and Alexander, 2023, p. 21), there is no consensus about to what end Israel should be taught in contemporary Jewish educational spaces. The lack of consensus reflects a plurality of perspectives about the goals of Israel education. This includes Barry Chazan's (2016, 2022) relational approach to Israel education, a model of pedagogy wherein the student and the student's relationship with Israel are the focus of the learning. For Chazan, what emerges from relational Israel education is a "personal connection with Israel" and "the creation of a relationship" rather than a rote memorization of Israel-related content (2022, p. 81). It is a model that "privileges the affective over the cognitive" (Zakai, 2024a, p. 12). A related approach has been offered by Alex Sinclair, Bradley Solmsen, and Clare Goldwater (2013). They concur with Chazan's end goal of student connectedness to Israel but believe that the way to accomplish this is by teaching students a more complex or critical history of Israel. Revealing some of the messier aspects of Israel allows students to see a 'realer' Israel which will in turn lead to a stronger association with the country. Jonah Hassenfeld (2023) has offered an alternative rationale for Israel education that is framed around collective belonging and national pride. This involves teaching all aspects of Israel's past—including the upsetting ones—not for the purpose of building a relationship but because "learning the stories of the groups to which one belongs is part of what belonging means" (p. 80). What emerges from this type of pedagogy is the production of narratives that "grapple honestly with the past but that . . . inspire students to achieve an Israel they can believe in" (p. 80). Hassenfeld's model is an aspirational Israel education that acknowledges the past but does not require students to passively accept it or actively try to synthesize it into their Israel schema; rather, it allows for a rejection of the past based on a belief that Israel can be better or different in the future. Only by knowing one's national past alongside feeling a part of the nation can one be able to articulate an alternative vision for the future.

In recent years, scholarship about how Israel is taught and learned in North American Jewish spaces has revealed a range of different student experiences and teacher practices. While it is outside the scope of this introduction to identify all of these works, I want to draw attention to ones whose conclusions speak more broadly to the considerations of the authors whose work is included in this volume. With regards to teaching, Sivan Zakai (2023) has written: "If all teaching is political, then teaching Israel is especially so" (p. 13). This is because, while Israel plays a central role in the lives of North American Jews, the ways in which it does so differs greatly amongst different Jewish communities, with Israel increasingly becoming a partisan topic (Waxman, 2016). Based upon interviews with liberal San Franciscan Jews, Ari Kelman and Ilan Zvi Baron (2019) concluded that, because Israel has become such a contentious topic, schools and synagogues were opting to avoid discussing it entirely in order to avoid dividing their communities. Kelman and Baron's conclusion is borne out by Karen Fraiman's (2023) study of Jewish educators, some of whom revealed that they would prefer to not be asked to teach courses about Israel in the Jewish day schools where they work. Fraiman identified four barriers that create educator reticence with regards to teaching Israel. First is knowledge; educators worried that they did not know enough content about Israel. Second is pedagogy: educators believed that they did not possess the requisite skills to facilitate conversations about Israel in their classes. Third was a concern that they were unable to provide enough social and emotional support to students who were affected by Israel-related content. Finally, there was a belief that administrators and parents were not sufficiently supportive of the ways in which educators taught Israel and that, by addressing fraught topics, the educators were making themselves vulnerable to professional repercussions.

The barriers that Fraiman writes about pre-date October 7, but October 7 did not make teaching Israel any easier. For example, twenty-first-century digital media culture and the constant barrage of new posts created teaching environments in which even the most prepared teacher could be confronted with breaking news in the middle of a lesson because a well-meaning and curious student was refreshing the *Times of Israel*'s liveblog and felt the need to announce it out loud so that everyone would be kept up to date. How to give space for news—which may not have even been verified—with no pre-planning or consideration for how to share the content poses myriad challenges for educators ranging from ceding control of the classroom to blogs to having students ask to stream the latest videos released by Hamas that were just posted online. These scenarios do not only present knowledge-based barriers. To show or not to show content from October 7 involves more than just deciding to click on a link on a smart board. This decision also relates to pedagogic, emotional, and stakeholder barriers. The pedagogic content knowledge (Shulman, 1986) possessed by Israel educators may not prepare them for teaching instantaneous news. Similarly, the graphic violence of October 7 has presented educators with dilemmas about how to sensitively and honestly discuss it in age-appropriate ways and also how to provide students with emotional support even as the educators themselves might be struggling with their own emotions. Lastly, any and all choices made by educators about what is shared and how it is shared may cause concerns for educators whose own administrations may not have policies in place that outline acceptable Israel-related discourse beyond statements of support for the country.

A second important consideration for educators in the wake of October 7 is with regards to the Israeli military's response to Hamas's terror attack and how to discuss instances where Israeli forces harmed Palestinians living in Gaza. Acknowledging these realities is demonstrative of being an honest broker and yet, as Zakai (2018) has documented, doing so poses challenges for some Israel educators. She writes of these educators that they have "beliefs about good history teachers [which] collide with their beliefs about what is required of good members of their own ethnic and religious communities, who cherish a particular heritage" (Zakai, 2018, p. 105). In her case study of two educators tasked with teaching aspects of Israeli history like the expulsion of Palestinians from Lydda in 1948, there was a clash between the types of narratives they were seeking to inculcate in their learners alongside fears about how the learning would impact students' conceptions of Israel. And while Zakai contends that skilled Israel educators are able to effectively navigate these dual commitments, the dilemma may be even more acute after October 7. This is because the topics that Zakai's educators wrestled with occurred in Israel's *past* (even though students were of course learning about them in the present), but the same cannot be said for Israeli military operations after October 7. In a study I conducted with twelfth graders about their learning of morally complex narratives in Israeli history, an answer offered by some of the learners was that those events happened many years ago and Israel has learned from its past in order to not make similar mistakes (Reingold, 2017). For some students, this approach to understanding Israel's past and present may no longer be true. How Israel educators respond to student concerns and teach about Israel's tactics and strategies for managing Gaza's civilian population in an era of immediate (even if inaccurate) news is a deeply challenging pedagogic dilemma.

With respect to learners themselves, much research over the last two decades has shown that students want to learn about both the good and messier parts of Israel's past and present (Reingold, 2017; Zakai, 2021; Zakai and Cohen, 2016), with students even suggesting that failing to do so represents a failure of their Israel education (Reingold, 2017 and 2021b). At the same time, October 7 is a watershed moment for North American Jewry and presents unique and unprecedented challenges for Israel educators. We know that October 7 has resulted in increased interest, curiosity, and care about Israel from adolescents (Reingold and Reznik, 2024; Reingold, 2024) and has led some who had previously not taken active stances about Israel when it was publicly disparaged to do so now (Reingold, 2024), but much still remains to be learned.

Teaching the Homeland in Diaspora Communities

As I observed above, teaching and learning about Israel in the diaspora during a period of heightened crisis in Israel has not been extensively studied prior to October 7 and therefore there is little literature from the field about how past crises in Israel can inform teaching about the present crisis. Such is not the case with other diasporic population groups whose educational experiences outside of the country of origin during a crisis (and also at other times) have received scholarly attention. These groups' experiences can inform how diaspora Jews respond to October 7 and provide a point of comparison for understanding how education systems transform in the wake of a crisis. Furthermore, as a volume dedicated exclusively to teaching and learning in the diaspora after the onset of a conflict, the chapters in this volume can inform how these non-Jewish diaspora communities teach and support students following instances of violence, terror, and war in their countries of origin.

When the teaching and learning of history in schools was introduced into curricula in the late 1800s, it was done so primarily to encourage students to read history through a prism of nationalism (Thelen, 1998). This approach was designed to strengthen nationalist sentiments amongst learners (Ramirez, 2012). The cataclysmic events of the twentieth and early twenty-first centuries—the World Wars, genocides, large-scale terror attacks—resulted in the waning of history for the purpose of inculcating nationalist sentiments, with some curriculum developers concluding that these events "gradually diminished the appeal of the nation-state . . . and undermined the kind of patriotic history that schools sought to teach" (Gross and Terra, 2018, p. 3). Such is not the case amongst diaspora communities. History remains a central pillar for retaining ties to countries and communities of origin and to also strengthening emotional bonds between people and with places.

A common link between many educational initiatives designed to strengthen the ties between diaspora youth and their historic countries of origins is a focus on native language instruction. Both Tibetan and Uyghur communities were subject to discriminatory policies and practices by Chinese governments that resulted in forced migrations by community members. While persecution of Tibetans began in the 1960s (Phuntsog, 2018) and intensified for the Uyghurs since 2009 (Abdulehed, 2024), both communities were also barred from speaking their indigenous languages. In the diasporas that were founded following emigration, efforts were made to retain ancestral languages and to pass them on to subsequent generations. Lenberg (2022) cites Uyghur Americans who, in response to Chinese efforts to remove Uyghur literature from bookstores, have begun teaching Uyghur poetry and literature to their youth as a form of cultural resistance. Afterschool programming and educational initiatives have also proliferated throughout the Uyghur diaspora. With their indigenous language forbidden in China, "children of the Uyghur diaspora have become the only inheritors of Uyghur language and culture" (Abdulehed, 2024, p. 77). The significance of this turn cannot be understated, because "the preservation of [their language and culture] rests on the shoulders of the Uyghur community living abroad." It is for this reason that Uyghur education is often predicated on the acquisition of the indigenous language, with community members locating in language an opportunity to perpetuate Uyghur culture (Abdulehed, 2024).

Attention towards culture, by way of language, is thus an act of resistance against genocide and persecution for the Uyghurs.

In the case of Tibetans, India has served as the primary site for their diaspora. Beginning in the 1960s, Tibetans began establishing their own schools with English and Tibetan as the languages of instruction for the thousands who live in the Tibetan diaspora (Phuntsog, 2018). Rather than their schooling being locally funded by grassroots organizations like the Uyghurs, Tibetans have benefitted from India allowing the Tibetan Government in Exile to fund their own school system, with the primary language of instruction being Tibetan (Phuntsog, 2018). Much like the Uyghur diaspora, the preservation of their distinct language has allowed the Tibetan diaspora to retain a strong connection to its indigenous land and heritage. Phuntsog explains the relationship between language, culture and national identity thusly: "The more the Tibetan language is repressed in Tibet, the more Tibetans within and outside mobilize to preserve and promote it. Considered to be one of the most resilient and successful refugee groups in the world, Tibetans in exile have created a cohesive community with a viable infrastructure to ensure the continuity of their culture, language, and national identity" (Phuntsog, 2018, p. 92).

Unlike the Uyghurs and the Tibetans whose diasporas were founded in response to persecution, segments of the Hungarian diaspora were formed following Hungary's acceptance into the European Union in 2004. This resulted in voluntary migration, especially amongst better-educated Hungarians who sought economic and vocational opportunities outside of Hungary (Papp, Kovács, and Kováts, 2023). Their decision to immigrate did not, however, result in a rejection of Hungarian national identity. With the financial support of the Hungarian government, weekend schools were established in places like the United Kingdom for the purpose of retaining and strengthening national identification. Here, too, the emphasis was placed on language instruction and retention, with classes offered in Hungarian (Papp, Kovács, and Kováts, 2023). The schools also focus on teaching Hungarian customs and culture, with these rituals often taking on new meaning in the diaspora as tools for identity formation. Thus, participation in traditional folk dances or the celebration of Hungarian holidays "may be interpreted as a channel for diaspora formation. In the diasporization process, the mutual sense of shared identity is often an innovative and transformative experience" (Papp, Kovács, and Kováts, 2023, p. 116).

In addition to strengthening students' feelings of national solidarity with their countries of origin, the formation of community amongst diaspora youth has also played a seminal role in diaspora education. In a study set amongst members of the Mexican diaspora living in the United States, Kovats Sanchez (2024) has identified *comunalidad,* community collectiveness and belonging, as a key feature of how the Mexican diaspora operates. Drawing upon the work of Ramirez (2007), she suggests that one way this is done is through the creation of native hubs, "mechanisms [built] to reinforce connection and positive reflections on Indigenous cultural identity away from a geographic center." These native hubs are purposefully designed "to transmit and nurture transnational belonging and comunalidad among growing diasporic Indigenous generations" (Kovats Sanchez, 2024, p. 11).

The Jewish diaspora and its connection to Israel bears both similarities to and differences from these other diasporic communities. Though Jews experience antisemitism, persecution of Jews today does not originate in their ancestral homeland. Instead, it primarily occurs outside of Israel. Furthermore, though the terms "Jews," "Judaism," and "Israel" are deeply intertwined, they are not synonymous with each other. Not all Jews are Israeli by citizenship. And yet, those residing outside of Israel are considered part of the Jewish diaspora. The concept of the Jewish diaspora, however, locates the land of Israel as the indigenous land. That indigenous land of Israel is where the modern nation-state of Israel is located. Furthermore, there also exists an *Israeli* diaspora, but this refers to Israeli citizens who reside outside of Israel. Thus, the Jewish diaspora extends beyond nationalist ties (which are often manifested in support for the nation of Israel) and is rooted in ethnic, cultural, or religious origins rather than any recent familial link to the country by way of physical presence or citizenship in the land.

Further complicating (and intertwining) the dynamics are studies that demonstrate that North American Jews feel a deep affinity and connection to the State of Israel as the national home of the Jewish people. The 2020 Pew Survey of American Jews revealed that caring about Israel is an essential or important part of what being Jewish means to them for 80% of the population. Additionally, 60% of American Jews report feeling an emotional connection to Israel (U.S. Jews' Connections, 2021). Amongst Canadian Jews, the most recent survey of attitudes towards Israel was conducted after October 7, revealing that 70% of respondents feel either connected or somewhat connected to Israel (Brym, 2024). Moreover, Israel and modern Hebrew are essential components of Jewish education in spaces like day schools (Zakai, 2014), supplementary schools (Kopelowitz and Pitkowsky, 2024), and camps (Bunin Benor, Krasner, and Avni 2020). Therefore, though October 7 took place in a country where most diaspora Jews do not possess citizenship, it had a profound impact on how diaspora Jews acted and reacted in response to the calamity because of their deep connections to Israel (Kravetz, Eisenman, and Manchester, 2024).

Highlighting the similar nationalist goals—national identification, relationships with the indigenous land, second language acquisition and retention—between the Jewish diaspora and other diaspora communities does more than just establish parallels between Israel education and other forms of diaspora education. Rather, it situates Israel education within a larger field of diaspora education and, through this, more ably allows for the exchange of ideas, practices, and concerns across nationalist divides. Each of the communities mentioned in this section are unique and perfect parallels do not exist. For example, unlike the Uyghurs and Tibetans who were forced into exile, the Hungarian diaspora studied by Papp, Kovács, and Kováts (2023) exists voluntarily, motivated by economic interests. Despite these differences, common educational interests intersect around nationalist, linguistic, and cultural pedagogies. Drawing upon these disparate communities' educational experiences situates the present volume in dialogue with how others go about teaching and learning while in the diaspora. This can deepen our understanding of Jewish students' and teachers' experiences after October 7 and help inform the educational decisions that Jewish communities make after October 7. Furthermore, as a volume dedicated exclusively to education in the Jewish diaspora following tragedy and trauma in the national homeland, the present work can serve as a resource for other diaspora communities who are similarly committed to preserving national identification in places of origin where violence and terror have shaped civil life.

This Volume

A recent demographic study, commissioned shortly after October 7, revealed a renewed interest in Jewish life from North American Jews of all backgrounds (Kravetz, Eisenman, and Manchester, 2024). Calling it "the surge," the study's authors document a sharp uptick in interest in Jewish and Israel education. Alongside this renewed interest in Jewish life amongst adults is an increased attention afforded to Jewish education, with enrollment in Jewish day schools rising in the wake of October 7 (Epstein, Rivkind, Adler, 2024), new educational imperatives being put forth (Bryfman, 2025), and curricular revisions being recommended (Gordon, 2023). *Education after October 7* examines these developments and considers how Jewish education in the diaspora evolved following the single-greatest tragedy in Israeli history.

The chapters in *Education after October 7* are united around three common elements. The first element is that the impetus for their composition is October 7, with all of the research studies and conclusions drawn about teaching and learning emerging following the initial terror attack. The second is that they are set in the Jewish diaspora. The ways that Israel will be taught about within Israel are of importance, but this volume is explicitly focused on how Jews *outside* of Israel learn about Israel. Lastly, the volume contains chapters concerned with how Israel is taught in the places where students learn about Israel during their years of compulsory schooling. Roughly corresponding to ages three to eighteen, it is a time period where individuals spend the majority of their time enrolled in school.

Focusing on the ages where Israel is taught in early childhood centers through secondary schools and also at summer camps recognizes that the nature of Israel education for adults (in college and afterwards) is very different from the education offered to children and adolescents. Whereas day school Israel education is often designed to foster an emotional connection to Israel as a component of a learner's Jewish identity (Horowitz, 2012), such is not the case when Israel is taught on campuses. There, Israel is an academic subject matter and is taught to learners with diverse religious, ethnic, and national backgrounds (Zakai, 2024a). Though the approach adopted for this volume does create a limitation wherein teaching and learning amongst adults is not considered, what emerges from the focused approach is a clearer picture of how October 7 affected teaching and learning with students engaged in compulsory schooling.

The first section of the book, "Worries and Anxieties: The Voices of Students, Parents, and Teachers," considers the psycho-social and educational impact of October 7. In the first chapter, Sivan Zakai and Lauren Applebaum write about the ways that elementary school children think about the initial terror attack, the plight of the hostages, and the ongoing war in Gaza. They conclude that, much like the adults surrounding them, the children demonstrate rich and diverse political thought. The second chapter, written by Rona Novick and Jenny Isaacs, is a quantitative study that examines the beliefs held by teachers and parents about the children in their midst. The authors demonstrate the changes in students' Jewish behaviors in response to concerns about antisemitism and the need to develop educational resources designed to support students during times of communal crisis. The third chapter is set in Germany and is authored by Maor Shani, Jana Gerber, and Marie Herb. Employing both quantitative and qualitative research methods, the authors write about the concerns held by Jewish parents about the future of German Jewry in the wake of October 7 and the ways that they use Jewish traditions to serve as a bulwark against the rise of anti-Israel and antisemitic public rhetoric.

The volume's second section, "Pedagogical Innovations: Teaching Anew after October 7," focuses on the curricular decisions made by educators after October 7. All three of the articles in this section present the perspectives of educators who realized that, in the wake of October 7, the ways that they had been teaching needed revising. The first chapter, co-authored by Meir Muller, Lyndall Miller, and Alana Rifkin Gelnick, is set in an early childhood center. The authors document the ways that the preschool teachers balanced preserving childhood innocence and teaching for resilience in response to their learners' desires to carve out space for October 7 in the classroom. In the second chapter, Benji Davis writes about the challenges that educators who were previously committed to teaching Palestinian stories in a dignified way faced after October 7. He reveals that educators adopted different strategies to manage previously held educational beliefs with their personal struggles vis-à-vis the Palestinian people following the terror attack. The third article, written by Vardit Ringvald and Sharon Schoenfeld, focuses on Hebrew teachers and how their classroom roles shifted. No longer only Hebrew language instructors, they also became Israel educators, a role that required new pedagogical considerations and strategies.

In the third section, "Teaching about Home: Israelis Abroad," the three chapters focus on *shlichim*, Israeli emissaries who teach about Israel and represent Israel to diasporic Jewish communities. The chapters in this section explore the unprecedented challenges that *shlichim* faced after October 7. Michal Shapira Junger's qualitative study reveals the complex decision-making processes that *shlichim* navigated as they tried to balance their personal needs and their professional responsibilities. The second and third chapters of this section are both set at summer camps but examine the Israeli experience from different vantage points. Tal Vaizman's ethnographic study of two overnight summer camps is primarily concerned with the experiences of Israelis themselves and how they worked to bring slices of Israeli life to American campers. In the third article, I write about the ways that camp leaders established new opportunities that allowed Israeli staff and campers to assume ownership over Israel programming.

The volume's concluding section, "After October 7: The Future of Jewish Education," is a collection of three articles that envision new models for Jewish education after October 7. Each of the articles offers a different vision for what the future of Jewish education might look like. Drawing upon survey data collected from Israel educators, Alex Pomson and Samantha Vinokor-Meinrath argue that Israel education needs to be better integrated into the larger field of Jewish education. Doing so will ensure that Israel education moves beyond being a reactive endeavor that responds to daily news cycles and becomes instead something more significant and valuable. Ezra Kopelowitz's article maps out three models of how educators taught after October 7 before concluding that none offer a satisfactory response to the crisis. Instead, he argues that an educational framework built around the notion of Jewish peoplehood is what will nurture in students feelings of collective Jewish belonging. In the section's third chapter, Jon A. Levisohn explores the significance of October 7 within a broader understanding of contemporary American Jewish civic life. He argues that Jewish education must adopt dual purposes: to prepare young people for encountering discomfort in contemporary America and to equip them with the skills to alter that uncomfortable reality in order to fashion a new society.

Each of the chapters in *Education after October 7* can stand alone and provide a window into one way that Jewish education has been changed by October 7. When read alongside other chapters, what becomes evident is that, in the aftermath of October 7, a series of tensions surfaced between the cognitive and emotional goals of education, between teachers' personal and professional identities, and over the philosophical and ideological purposes of Jewish and Israel education. In the volume's conclusion, I adopt a zoomed-out lens to weave together these strands of tension before using them to offer a series of practical next steps that institutions can adopt for improving teaching and learning in their spaces.

References

Abdulehed, M. (2024). Role of teaching Uyghur language in shaping cultural identity of children of Uyghur diaspora. In R. Clothey and D. Mahmut (Eds.), *Uyghur identity and culture: A global diaspora in a time of crisis* (pp. 77–88). Routledge.

Benor, S. B., Krasner, J., and Avni, S. (2020). *Hebrew infusion: Language and community at American Jewish summer camps*. Rutgers University Press.

Bryfman, D. (2025). Redeeming the hostages is the Jewish educational imperative of our lifetime. *eJewishPhilanthropy*, January 9. https://

ejewishphilanthropy.com/redeeming-the-hostages-is-the-jewish-educational-imperative-of-our-lifetime/

Brym, R. (2024). Jews and Israel 2024: A Survey of Canadian Attitudes and Jewish Perceptions. *Canadian Jewish Studies / Études Juives Canadiennes*, 37. https://doi.org/10.25071/1916-0925.40368

Chazan, B. (2016). *A philosophy of Israel education: A relational approach*. Palgrave Macmillan.

Chazan, B. (2022). *Principles and pedagogies in Jewish education*. Palgrave Macmillan.

Davis, B., and Alexander, H. (2023). Israel education: A philosophical analysis. *Journal of Jewish Education*, 89(1), 6–33. https://doi.org/10.1080/15244113.2023.2169213

Epstein, O., Rivkind, B., and Adler, A. (2024). Enrollment trend report: Families turn to Jewish day school post 10/7. *Prizmah: Center for Jewish Day Schools*, June 11. https://prizmah.org/knowledge/resource/enrollment-trend-report-families-turn-jewish-day-school-post-107

Fraiman, K. (2024). Barriers to entry exploring educator reticence for engaging with the Israeli–Palestinian conflict. In S. Zakai and M. Reingold (Eds.), *Teaching Israel: Studies of pedagogy from the field* (pp. 229–253). Brandeis University Press.

Golden, J., and Kadden, Y. (2024). Knowledge, connection, and stance: Toward a more enduring Israel engagement. In S. Zakai and M. Reingold (Eds.), *Teaching Israel: Studies of pedagogy from the field* (pp. 151–176). Brandeis University Press.

Gordon, S. (2023). Israel education in a post-October 7th world. *Jewish Education Innovation Challenge*, December 14. https://www.jewishchallenge.org/insights/2023/12/14/israel-education-in-a-post-october-7th-world

Gross, M. H., and Terra, L. (2018). Introduction: What makes difficult history difficult? In M. H. Gross and L. Terra (Eds.), *Teaching and learning the difficult past* (pp. 1–8). Routledge.

Hassenfeld, J. (2016). Negotiating critical analysis and collective belonging: Jewish American students write the history of Israel. *Contemporary Jewry*, 36(1), 55–84. https://doi.org/10.1007/s12397-016-9157-6

Hassenfeld, J. (2018). Landscapes of collective belonging: Jewish Americans narrate the history of Israel after an organized tour. *Journal of Jewish Education*, 84(2), 131–160. https://doi.org/10.1080/15244113.2018.1449482

Hassenfeld, J. (2023). What's love got to do with it: Reevaluating attachment as the goal of Israel education. *Journal of Jewish Education, 89*(1), 75–81. https://doi.org/10.1080/15244113.2023.2169514

Horowitz, B. (2012). *Defining Israel education*. Jim Joseph Foundation. https://jimjosephfoundation.org/wp-content/uploads/2012/01/iCenter_Bethamie.pdf

Kelman, A. Y., and Baron, I. Z. (2019). Framing conflict: Why American congregations cannot not talk about Israel. *Contemporary Jewry, 39*(3–4), 497–522. https://doi.org/10.1007/s12397-019-09305-2

Kopelowitz, E. and Pitkowsky, A. (2024). Nurturing Jewish consciousness: Utilizing values at synagogue supplementary schools to teach Israel. In S. Zakai and M. Reingold (Eds.), *Teaching Israel: Studies of pedagogy from the field* (pp. 309–332). Brandeis University Press.

Kovats Sánchez, G. (2024). Cultivating kinship and refusal in Indigenous diaspora. *Diaspora, Indigenous, and Minority Education: Studies of Migration, Integration, Equity and Cultural Survival*. https://doi.org/10.1080/15595692.2024.2337940

Krasner, J. (2005). Jewish education and American Jewish education, part II. *Journal of Jewish Education, 71*(3), 279–317. https://doi.org/10.1080/00216240500341906

Krasner, J. (2006). Jewish education and American Jewish education, part III. *Journal of Jewish Education, 72*(1), 29–76. https://doi.org/10.1080/00216240600581591

Kravetz, M., Eisenman, S., and Manchester, D. (2024). 'The surge,' 'the core' and more: What you need to know about the explosion of interest in Jewish life. *eJewishPhilanthropy*, May 9. https://ejewishphilanthropy.com/what-you-need-to-know-about-the-surge-of-interest-in-jewish-life/

Lenberg, L. (2022). Uyghur diaspora activism in the face of genocide. *International Journal of Human Rights Education, 6*(1). https://repository.usfca.edu/ijhre/vol6/iss1/7

Papp Z., A., Kovács, E., and Kováts, A. (2023). Unpacking the functions of institutions in an emerging diaspora: Hungarian weekend schools in the UK. *Diaspora, Indigenous, and Minority Education, 18*(2), 107–120. https://doi.org/10.1080/15595692.2022.2164271

Phuntsog, N. (2018). Tibetan language at home in the diaspora: The mother tongue-based bilingual schooling of Tibetans in India. *Minority Education, 12*(2), 82–94. https://doi.org/10.1080/15595692.2017.1398141

Ramirez, F. O. (2012). The world society perspective: concepts, assumptions, and strategies. *Comparative Education, 48*(4), 423–439. https://doi.org/10.1080/03050068.2012.693374

Ramirez, R. K. (2007). Native hubs: Culture, community, and belonging in Silicon Valley and beyond. Duke University Press.

Reingold, M. (2017). Not the Israel of my elementary school: An exploration of Jewish-Canadian secondary students' attempts to process morally complex Israeli narratives. *The Social Studies, 108*(3), 87–98. https://doi.org/10.1080/00377996.2017.1324392

Reingold, M. (2018). Broadening perspectives on immigrant experiences: Secondary students study the absorption difficulties faced by Mizrachi immigrants in Israel. *Journal of Jewish Education, 84*(3), 312–329. https://doi.org/10.1080/15244113.2018.1478531

Reingold, M. (2021a). Changing students' perceptions by humanizing Dati Israelis through comics. *Religious Education, 116*(3), 278–295. https://doi.org/10.1080/00344087.2021.1917848

Reingold, M. (2021b). Confronting BDS in the classroom: Jewish high school students build community by watching BDS demonstrations on university campuses. *Canadian Jewish Studies / Études Juives Canadiennes, 31,* 69–88.

Reingold, M., Pomson, A., and Zakai, S. (2025). The ages and stages of learning about Israel: A developmental review of the literature on Israel education. *The Journal of Jewish Education.*

Reingold, M., and Reznik, S. (2024). Navigating crisis together: Canadian Jews, Israel, and October 7. *Contemporary Jewry, 44*(4), 885–902. https://doi.org/10.1007/s12397-024-09572-8

Shulman, L. S. (1986). Those who understand: Knowledge growth in teaching. *Educational Researcher, 15*(2), 4–14. https://doi.org/10.2307/1175860

Sinclair, A., Solmsen, B., and Goldwater, C. (2013). *The Israel educator: An inquiry into the preparation and capacities of effective Israel educators.* Israel Education Research Briefs. Consortium for Applied Studies in Jewish Education (CASJE).

Thelen, D. (1998). Making history and making the United States. *Journal of American Studies, 32*(3), 373–397. http://www.jstor.org/stable/27556475

U.S. Jews' connections with and attitudes toward Israel (2021). *Jewish Americans in 2020.* Pew Research Center. https://www.pewresearch.org/religion/2021/05/11/u-s-jews-connections-with-and-attitudes-toward-israel/

Waxman, D. (2016). *Trouble in the tribe: The American Jewish conflict over Israel*. Princeton University Press.

Zakai, S. (2014). "My Heart is in the east and I am in the west": Enduring questions of Israel education in North America. *Journal of Jewish Education, 80*(3), 287–318. https://doi.org/10.1080/15244113.2014.937192

Zakai, S. (2015). The stories of our national past: History and heritage in a Jewish high school. *Curriculum Inquiry, 45*(2), 219–243. https://doi.org/10.1080/03626784.2015.1011042

Zakai, S. (2018). When past and present collide: Dilemmas in teaching the history of the Israeli-Palestinian conflict. In M. H. Gross and L. Terra (Eds.), *Teaching and learning the difficult past* (pp. 104–118). Routledge.

Zakai, S. (2021). "It makes me feel many different things": A child's relationships to Israel over time. *Journal of Jewish Education, 87*(2), 120–143. https://doi.org/10.1080/15244113.2021.1926375

Zakai, S. (2022). *My second-favorite country: How American Jewish children think about Israel*. NYU Press.

Zakai, S. (2024a). Introduction. In S. Zakai and M. Reingold (Eds.), *Teaching Israel: Studies of pedagogy from the field* (pp. 1–32). Brandeis University Press.

Zakai, S. (2024b). "We're not friends anymore because I support Israel": Evolving beliefs about Israel politics from elementary to middle school. *Contemporary Jewry, 44*(1), 83–105. https://doi.org/10.1007/s12397-024-09549-7

Zakai, S., and Cohen, H. T. (2016). American Jewish children's thoughts and feelings about the Jewish state: Laying the groundwork for a developmental approach to Israel education. *Contemporary Jewry, 36*(1), 31–54. https://doi.org/10.1007/s12397-016-9160-y

Section One

WORRIES AND ANXIETIES: THE VOICES OF STUDENTS, PARENTS, AND CHILDREN

"A Lot of Horrible Things Have Happened": Jewish Children's Beliefs about October 7 and Its Aftermath

Sivan Zakai and Lauren Applebaum

Introduction

Dalia Cohen and Addison Price[1] have been friends since the start of elementary school. Now that they are big kids in fourth grade, they continue to sit side by side in their Jewish day school. They both like *Hamilton* music, both wear rubber bracelets around their wrists, and are both eager to share their thoughts about current events. They also both spend a lot of time worrying about the state of the world, and they are both horrified when they think about the events of October 7. Despite these similarities, Dalia and Addison have radically different beliefs about the events that have unfolded since October 7.

Dalia is "really, really worried about Israel crumbling" after "Hamas's attacks [on] Israel." She fears for the safety of her "family in the [Israeli] army" and other Israelis who are living under the constant threat of "bombs and missiles and explosions." She thinks about hostages "of all ages being taken" and about family friends who narrowly escaped the Nova "concert where [others] were killed." "What's going on in Israel has definitely changed me," she laments. "My heart just feels heavy."

---

[1] All children's names are pseudonyms.

Addison is also deeply worried, but her primary concern is for the civilian population of Gaza. She explains, "Israel has blocked [them in]. It has already bombed their airports and is bringing in soldiers to bomb them. So they have no home, and they have nowhere to go. They're out of water, possibly out of food, and they're just there waiting to die." She reflects that "if I were in their shoes, I wouldn't be comfortable," and she reports feeling "very sad."

In this chapter, we examine the ideas and beliefs that Jewish children like Dalia and Addison have about October 7 and its aftermath. Drawing upon a study of eighty-five fourth- and fifth-grade children, roughly equally split between those attending day schools and those attending synagogue-based supplementary schools, we investigate children's views about the events of October 7, the ensuing war, and the ongoing hostage crisis. We argue that elementary-age Jewish children—regardless of the denominational or political commitments of their families, and irrespective of whether they attend day or supplementary school—share a common set of characteristics: they know about the horrors of October 7, they express deep concern about the hostages, and they claim that events in the Middle East matter deeply to them. At the same time, Jewish children have profound disagreements about Israel's conduct in the war. Their conceptions of the war are overtly political, demonstrating the ways that even young children make sense of the world with a political valence. Children with radically different beliefs about Israel's role in the war, like Addison and Dalia, often sit side by side in their Jewish day and Jewish supplementary schools.

Methodology

In the fall of the 2023–2024 school year, we launched the Learning and Teaching about What Matters Project,[2] a research project aimed at better understanding how Jewish children and their educators think about "what matters" in the world and the educational implications of those ideas. We wanted to understand: (1) What issues in the contemporary world matter most to Jewish children? (2) How do Jewish children make sense of those

---

2   The Learning and Teaching about What Matters Project is a research project at the Jack, Joseph and Morton Mandel Center for Studies in Jewish Education at Brandeis University. The data collected for this chapter was funded by an award from CASJE (Collaborative for Applied Studies in Jewish Education) at the George Washington University.

issues? (3) How do educators make sense of their role of thinking with children about these issues?

To answer these questions, we partnered with five synagogues on the West Coast of the United States. Each of these synagogues contains *both* a Jewish day school *and* a supplementary school. As the school year began, we recruited fourth- and fifth-grade children and educators at each of the ten schools. A total of eighty-five children and thirty educators, who hold a range of political ideologies and denominational affiliations, enrolled in the study. Forty-five children and twenty educators were situated in synagogue-based day schools, and forty children and ten educators were part of synagogue supplementary schools. Because the research was an attempt to understand the thinking of Jewish children rather than analyze specific types of Jewish schooling, we included children from both school types.

The research study was designed long before the events of October 7, but because our questions were designed to capture issues that "matter" to Jewish children and their educators, we were able to "catch" data about the ways that Jewish children were thinking and feeling about a range of issues that the children themselves identified as important. They included the massacres of October 7, the ensuing war, the ongoing hostage crisis, rising antisemitism in the US context, and more.

While children spoke with us about a range of contemporary issues, and while we also collected data about teachers' ideas and beliefs, this chapter focuses solely on uncovering the ways that Jewish children spoke about events related to October 7 and its aftermath. To understand the context in which children shared these ideas and beliefs, readers need to know what we asked the children, when, and why.

In the first phase of the study, we interviewed each child participant some time between November 2023 and January 2024. We asked children broad, open-ended questions intended to capture a) what issues mattered to them, and b) how they spoke about those issues and their import. These questions were both playful in nature (e.g., *If you had a magic wand and could solve any one problem with our world today, what problem would you want to solve and why?*) and serious (e.g., *What do you think adults need to know about how children think about important issues in our world?*) After that, each interview narrowed to probing questions when children themselves raised troubling issues, always mirroring the language that children themselves used (see Zakai, 2019). Ethically, this type of design respects both children's thinking and the decisions of parents who may have chosen not to discuss particular issues with their young children. Methodologically, it aims to avoid providing images and language to children, striving instead to capture what children themselves know and think about current events.

In a later phase of the study, after having learned that all of the children were clearly aware of the events of October 7, and after working with the children's educators to determine what else would be useful to know about children's thinking, we returned to each of the children for a second one-on-one conversation about a range of issues including the ongoing war between Israel and Hamas. Between April and May 2024, we asked children another set of open-ended questions that once again ranged from serious (e.g., *Where have you learned about the Israel-Gaza war? If you talk about it at school, can you give me one example of a conversation or lesson you've had?*) to fanciful (e.g., *If you were the principal of your school, would you tell teachers to talk more about the Israel-Gaza war than they already do, less about the Israel-Gaza war than they already do, or the same amount about the Israel-Gaza war as they already do? Why?*). Then we conducted a "think aloud" exercise, a method that invites participants to voice aloud their internal thoughts as they read and attempt to make sense of a text (Wineburg, 2001). In this "think aloud," we asked children to read a written-for-children article titled "The Israel-Hamas War" from the *New York Times for Kids*. After each paragraph, we asked the children: *What are you thinking, feeling, or wondering about what you just read?* After they had read the entire article, we asked follow-up questions such as: *What do you know about what's happened since the article was written?* and *What else do you want teachers to understand about how you think about the war?*

All of the data from the interviews and think aloud exercises was coded in the traditions of grounded theory (Charmaz, 2006; Glaser and Strauss, 1967) and collaborative data analysis (Cornish et al., 2013). We attempted to make sense of the patterns in children's words and ideas. What follows is an analysis of children's ideas, thoughts, and beliefs about October 7 and its aftermath, highlighting both the agreements and the profound differences among Jewish children.

Findings

Children construct an understanding of current events much like an artist crafting an elaborate mosaic. They gather small pieces of different sorts from a wide variety of sources and work to put them together into a larger image.

Children's conceptual mosaics are often marked by both a sense of coherence *and* missing pieces.

The children in this study reported gathering the "tiles" to form their "October 7 mosaics" from a wide variety of sources: conversations with parents, grandparents, peers, teachers, and rabbis; television, radio, and online news sources; social media; signs, posters, and protests in their neighborhoods; and elsewhere. In a particularly cogent explanation of children's ways of sensemaking, fourth grader Eve explained how she built a mental image of the events of October 7 by gathering initial bits of information from watching the news and hearing her parents talk. "I'm pretty sure that I know this, or I know this, but I'm not positive," she elucidated. "And then some kids talk about it at school. And then I was like, 'oh, right, I'm right about that.' Or, 'oh, I have to change this piece in my head to this because that's incorrect.'" Over time, by checking herself and adjusting her understanding, she was able to construct an evolving and ever clearer picture of October 7 and the ensuing war.

There were both striking similarities and key differences among the children's "images" of October 7 and its aftermath, and in the pages that follow we map out both the commonalities and the diversity of children's ideas and beliefs. All quotations are verbatim transcriptions of children's words, though the children themselves are referred to by pseudonyms to protect their identities.

Children's Ideas and Beliefs about October 7

The eighty-five children in this study came from a wide variety of denominational, ethnic, and educational Jewish backgrounds. Yet, despite the differences in their families, schools, and upbringings, the children were united by two core commonalities: they knew about the tragic events of October 7 and the ensuing war, and they worried about these events. As Ian explained, "I actually knew a lot about Israel, Gaza, and what happened on October 7 and the hostages. I feel scared and anxious." "I know basically all of it," insisted Toby, "and I think it's not okay to kill innocent people."

Approximately a quarter of the children knew about October 7 only in broad brushstrokes. "I wish for October 7 never to have happened," said Emilia, who clearly knew that "there's a lot of terrible things going on" but offered no details. "I know a war started on October 7, right?" offered Layla. "Hamas attacked Israel on October 7. I feel like they just stormed in," said Luke.

"October 7 is ugly!" insisted Brian. These children clearly knew "October 7" as a key term, and they associated the day with "terrible things," but, if they knew specific details about the atrocities of that day, they did not share them with the interviewer. This group of children included both day school (e.g., Emilia) and supplementary school students (e.g., Brian). No matter what type of Jewish education they were receiving, this group of children clearly knew *that* October 7 was "ugly" but offered very little explanation of *what*, specifically, happened on that terrible day.

Most children, however, expressed not only detailed knowledge of the events of October 7 and its aftermath but also strong beliefs and emotional reactions. These children, regardless of whether they attended a Jewish after school program or a Jewish day school, shared particular details about the tragedies of October 7 and expressed a clear sense of moral outrage. "I feel sad that in just one day Hamas killed like 1,200 people," explained Darya. "If you attack someone–which of course is something I never want–then attack someone in a position of power. But to attack ordinary people who aren't in the army or trying to fight a war is really bad." In the words of Piper, "They attacked the Nova festival. There were people who lost family. There were injured people. Hamas, guys, you don't take kids! You don't take two-month-old kids away from their mothers. You don't separate them. You don't take elderly people. They took mothers away from children." These children's accounts were peppered with more specific information, at times about the Nova festival but more commonly about the attacks on the southern kibbutzim. They were clearly horrified about particular, not generalized, tragedies.

Several of these children used language that suggested they viewed themselves as personal witnesses to the events of October 7. They frequently used phrases like "I saw" or "I watched" to describe their understanding of that fateful day. "I watched it on October 7," insisted Oaklie. She continued, "I watched it happen in the morning. It was super emotional. I knew the whole time what was going on." Similarly, Dalia explained, "I saw on the screen there were bombs and missiles and explosions. And news reporters and people behind the news reporters running and taking shelter. And it was just creeping me out. I was like, please just turn it off. I can't bear to see this." This phenomenon, which we call "remote trauma," mirrors the experiences of other elementary-age Jewish children who watch from afar as violent events unfold in the Middle East and believe they have personally seen these events (Zakai, 2022). Unlike older teens who often make careful choices about their social and digital media choices (Reingold and Reznik, 2024), these children generally do not have their own social media accounts and instead are seeing the digital choices made by their parents and others in their environments. Although the children are physically remote, they use tv remote controls and computer trackpads to "witness" the horrors. "I saw it," declared Eve, "and in my head I kind of pieced together what I had learned."

Children's Ideas and Beliefs about the Hostages

As much as the children clearly knew about the horrors of October 7, they commented both most frequently and most intensely about the hostage crisis. "There's so many hostages, and it's not really a fair deal," explained Sage, giving voice to a belief that the children clearly shared. "Obviously I don't like hostages," she explained. "It's not a good thing and people should be with their family and not being held captive."

Many of the children seemed to have an explicit belief that there is a "right way" to wage war, and that the taking of hostages—and especially children as hostages—violates the "rules" of warfare. "War is only supposed to be men versus men," insisted Kai, "and it's like taking me or my brothers to hostage with not really great people. I don't really think it would be right to take older or younger kids, or women or girls." "The way that they took hostages," reflected Leo, "they took young kids and elderly people. If you think about it, adults are the ones who really fight in the army, not kids." "How could an adult do that to a young kid? And also, like, an elderly person?" Jamie raged. Darya lamented, "Kids, like, just being held hostage! Like no food or water! What did they do to deserve that?" These children believed that it was morally wrong to take people, and especially children, hostage. As Paz explained, "You don't capture people, hold them hostage." Or, in the words of Eden, "That's just so wrong!"

Another striking aspect of the children's reflections was that many of the children imagined *themselves* in the place of the child hostages. Like Kai in the paragraph above, they thought about an alternate reality in which Hamas was "taking me or my brothers to hostage." Eden explained, "I'm Jewish, and I can't even imagine what it's like, if I was a hostage." But she clearly did spend a considerable amount of time imagining exactly this scenario. She explained, "I'd be like sitting there in a cell without food or anyone to talk to you. And I'd be traumatized." Otis believed that *many* Jewish children spent time thinking "it could happen to them, or they could be held hostage." Children like Kai, Eden, and Otis didn't only empathize with the child hostages; they actively imagined themselves in the place of these other Jewish children.

Most of the children in this study reported having encountered information about the hostages in their own neighborhoods. "I have seen many photos, like going out to lunch with my dad," explained Gwen. "I was going to a museum," recounted Jeremiah, "and there was an entire wall that was filled with 240 posters of everyone who was taken. It felt like a memorial, especially in the Jewish communities." "Tonight," said Ian, "I'm going to hear one of the siblings of a hostage speak. They're visiting LA to do some speaking engagements... I think it's going to be a really upsetting thing to hear about, but I'm interested in hearing their story." Dalia encountered "the kidnap posters" in her school, and Jamie recounted seeing the posters "everywhere." For these children, all of whom lived in neighborhoods with large Jewish populations, encountering images or stories of the hostages had become part of their everyday lives.

Some children told generic stories about how "Hamas waltzed into Israel and grabbed 240 people" (Jeremiah), but other children told specific stories about particular hostages. For example, Meital felt especially worried about "two children, a baby and a little boy" who were clearly Kfir and Ariel Bibas. Boaz told a story about "a video of a kid who was a hostage" that matched the videos of Ohad Munder's return to Israel after his time in Hamas captivity. In Leo's words, "He got released and was running back to his family in Israel." Multiple children told stories about Alon Shamriz, Yotam Haim, and Samer Talalka, Israeli hostages who were tragically killed by the IDF. Adam explained, "I know something really sad happened when hostages were trying to escape. They were shot by Israeli soldiers." In Darya's telling, "I also know that a lot of horrible things have happened, like the soldiers who accidentally killed hostages because they thought that they were Hamas but they were actually just coming because they wanted to be rescued." Other children told stories that were likely about hostages Emily Hand and Hersh Goldberg-Polin. The children never referred to these hostages by name, but they clearly knew particular and disturbing details of specific hostages' stories.

Regardless of whether the children knew particular or generic details about the hostages, it was clear that all of the children felt the suspended state of uncertainty of the ongoing hostage crisis. Adam explained that while some hostages had been released and some had died, "the rest are still being held captive. We've been praying every day, particularly for the hostages, and saying special prayers." Eden reflected, "It's been [a long time], and that's crazy! And these kids and the adults are never going to recover. And we don't even know how many of them are alive." The children expressed a deep sense of concern over these remaining hostages. "What are the hostages eating?" worried Alex. Shlomit feared that even if these hostages were freed, they would be "traumatized for the rest of their life." These children reported spending considerable time thinking or talking, in Mason's words, "about how many hostages there are and how sad it is."

Children's Ideas and Beliefs about the War

Without fail, the children knew about the war between Israel and Hamas, and many (though not all) children also understood that other countries like Iran and Lebanon also played a role in the war. In response to open-ended questions about the issues that they believed were most important, children repeatedly made claims like Bryce, who exclaimed, "I care a lot about this war!" "The war is important to me," insisted Jeremiah.

Why did these children, whose own lives in the United States were physically far away, care so deeply about a war in the Middle East? The children in this study typically gave one of three answers. One subset of the children said they care about the human costs of *any* war, including the war that followed October 7. "When there's a war," explained Ty, "a lot of people die or get hurt, and it makes me and everyone in the world sad." Shlomit stated, "It's sad to see Israel in a war [because] it's sad to see a country, any country in general, have to go to war with another country." For children like these, "*any* war matters" (Leo), because "a lot of innocent people die from war" (Dina).

A second group of children, by contrast, explained that they care about the war because of its particular meaning to them as Jews. "The war matters to me because I'm Jewish," said Bryce. "Israel is a Jewish home for the Jews. I'm proud to be Jewish. But I hate to say, lots of Jews are dying from this, lots of Jewish kids are getting kidnapped for doing nothing." "It matters deeply because I'm Jewish," said Gideon, "and the war on Israel is hitting my roots." "Because I'm Jewish and it's my religion, I really pay attention to it," explained Otis." "It matters a lot to me because I'm Jewish," explained Piper. These children repeatedly insisted that the war was important to them as Jews.

A third group of children had even more personal ties to the war, explaining that they cared deeply about it because they have family, friends, or acquaintances who had been personally impacted by the war. Dalia explained, "This war really matters to me because I have a lot of family in Israel in Tel Aviv and Jerusalem and Haifa. And we're contacting our family weekly or daily to see how they're doing." In the words of Mark, "Israel is where my family came from, so it's devastating for me. I don't want my family in Israel to die." "My uncles and aunties still live there," said Stella, "so it matters to me a lot because it's just sad to see my family getting attacked." These children expressed deep concern for people they personally knew.

All three groups of children—those who cared about the war out of a universalist concern for human life, those who cared about the war out of a particularist concern for Jews, and those who cared about the war because of their personal connection with loved ones in Israel—agreed that "the Israel-Gaza war is important to me" (Darya). Summing up the shared position of all of the children, Danny explained, "There's a war, and I really don't like it!"

Yet, although all of the children agreed about the *existence* of war, the children had vastly different beliefs from one another about the *nature* of this particular war. Just like American Jewish adults who generally agree that the events of October 7 were heinous and tragic but are starkly divided about Israel's response, these American Jewish children disagreed about Israel's actions in the unfolding war even as they agreed that "a lot of horrible things" (Darya) happened on October 7.

Some children believed that, because Hamas started the war, Israel's actions since October have been—by definition—right and necessary. "Everything that happens in the war is not Israel's fault, because Hamas attacked first," explained Gideon. "Hamas is a terrorist group," stated Keaton, "and the [Israeli] army didn't even want to engage in the war, but now they have to because the Hamas terrorists started it." In Gala's view, "Israel has a right to defend themselves because that was pretty trashy of Hamas to kill 1,200 people [on October 7]. I don't really blame Israel for getting them back." Otis believed that once it was attacked on October 7, "I think Israel had no other choice." These children were convinced that "Israel is doing the correct thing" in fighting the war (Naomi).

All of the children in this group believed that "Israel did the right thing to fight back" (Mia), and some also believed that, in exercising its right to self-defense, Israel needed to make painful but necessary ethical "tradeoffs" (Mia) in the midst of a difficult situation. Paz, for example, believed that Israel's actions have all been "to defend themselves" even at moments where it, too, has "killed a lot of civilians." In her view, "Israel didn't attack them [and didn't] just decide to kill civilians. They decided to fight back [and civilians have died]." Paz saw no moral equivalence between the Israeli civilian deaths on October 7 and the Palestinian civilian deaths from Israel's response. In her view, Israeli civilian deaths were unprovoked and unjustified, whereas

Palestinian civilian deaths were a tragic but necessary response to Hamas aggression. Raymond explained that even the tragic killing of seven World Central Kitchen aid workers in April, 2024 was necessary. In Raymond's view, "The US told Israel not to fire on the Gaza food aid, but Israel did . . . I think Israel must be doing it to stop the war. Israel has to get their food. So they don't have any food. That's how they're going to stop the war." In Raymond's ten-year-old mind, the ends justify the means; even Israel's horrific killing of aid workers was evidence of Israel's mandate to pursue a sustainable future free of Hamas.

Another group of children, by contrast, expressed deep skepticism about Israel's conduct in the war out of concern for the safety of civilians in Gaza. "It's an ethical issue that Israel's also bombing and killing a lot of people in Gaza," claimed Lucy, "and that's not fine because killing civilians either way is a terrible thing." Darya explained, "It makes me sad that women and children in Gaza have died because I know that Gaza people, they're not Hamas. They didn't deserve to die." These children insisted that "I feel bad for everyone, both sides" (Naftali), and this concern made them profoundly upset by Israel's actions in the war. As Addison explained, "I wish that Israel would stop bombing them. I'm not convinced Israel is doing the right thing about Gaza."

None of the children who held this position claimed that Hamas was justified on October 7 or in the ensuing war. Instead, these children expressed horror at the actions of *both* Hamas *and* Israel because they believed that each side wrought terrible human suffering. In the words of Jamie, "I think that Israel has a right to be angry with Hamas for taking their people, but I think the whole entire [war] could have been avoided without killing people." Similarly, Sage insisted that she did not support Hamas, but neither did she support Israel's actions in the war. "I know that a lot of Palestinians are starving right now in Gaza," she explained, "and I also don't support that." Children in this group shared a belief, expressed by Jacqueline: "If you're going to be in a war, it's not like the civilians are the people that are fighting in the war. If you're going to kill anybody, don't kill the people that didn't do anything. But don't kill anybody at all if you can."

These two different groups of children—those who believed that Israel's actions in the war have been justified, and those who expressed deep concern about Israel's conduct in the war—sit side by side in their Jewish day and supplementary schools. Their differing beliefs make clear that even elementary-age Jewish youth have emerging political ideologies, and those ideologies are rooted in disparate beliefs about the nature and ethics of warfare.

Children's Ideas and the Practice of Jewish Education

Upper-elementary-age Jewish children, regardless of whether they attend a day school or a supplementary school, know that "a lot of horrible things have happened" (Darya) on and since October 7. Children with different denominational, ethnic, and educational Jewish backgrounds share a basic understanding that "on October 7, a lot of people died" (Lucy) and share a sense of outrage that "it's just so wrong!" (Eden) that "Hamas started the attack [and] Hamas killed civilians" (Mia). These children, regardless of the families or synagogues in which they are being raised, also share a deep desire "for the Hamas people to give all of our hostages back" (Kai) and a hold common belief that "the most important to get out of being hostages is children, because, like, they still have a lot of more life and they don't want to be, like, traumatized for the rest of their life" (Shlomit).

Lest Jewish educators assume that thinking about the horrors of October 7 or worrying about the ongoing war and hostage crisis are the exclusive domain of teens and adults, this research clearly demonstrates that even Jewish children know and deeply care about terrible and tragic events. Educators who work with elementary age students should be particularly cognizant of the fact that many Jewish children appear to be imagining themselves in the place of the hostages, and many have a shattered sense of their own security in the wake of October 7 given their understanding that "Jewish kids are getting kidnapped" (Bryce). Long after the vast majority of child hostages had been released, children like Bryce continued to speak in the present tense about "Jewish kids getting kidnapped" and continued to imagine themselves in the place of the hostages.[3]

Yet, despite the many similarities among Jewish children, the greatest challenges that Jewish educators will face will no doubt be in managing the profound *differences* among Jewish children. The fourth and fifth graders in this study very clearly demonstrated a range of explicitly political beliefs about Israel's conduct in the war. Some children believe that "Israel is just [in its attempts to] protect itself and eliminate Hamas" (Alex), while other children "feel like Israel isn't doing the right thing" (Eve). While all of the children agree that "Hamas started the war" (Layla), they have profoundly different beliefs about whether what "happened to the Palestinian civilians"

---

3   Shlomit, like many of the other children in this study, were especially concerned about the child hostages at a time when the tragic fate of the Bibas children was still unknown.

(Sadie) since the war began is "not Israel's fault because Gaza attacked first" (Aliza) or whether "it's terrible that Israel is also killing civilians" (Eden). The children also have profoundly different ideas about whether, ultimately, "it's Israel's land, it's our land" (Piper) or whether both "Israelis (my people) and Palestinians deserve freedom" (Toby) in the land. Children—like the participants in this study who expressed this range of ideas—are in every classroom, and they are sitting side by side with each other.

Jewish educators ought not mistake children's similar ways of understanding the horrors of October 7 and the hostage crisis for a sort of apolitical naïveté; their differing ways of understanding Israel's role in the war clearly demonstrate that even young children have emerging political viewpoints. Children's developing political stances may or may not match those of their teachers, parents, or peers. Either way, educators ought to recognize children as political—not pre-political—beings. Treating children as full members of the Jewish community who are, like Jews of all ages and political persuasions, attempting to make sense of unfolding events in the world, more accurately recognizes children's capacity for sense-making. It also broadens and deepens the types of classroom discourse that educators can employ with elementary age students.

Challenging Common Assumptions

The data from this study challenge two commonly held assumptions in Jewish education. The first is a common belief about what kinds of children have deep Jewish knowledge, assuming that day school students typically have more sophisticated understanding of contemporary Jewish life than supplementary school students. The second is a prevailing idea about children's capacity for political engagement, imagining elementary-age children as not yet ready to engage with contentious political issues. The ideas and beliefs of children in this study reveal a much more complicated picture.

Because day school students are studying in a more immersive Jewish environment than supplementary school students, a casual observer might assume that Jewish children in a synagogue supplementary school setting would know less about the events of October 7 than Jewish children in a Jewish day school. This study clearly demonstrates that this is not the case: "low information" and "high information" children are found in both settings. While all of the children in this study shared a basic understanding of the events of October 7, some children—in both day and supplementary schools—knew only broad brushstrokes, and some children—in both supplementary and day schools—had detailed knowledge of specific October 7 atrocities, specific hostages, and specific events in the ensuing months of war. The type of school that children attended seemed to have very little bearing on the depth and level of their understanding of October 7 and its aftermath.

This is because Jewish education, no matter how immersive, is only one setting where children are learning about the events of October 7. Children are in conversation with their parents and grandparents, overhearing the radio (set to a wide variety of channels) during carpool, browsing all over the internet, and encountering protests and counter-protests in their neighborhoods. Children report stitching together a larger understanding from a patchwork of sources, most of which occur *outside* of Jewish institutions. Assuming that the school type—no matter whether it is a day or a supplementary school—is the primary influence on a child's understanding of October 7 ignores children's agency in constructing an understanding of events based on the wide variety of inputs they encounter in their daily lives. As Kelman (2024) explains, "education is everywhere" (p. 139), and children learn both in their schools and from a wide variety of sources and experiences that they encounter. A teacher walking in to a day school classroom who assumes incorrectly that all children have high levels of knowledge may be ill-prepared to engage in conversation with the children who only have hazy details of events, while a supplementary school teacher assuming her students won't know very much may be blindsided by the disturbing details that may come up in conversation.

The assumptions about what children *do* know are complicated even further by differences in the underlying beliefs about what children *should* know. Another, equally problematic, common assumption is that children are just too young to understand or grapple with the highly politicized nature of the post-October 7 world. Contested questions about the ethics and strategies of warfare are relegated to the teen years, and children are "protected" from having to grapple with these matters in their Jewish classrooms. Yet the data in this study show that children are *already* thinking about the horrors of October 7, the ongoing hostage crisis, and the continued violence and war. They are *already* grappling with profound questions about communal responsibility and morality. When they do so, Jewish children—much like the adults in their communities—are drawing vastly different conclusions about Israel's role in the unfolding war.[4]

---

[4] This is both similar to previous work that has shown that young children are capable of thinking about war, and also strikingly different in that children's beliefs about war are more explicitly political than previously understood. See Zakai (2019, 2022).

Despite their shared concern about the state of the hostages, Jewish children do *not* hold a uniform set of beliefs and commitments as they think about the war. Children's conceptions of the war are overtly political, and there are children who attend both day and supplementary schools who take right-leaning positions as well as children from both school contexts who take left-leaning positions. The former prioritize Israeli security, the eradication of Hamas, and the return of the hostages. The latter privilege the safety of civilians of all nationalities, the cessation of violence, and the return of the hostages. Perhaps most striking of all, children's political beliefs about the nature of the war do not always mirror the predominant adult culture of their schools and communities. Schools embedded in synagogue communities with predominantly left-leaning adult discourse include children who express right-leaning positions, and vice versa. These children are developing their own beliefs about the ethics of war and the rights of Israelis and Palestinians, and these beliefs have an explicit political valence. Thus, educators should not assume that children hold beliefs that align with their own or with the loudest or most commonly held positions of the community's adult population.

Conclusion

As a whole, Jewish children appear to be united by two common positions: a belief that October 7 and its aftermath "really matters to me" (Dalia) and a conviction that "it's just so wrong" to hold civilians—and especially children—as hostages. All of the children we have interviewed, regardless of the homes and schools in which they are being raised, are worried about and are paying attention to October 7 and the ensuing events. All of these children express deep concern for the hostages, and many spend considerable time imagining what it would be like if they or their loved ones were held in captivity. Some children understand broad brushstrokes about the atrocities of October 7 and the ongoing war, and others can recount specific, disturbing details. Both of these types of children are present in the classrooms of both Jewish day and Jewish supplementary schools. Jewish educational institutions that are committed to caring for the emotional well-being of children will need to account for the fact that Jewish children are grappling with the atrocities and ongoing reverberations of October 7, even as they do so with varying degrees of detail.

Despite their shared commitments, Jewish children are also deeply divided about the morality of Israel's conduct as the war has unfolded. American Jewish children—much like American Jewish adults—differ in both their political ideologies and their beliefs about the ethical use of military force. Children with a range of beliefs about the war sit together in the same supplementary and day school classrooms. Political disagreements are alive not only in the broader society and on the campuses of universities, but also within the walls of Jewish elementary school classrooms. Jewish educational institutions that aspire to support children's intellectual growth along with their emerging Jewish commitments will need to make space for children to express and listen to each other's stances about the ongoing war. This will require educators to interpret children's differing ideas not just as a way of making sense of current events but also as an expression of their nascent visions of a more just and peaceful world.

References

Charmaz, K. (2006). *Constructing grounded theory: A practical guide through qualitative analysis.* Sage.

Cornish, F., Gillespie, A., and Zittoun, T. (2013). Collaborative analysis of qualitative data. In U. Flick (Ed.), *The Sage handbook of qualitative data analysis* (pp. 79–93). Sage.

Glaser, B. G., and Strauss, A. L. (1967). *The discovery of grounded theory: Strategies for qualitative research.* Aldine Transaction.

Kelman, A. Y. (2024). *Jewish Education.* Rutgers University Press.

Reingold, M., and Reznik, S. (2024). Navigating crisis together: Canadian Jews, Israel, and October 7. *Contemporary Jewry, 44*(4), 1–18. https://doi.org/10.1007/s12397-024-09572-8

Wineburg, S. (2001). *Historical thinking and other unnatural acts: Charting the future of teaching the past.* Temple University Press.

Zakai, S. (2019). "Bad things happened": How children of the digital age make sense of violent current events. *The Social Studies, 110*(2), 67–85. https://doi.org/10.1080/00377996.2018.1517113

Zakai, S. (2022). *My second-favorite country: How American Jewish children think about Israel.* New York University Press.

Trauma Reach and Response: Teacher and Parental Reports of the Impact of October 7 and School Programming on North American Jewish Day School Students

Rona Milch Novick and Jenny Isaacs

Introduction

The terrorist attacks on Israel on October 7 were immediately and widely recognized as having a significant impact on Jews in the diaspora (Diaz, 2024). In the months after October 7, many North American day schools added to their regular curricula and co-curricular activities a variety of opportunities for students to respond to the horrific events (Cochran, 2023; Reingold and Reznik, 2024). This included special prayer services, participation at rallies and in charity events, and lessons on Israeli history. Schools were challenged to do so in the face of their varied constituencies which might include Israeli families, families with strong connections to Israeli relatives, anxious and vulnerable students and adults, individuals with differing ideological and political views as well as the relatively unaffiliated. Decisions made about how to respond to the unfolding situation, and considerations of which educational approaches were most appropriate were, out of necessity, made with little or no information about the impact the events of October 7 had on Jewish day school students. The authors of this research project were interested in contributing to our understanding of the North American Jewish student experience of the events and the approaches of their schools, as seen by both parents and teachers.

While educators and educational leaders sensed that North American Jewish students were impacted, there was little data available. One study of Jewish students aged from nine to eleven years in ten Jewish day and supplemental schools in California reported students stated that they feel scared and worried; and were emotionally concerned about the news they were hearing (Applebaum and Zakai, 2024).They voiced particular distress about Hamas's attacks on civilians and could imagine themselves in that horrific situation, especially given that children had also been taken hostage. Similarly, an exploration of a select group of Canadian Jewish day school students and young alumni documented experiences of being "overwhelmed" by both media coverage and anti-Israel and antisemitic social media responses, as well as a strong appreciation for the sense of community that their Jewish school (students) or dedicated WhatsApp social media group (alumni) provided (Reingold and Reznik, 2024).

Trauma From a Distance: Research Background

The phenomena of vicarious traumatization have been well documented, but largely for adults and most frequently referring to the traumatization that caretakers (i.e., therapists, teachers, emergency personnel) experience in providing post-trauma care (Motta, 2012). Research has documented transmission of trauma from family members to children, including Holocaust survivors (Greenfield et al., 2022, Kassai and Motta, 2006), veterans (Suozzi and Motta, 2004), family members of those with a serious illness (Libov et al., 2002), and children of parents with serious emotional disturbance (Lombardo and Motta, 2008). Motta (2012) defined secondary trauma, as opposed to the vicarious trauma which often refers to that of professional caregivers, as the transfer and acquisition of negative affective and dysfunctional cognitive states as a function of prolonged and extended contact with others who directly experienced the trauma. This definition includes more than helping professionals, but still involves close contact with those in the trauma epicenter.

Research following the 2011 terrorist car bombing in Oslo found evidence of secondary or vicarious traumatization without direct contact with victims. Even amongst those not present at the time of the car bombing, those who perceived their life in danger reported higher degrees of PTSD (post-traumatic stress disorder; Heir et al., 2016). Another agent of potentially indirect trauma impact has been identified as moral injury. Studying protesters' exposure to potentially morally injurious events (PMEIs), including a sense of betrayal by once trusted leaders, Levi-Belz and colleagues (2023) found over ten percent of frequent protesters met criteria for PTSD. An expanded view of PMEIs includes indirect exposure to the transgressive behaviors of others, including their immoral actions (Zerach and Levi-Belz, 2020), for which the October 7 acts of Hamas would qualify.

Trauma impact may also be generalized across those with shared culture or identity. Studies of US emergency personnel post the 9/11 World Trade Center attacks demonstrated a powerful impact regardless of whether such workers were present (Lee and Olshfski, 2002). Morrison and Morrison (2024) suggest that shared identity with those directly impacted facilitates the transmission of trauma to others, creating a communal or cultural pathway for traumatization, and urge that trauma be understood not only as an individual but a communal phenomenon.

An additional mechanism for spreading trauma beyond those present is media exposure. Popper and colleagues (2007), studying media exposure after the 9/11 attacks, provide evidence for a direct association between television viewing and increased stress and trauma. Other research, while recognizing that with children the issue includes the role of parental monitoring and overall exposure to violence and trauma, indicates that media exposure has a substantial impact on traumatization (Singer et al., 2004). Perhaps the most compelling finding is that trauma and fear results when rhesus monkeys watch videos of other monkeys displaying fear, even if they have no prior contact with either the fearful monkeys themselves, or with the object of their fear (Mineka and Zinbarg, 2006).

Trauma from a Distance: The Jewish School Perspective

For all the above reasons, it would seem reasonable to assume that North American Jewish day school students could experience the events unfolding in Israel on October 7 and the three months following as traumatic. In many cases they witnessed their parents' and teachers' stress and trauma. Many Jewish schools hire Israeli teachers through organized programs that aim to build Israel-diaspora connections such as the World Zionist Organization Shlichut Program. Others may recruit Israeli expats because of their fluency in and ability to teach Hebrew. It is also likely that students were exposed to media stories and images directly or heard about them from peers or adults. Applebaum and Zakkai (2024), in their interviews with Jewish students in the months following October 7, quote one student who said she "can't bear to see" what's happening and voiced her desire that at school and home adults would provide her safe spaces where she need not think about it. One participant in the qualitative research of Reingold and Reznik (2024) echoed this sentiment, saying; "the news is terrifying, and I don't like watching it." The same student, who had seen social media as a safe space to connect and unwind, then commented "nothing was censored, and I would watch videos not realizing how traumatizing they were to watch." This sentiment was shared with the first author, on an educators' mission to Israel in January 2024. On a visit to Ofakim, a community that suffered significant attacks and loss of life on October 7, a teenager spontaneously offered that, if he were a parent, he would not allow his children or teens to have cell phones because of the horrible and distressing images regarding the attacks and war that were often disseminated.

Most certainly, Jewish students struggled also with the moral injury of hearing about the brutal violence perpetrated and threatened against their cultural group. Although the antisemitism and pro-Palestinian rhetoric and demonstrations became extremely prominent in the spring of 2024, as early as January, the American Jewish Congress survey of American adults found over forty percent reported feeling less safe as a Jew (AJC, 2024). Brym's 2024 survey of Canadian Jews similarly found a pervasive sense of feeling unsafe and victimized. The general perception was that negative attitudes toward Jews have escalated and are unlikely to improve.

In addition to exposure through family connections and media, Jewish schools' actions may have kept the October 7 attacks and their after-effects in students' consciousness. Schools rightly understood the healing and protective properties of community, agency, and spirituality in times of trauma (Hobfoll et al., 2007; Worthington et al., 2024) and engaged students in communal prayer, charity projects, and advocacy. These school approaches were consistent with research on effective community trauma interventions, however, Hobfoll and colleagues (2007) also identify the potential downside of what they dub the "pressure-cooker phenomenon" which occurs when too much discussion and repetitive presentation of horrific acts can increase anxiety or depression.

The current authors sought to explore several areas of potential impact of the October 7 terrorist attack on the North American Jewish day school and supplemental school population. In addition to quantifying the extent of secondary traumatization in the form of increased anxiety, fearfulness, and other mental health indicators, we hoped, through parent and teacher reports, to get a sense of the impact on students' Jewish identity, spiritual beliefs, and connection to Israel. We also collected information about school responses, including the variety and amount of programming offered, in order to explore the nature and breadth of school approaches.

Methodology

The current study asked parents of Jewish children and teachers of students in United States or Canadian Jewish day schools to report on the impact that the events of October 7, 2023, had on their children and students, respectively. Quantitative surveys with several open-ended questions were completed between January to early February 2024. Data were collected from 368 parents reporting on their most impacted child and 116 teachers (47% Jewish Studies, 36% general studies, and 17% both) who reported on their overall student body. The sample was comprised mostly of parents and teachers of students attending Orthodox Jewish day schools, by their self-report (over 85% of the sample). Table 3.1 displays the grade distribution of children rated by parents and the grades of the students rated by teachers. Parents reported on male and female children equally, focusing the least on children pre-K or younger, but they selected children more evenly distributed across the remaining grades. Teachers often taught across multiple grades; and, like parents, they taught and rated fewer pre-K or younger children, but the vast majority of students were more evenly allocated across kindergarten to twelfth grade.

Parents reported on their connections to individuals in Israel and home activities including the frequency of their child's engagement in prayers, communications, advocacy, and charity activities at home or in the community, particularly related to October 7, Israel, or antisemitism. Teachers also were asked about their students' engagement in similar activities at school.

The remaining measures were given to both parents and teachers in a similar manner, focusing on the child or children they were reporting on. The first set of questions focused on the impacts of the events of October 7, the ongoing situation in Israel, and antisemitism, as well as how the children's responses changed over time (i.e., lessened or increased).

A series of measures focused on problematic behavior and experiences among the children. Five questions addressed children's media consumption regarding the events in Israel and antisemitism, focusing on excessive engagement or "doom scrolling." Ten questions were included assessing trauma reactions such as symptoms of worry, obsession, and avoidance related to the events in Israel and antisemitism. In addition, a twelve-item symptom checklist assessed how children's behavior has changed since October 7, evaluating anxiety, somatization, depression/hopelessness, attention/concentration/hyperactivity, withdrawal, and anger/irritability symptoms.

The research also sought to understand the impact of October 7 and the following events on religion and spirituality, as well as Jewish identity and connection to Israel. Seven items were created to assess perceptions of changes in children's concerns and questions about religion, as well as their engagement in prayer and other religious practices since October 7. Finally, we examined positive and negative aspects of Jewish identity and connection to Israel with seven items tracking changes in student views of antisemitism, Jewish identity, and Israel.

Results

Connected Communities

The sample included families with strong connections to Israel. Among the parents, 59% indicated they had immediate family living in Israel (i.e., parent, sibling, and/or child) and 33% indicated they had extended family there (i.e., aunt/uncle and/or cousin), totaling nearly 80% reporting they had family members living in Israel. In addition, several parents indicated they had grandparents, friends, or much of their extended family residing in Israel, highlighting how directly impacted their families were by events in Israel.

On the global measures (i.e., how impacted were children/students), both parents and teachers reported a notable impact of the events in Israel on October 7, the ongoing situation in Israel, and antisemitism. When teachers were asked to share their perception of how many of their students were impacted 30% said that many or virtually all students were impacted, 56% said few or some, and only 14% said that none were. Regarding the degree of impact, around half of teachers and parents said their sense was that children were moderately to significantly impacted, while only 19% of teachers and 12% of parents perceived the children were barely impacted.

Broad Effects

Parents often commented on the effect of the events of October 7 on their children. One parent indicated that they felt "sad because I don't want [my child] to not have an *aba* [dad] . . . We also sheltered a family from Israel for two months, so our house was impacted in a unique way." Another parent indicated that

> My child was in Israel on October 7 with the family. He always had a fear of war breaking out even though we visit frequently. The morning of October 7 was a nightmare come true. He began to vomit after the third siren and had a panic attack. It was a very difficult couple of days for him. Since then both my husband and myself have been back to Israel multiple times. He was extremely nervous while we were there. He also has a sister who is there and expresses concern for her.

Quotes like the one above highlight the amount of worry that children and their families expressed. This sentiment was echoed in both parents' and teachers' responses. Table 3.2 shows the breakdown in parent and teacher reports of their sense of the extent that children were experiencing worry. Nearly 75% of parents indicated that their most affected child expressed worry about the events in Israel, 80% reported their child worried about the safety of individuals in Israel, and over half said their child expressed worry about their own safety or the safety of their family or local community, even outside of Israel. Regarding teacher reports, 34–38% said some of their students reported the three concerns above, while over a third of teachers thought many or most of their students expressed worry about the events in Israel and the safety of individuals in Israel, and 13% thought many or most of their students expressed worry about their own safety or the safety of their family or local community.

Parents and teachers rated children regarding the religious and spiritual effects October 7 had on children. The breakdown of ratings is displayed in Table 3.3. Four items reflected more conflicted attitudes about God and prayer. Both parents and teachers failed to see reductions in these negative experiences and a majority thought no change had occurred since October 7. However, 30% or more of parents and teachers thought children had shown increases in asking questions about God's role in the world and why bad things were happening to good people. They did not perceive similar escalation in children's feelings that prayer was not helpful or in children's expression of anger towards God, with both remaining fairly stable. When examining positive religious and spiritual effects, 39–56% of parents and teachers thought children had not changed since October 7, but around 40–60% of parents and teachers stated that children were increasingly expressing that prayer was helpful and they perceived the children as more committed to prayer and other religious practices.

Parents and teachers also rated children regarding their negative and positive sense of Jewish identity and connection to Israel since October 7. The breakdown of ratings is displayed in Table 3.4. Both parents and teachers believed children generally either showed no difference or became more likely to talk about antisemitism, show fear of identifying or being identified as Jewish, and fear about visiting Israel. Most notably, well over half of parents (63%) and teachers (75%) indicated that children were remarking or talking about antisemitism more than before October 7. However, regarding expressing negative views of Israel, parents (82%) and teachers (65%) mostly reported no difference since October 7, with the remaining parents and teachers being somewhat more likely to say children had expressed less negative views of Israel, compared to escalating negative views of Israel. For the positive items regarding Jewish identity and connection to Israel, both parents and teachers often felt children demonstrated no changes or they had an increasing sense of pride in their Jewish identity, positive views of Israel, and desire to visit Israel. In fact, over half of parents (60%) and teachers (75%) agreed that children were expressing a more positive view of Israel since October 7. This demonstrates that children may have complex views of their Jewish identity and connection with Israel, concurrently experiencing both fear and connection, pride and apprehension.

Understanding the Correlation between Impact, Exposure, and Adjustment

Teacher and parent reports of impact and exposure correlated significantly with many of the adjustment measures. Table 3.5 displays the correlations of teacher and parent reported impact measures and media exposure with home and school activities and child adjustment.

Teacher reports of the number of students that were impacted and the degree of impact were moderately positively correlated with the amount of school activities offered related to the events of October 7, Israel, or antisemitism, and students' positive views of their Jewish identity and connection to Israel. This suggests that, when teachers believed more students were impacted and the impact was more pronounced, that schools tended to engage their students more in prayer, communications with individuals in Israel, advocacy, and charity to support individuals in Israel. With regards to Jewish identity and connection to Israel, teacher reports of more widespread and intense impact were also related to teachers indicating their students felt more pride in their Jewish identity and an increased positive view and desire to visit Israel.

Simultaneously, teachers reported that both the breadth and intensity of impact among their students was strongly positively related to social or other media use and trauma symptoms, and, to a lesser extent, negative problematic mental health symptoms. This meant that, when teachers believed many students were impacted and the impact was more intense, students were much more likely to be engrossed in media coverage of the war and preoccupied with thinking about and discussing the war. Teachers who reported greater impact also thought students were more traumatized by the events of October 7, Israel, or antisemitism, displaying notably higher levels of excessive worry, obsession, and sometimes even avoidance of the topic. Although less pronounced, teacher reports of greater impact on their students were associated with some elevations in mental health symptoms like anxiety, somatization, depression, and inattention. One notable exception was that teacher reports of impact were not correlated with their perceptions of challenges to student's religiosity (e.g., feeling prayer is not helpful or expressing anger towards God) or Jewish identity and negative connection to Israel (e.g., being fearful of being identified as Jewish or visiting Israel). The strongest correlations were between teacher reports of impact with media exposure and trauma ($rs \geq .55$).

Parent reports of the degree of impact the events of October 7, Israel, or antisemitism had on their most impacted children were similar to teachers' reports in many ways. Like teachers, parents also believed that, when their child was more profoundly impacted, they engaged in more pro-Israel supportive activities (in the home and community), had more intense media usage, and strongly displayed more trauma symptoms. However, parents reported that more severely impacted children had even more intense mental health symptoms, but the association with positive views of their Jewish Identity and connection to Israel were no longer evident. In contrast to the teacher reports, parents with children they believed were more intensely impacted reported that their children tended to have more negative views of their Jewish identity and connection to Israel, as well as more challenges to their spiritual and religious beliefs. The strongest correlation with parent reports of impact was with trauma ($r = .53$).

Both teacher and parent reports of media exposure to events related to October 7 were significantly positively correlated with all measures of adjustment. This includes positive aspects like home- or school-based activities meant to support Israel's efforts, positive spirituality and religiosity, as well as a positive Jewish identity and connection to Israel. Conversely, greater media exposure was also related to observed increases in trauma, mental health symptoms, challenges to spirituality and religiosity, and increased negative Jewish identity and connection to Israel, whether rated by teachers or parents. The strongest correlations were between teacher reports of media exposure and trauma symptoms ($r = .73$), followed by parent reports of the same ($r = .52$).

Discussion

The findings of the current study certainly underscore the need to recognize that students attending Jewish day schools are part of a global Jewish community and may be significantly impacted by events that happen at a great distance. They add to the body of research that documents the impacts of vicarious trauma, even when individuals are not present at the site of the traumatic event (Heir et al., 2016; Motta, 2012). As Lee and Olshfski (2002) found in assessing trauma impact among first responders after 9/11, belonging to a specific community is sufficient to create vicarious traumatization. The respondents in the current study were members of a unique "community," in that families choosing to send their child to a Jewish school are likely more connected to Jewish communal, national, and international issues than the general Jewish population and view their identity as being part of the Jewish community. A further unique characteristic of the current sample was the rather striking percentage of survey participants with first degree relatives in Israel. This suggests a blurring of the Israel/diaspora distinction and the globalization of Jewish connections that may contribute to strong ties of community and belonging but also create vulnerabilities for vicarious traumatization.

Broad Impact

Whether reported by parents or teachers, there was broad and significant observed impact of the events of October 7 and its aftermath on North American students. The authors made a deliberate choice to have parents describe their most impacted child, while teachers reported on their students, in the aggregate. This allowed for consideration of those most affected, as well as a sense of overall impact. It is not surprising therefore that over half of the responding parents indicated that their child had significant worry, and that it extended not only to the Israel situation, but to safety of themselves, their family, and the local community. That teachers found more than a third of students were concerned about Israel, and only thirteen percent were worried about local issues may be an artifact of parents' instruction to consider their most impacted child while teachers rated students on average. It should also be noted that the data collection was completed prior to the end of February 2024. The escalation of antisemitism and highly public and vocal pro-Palestinian events across North America might result in quite different findings. This limitation will be discussed further below.

Antisemitism, Connection to Israel, Spirituality, and Jewish Identity

Not surprisingly, the horrific events of October 7 and the ongoing violence may have affected children's beliefs about themselves, about Israel, and about religious concepts, in both negative and positive directions. Although both parents and teachers reported mild or major increases in children's discussions of antisemitism (over 60%) and fears of visiting Israel (over 45%), children's expression of negative views of Israel were reported by relatively few parents and teachers. Concurrently, increases in positive views of Israel and a desire to visit Israel were reported for a large percentage of the sample. Children's Jewish identification was similarly affected in multiple directions. The increase in fearfulness at identifying or being identified as Jewish that both parents and teachers reported was not as large as the number of parents and teachers who reported children's increased statements of pride in their Jewish identity. The experiencing of two seemingly conflicting reactions concurrently speaks to the complexity of children's Jewish identity, and is consistent with other research on the response to antisemitism. Leets (2002) found college students response to anti-group hate speech (either antisemitic or anti-gay) was equally divided amongst those who engaged and those who assumed a non-assertive or withdrawn stance. The engaged responses included statements affirming and defending their identity. Similarly, Creese (2024) found antisemitism amongst an Australian community correlated with increased Jewish identity. She posits a mechanism akin to cognitive dissonance at play as follows: If being identified as Jewish entails a risk, and yet people continue to choose to so identify, Jewishness must be something that is seen as intensely valuable and worthy! The findings of positive identity shifts are echoed in recent news reports of strong and growing Jewish identity in the face of antisemitism (Ouzan, 2024). Whether these phenomena were operating for the students in this sample, or the holding of two divergent views simultaneously is developmentally normative, or indicative of identity and concept formation in process in times of intense experience, is unclear. What is important is for future research and intervention to assess and address both fears and affinities, negative concerns and positive connections.

This pattern of bi-directional change held true in assessing spiritual effects of October 7. There were fairly widely endorsed escalations in children's religious questioning of God's role, of bad things happening to good people, and more moderate indications of seeing prayer as unhelpful or feeling angry towards God. At the same time, almost half the parents and teachers saw children as more interested in and committed to prayer since October 7, and reported children increasingly expressed that prayer was helpful. While both parents and teachers reported an increase in commitment to religious practices, teachers did so at greater levels, perhaps because such practices are more readily observed in the school setting. This increase in spirituality and religious practice is consistent with research on spiritual interventions in response to trauma (Captari et al., 2018; Smith et al., 2000; Worthington et al., 2024) which find such interventions support mental health and adjustment outcomes, but also facilitate increased spiritual connections and feelings of belonging and closeness to God. These are outcomes that would both promote student resilience and be mission aligned for Jewish day schools.

Relationships between Impact and Adjustment Outcomes

The many correlations between teacher and parent reports of impact and child adjustment are to be expected, given that teachers and parents would likely gauge the degree and extent of impact based on trauma and mental health effects in similar ways. It is interesting that teacher reports of breadth and severity of the impact did not correlate with negative measures of religious or Israel and Jewish identity. Teacher reports of impact did correlate with positive religious and Israel and Jewish identity, which might be a result of schools with a preexisting strong approach to these areas experiencing more impact, or, as will be discussed below, may relate to how schools and communities addressed the events of October 7.

In addition to adjustment measures, school and home responses to October 7 also related to the degree of impact. Whether there is any causal relationship, or its direction, is impossible to determine from the current data. Did schools and families, sensing their students/children were significantly impacted, offer more programming, or did the engagement in post-October 7 programming facilitate increased or continued impact?

Recipe for Resilience: A Balancing Act

The events of October 7 and its aftermath presented a significant challenge to Jewish day schools. Among their curricular goals is often creating connection with and empathy for Jews worldwide, as well as facilitating connections with Israel and fostering Jewish identity. In offering October 7 related programming, they aim to promote these goals but are also concerned about the potential of escalating students' anxieties and worries. This dilemma is illustrated in the statements of teachers on the open-ended survey questions:

> The students that were in Israel when the war broke out are much more affected by the trauma that came along with it. Students who were in the US seemed to have coped much quicker with more ease and they almost enjoy speaking about it because it gives them purpose.

Another teacher remarked:

> In general, we tend to focus on Israel and the situation only at certain times. We try to emphasize normalcy and control over our surroundings. We do not want to traumatize the students. That said, if the topic of Israel does come up, the conversation can be loud and difficult to end. There are a lot of pent-up thoughts and feelings and the students are holding them inside.

Reflecting on the change in students and school response, one teacher in an all-girls school wrote:

> I think, in October, the reactions were much stronger. We had regular Kumzits [spiritual singing sessions] and I saw tears almost every day for the first week or two. Obviously, now, three months into the war, that's changed. But our girls are still very concerned about their friends and relatives in Israel and their Davening [praying] has been incredible.

Parents had a unique view of the potentially negative impact of well-intentioned school activities, as indicated by this mother who said her child:

> was particularly affected by large posters of hostages put up at her school. She had a panic attack and was scared to go to school because looking at all the images of all 250 hostages was so upsetting.

That schools were aware of the need to consider the impact of their approaches was demonstrated when a school leader informally shared that, in planning for the one-year anniversary of October 7 and Simchat Torah festivities, a conscious decision was made to avoid including hostage pictures, which might be overwhelming, especially for young students, and instead one yellow chair would be placed at the school assembly.

Schools were challenged to strike the right balance as they provided programming that would be consistent with best practices in communal trauma situations. Hobfoll and associates' (2007) review of communal post-traumatic approaches recognizes the critical role schools can and should play. They identify five critical elements, not specific to schools, distilled from the literature on effective interventions which includes promoting 1) a sense of safety, 2) calming, 3) a sense of self– and community efficacy, 4) connectedness, and 5) hope. Considering how this applies with children and the unique role of schools, Saltzman and colleagues (2006) explain that schools allow children to participate in age-appropriate rituals with adult guidance, to see grief modeled appropriately, and to gain some agency in planning and implementation of activities.

Jewish schools, in addition to responding to the trauma as it unfolded and continued, have a clear mission to foster Jewish identity, often including a connection to the global Jewish community and Israel, in particular. Schools were tasked with the delicate balancing of these mission driven goals with the evidence of student impact they were witnessing.

The Benefit of Multiple Perspectives

The overall pattern of responses from parents and teachers were largely similar, with two important differences. First, parents reported more intense mental health symptoms. This may be an artifact of parents reporting on their most impacted child vs. teachers reporting on students in general, or it may reflect parents' greater observation of mood changes, anxiety, and sleeping and other difficulties that may be difficult for teachers to assess. Second, there were instances in which parents' comments revealed that they witnessed some powerful impacts of trauma on children's behavior during non-school times:

> My child refused to wear a kippah (which every male in our family always wears) when we went to a museum and took the subway. He expressed that he was afraid. He walks to his yeshiva every morning from our house and will not put on his kippah until he gets to school. He did not ever express this concern until after October 7.

One parent noted the challenge of their child's exposure to heated rhetoric:

> He is very strong and proud Jew, but it is hard for a frum [religiously observant] kid who has been in a Jewish school since kindergarten to suddenly have to walk into the science building where a bunch of ne'er-do-wells are pumping their fist in the air calling for the death of the Jews.

Another parent provided evidence of her child's increasing apprehension about the safety of being Jewish:

> My child (8 yr old) wears a Jewish star necklace my in-laws bought her. I see her tuck it under her shirt in public places. And the first time she tucked it under, she commented, "I think I should hide it because people don't like Israel" [after October 7].

The unique perspectives of parents can play an important role as schools navigate the challenge of providing programming that drives their mission of fostering Jewish identity and serves to lessen trauma impact.

A Shared Concern: Media Exposure

One area of clear agreement between parents and teachers was the impact of media exposure. Consistent with earlier research (Propper et al., 2007; Singer et al., 2004), there was a strong correlation between engagement with media and increased mental health and trauma symptoms. Hobfoll et al. (2007) discuss how media reports' sensationalization decreases sense of safety; perhaps a deliberate choice as market research has documented that such an approach increases viewing. Pfefferbaum and colleagues (2001) suggest that those children most impacted by a trauma are most likely to spend more time engaging with trauma-related media coverage. In the current study, although media engagement related to children's religious beliefs and behavior, their Jewish identity, and connection to Israel, it correlated with both positive and negative items in those areas. Children's increased media consumption may have both increased their concerns and fearfulness and fostered their identity and connection to Israel. Perhaps, the same mechanisms proposed by Creese (2007) were at play, i.e., children consider it must be very valuable to be Jewish given that, despite the danger, many proudly continue and celebrate their Jewish identity. Another possibility is that perception of media as anti-Israel or anti-Jewish may have invoked children's impetus to "own" and defend Israel and Jewish connections.

Limitations

The current study provides a view of a specific population at a specific point in time during a trauma that has continued beyond what most would have hoped. As such, generalizability to other populations, or assumptions that the findings would be replicated today are not assumed. The data is also comprised of teacher and parent reports; two important sources of information about children's well-being. However, without responses from children directly, there is a risk of both under- and over- or misreporting children's experiences and certainly their inner feelings. Despite these limitations, the authors believe there is significant value in the snapshot this data provides. In the near aftermath of trauma, any information that can inform parent and school choices and add to an understanding of children's experiences can be extremely useful.

Conclusions

This exploration of the impact of October 7 on North American day school students, as expressed by their parents and teachers, provides a snapshot of a moment in global Jewish history. Clearly, parents and teachers viewed students as significantly impacted in ways that affected their local sense of safety as well as their concern for their family, friends, and Jews in the State of Israel. Schools provided an array of curricular and co-curricular vehicles for resilience building and development of positive Jewish identity, spirituality and connection to Israel. A delicate balance is likely necessary as schools are comprised of varied constituencies with diverse vulnerabilities and needs. Perhaps approaches which allow students and families to "opt in" to participate, or choose from a variety of activities will be most helpful. Given that schools are not observing the same religious and identity challenges or mental health impacts that parents are, a more integrated and holistic approach may prove worthwhile. Clearly, communication between home and school will be important in understanding all students' responses and needs, and in titrating the dose of information and programming provided to benefit all.

The current study offers a static, snapshot view of North American Jewish day school student responses to October 7. At the time of this writing, it is over 450 days since the initial trauma of October 7, and the trauma of unreturned and in some cases murdered hostages and war casualties continues. Students have likely been unable to avoid uncomfortable images, and may have experienced directly, either on visits to Israel or in their home communities, difficult and painful situations. The impact of this ongoing trauma certainly requires further study.

In addition to personal exposure, students have also been unlikely to escape media coverage, sometimes sensationalized and hostile. The current findings align with prior research regarding the role of media consumption in trauma situations (Motta, 2012; Singer et al., 2004). A greater understanding of the role of media in traumatic impact for children, as well as the potential of media-literacy or similar training to mediate such impact will be critical. Such research could inform parental and school efforts to educate students about media exposure and contribute to creating home and school spaces for children to process what they see, hear, and experience in developmentally appropriate ways.

Jewish day schools and Jewish families will, unfortunately, likely face future traumas and tragedies. They will do so as part of an interconnected global community in the context of a media system that is virtually impossible to avoid. Understanding the impact of even distant trauma on students, and providing varied approaches to meet diverse needs, will be important in supporting students' growth.

References

American Jewish Congress (2024). Majority of American Jews feel less safe after October 7 Hamas terror attack. *American Jewish Congress Global Voice*, January 11. https://www.ajc.org/news/majority-of-american-jews-feel-less-safe-after-october-7-hamas-terror-attack

Applebaum, L., and Zakai, S. (2024). Learning from children's ideas about October 7th and the Israel-Hamas war. *Jewish Educational Leadership*, 23(1), https://www.lookstein.org/journal-article/f_24/learning-from-childrens-ideas-about-october-7th-and-the-israel-hamas-war/

Brym, R. (2024). Jews and Israel 2024: A Survey of Canadian attitudes and Jewish perceptions. *Canadian Jewish Studies / Études Juives Canadiennes*, 37, 12–19. https://doi.org/10.25071/1916-0925.40368

Captari, L. E., Hook, J. N., Hoyt, W. T., Davis, D. E., McElroy-Heltzel, S. E., and Worthington, E. L., Jr. (2018). Integrating clients' religion and spirituality within psychotherapy: A comprehensive meta-analysis. *Journal of Clinical Psychology*, 74(11), 1938–1951. https://doi.org/10.1002/jclp.22681

Cochran, L. L. (2023). Jewish day schools in US take up mantle for both Israeli and American students amid Gaza conflict. *The Hill*, December 15. https://thehill.com/homenews/education/4358271-jewish-day-schools-israel-hamas-gaza/

Creese, J. (2024). "We're alone in this together": The anthropology of fear and Jewish attitudes to anti-Semitism. *Journal of Modern Jewish Studies*, 23(1), 5–25. https://doi.org/10.1080/14725886.2022.2142774

Diaz, E. (2024). How Oct. 7 Changed American Jews. *New York Times*, October 6, A, 7.

Greenfeld, D., Reupert, A., Harris, N., and Jacobs, N. (2022). Between fear and hope: The lived experiences of grandchildren of holocaust survivors: A qualitative systematic literature review. *Journal of Loss and Trauma*, 27(2), 120–136. https://doi.org/10.1080/15325024.2021.1905320

Heir, T., Blix, I., and Knatten, C. K. (2016). Thinking that one's life was in danger: perceived life threat in individuals directly or indirectly exposed to terror. *British Journal of Psychiatry*, 209(4), 306–310. https://doi:10.1192/bjp.bp.115.170167

Hobfoll, S. E., Watson, P., Bell, C. C., Bryant, R. A., Brymer, M. J., Friedman, M. J., Friedman, M., Gersons, B. P., de Jong, J. T., Layne, C. M., Maguen, S., Neria, Y., Norwood, A. E., Pynoos, R. S., Reissman, D., Ruzek, J. I., Shalev, A. Y., Solomon, Z., Steinberg, A. M., and Ursano, R. J. (2007). Five essential elements of immediate and mid-term mass trauma intervention: empirical evidence. *Psychiatry*, 70(4), 283–369. https://doi.org/10.1521/psyc.2007.70.4.283

Kassai, S. C., and Motta, R. W. (2006). An investigation of potential Holocaust-related secondary traumatization in the third generation. *International journal of emergency mental health*, 8(1), 35–47.

Lee, S.-H., and Olshfski, D. (2002). Employee commitment and firefighters: It's my job. *Public Administration Review*, 62(s1), 108–114. https://doi.org/10.1111/1540-6210.62.s1.19

Leets, L. (2002). Experiencing hate speech: Perceptions and responses to anti-Semitism and antigay speech. *Journal of Social Issues*, 58(2), 341–361. https://doi.org/10.1111/1540-4560.00264

Levi-Belz Y., Groweiss Y., and Blank, C. (2023). Moral injury and its mental health consequences among protesters: findings from Israel's civil protest against the government's judicial reform. *European Journal of Psychotraumatology*, 14, 2–12. https://doi:10.1080/20008066.2023.2283306

Mineka, S., and Zinbarg, R. (2006). A contemporary learning theory perspective on the etiology of anxiety disorders: It's not what you thought it was. *American Psychologist*, 61(1), 10–26. https://doi.org/10.1037/0003-066X.61.1.10

Morrison, N. M. V., and Morrison, B. W. (2024). Evaluating the evidence for interventions directed at healing collective trauma: A systematic review. *Traumatology*. Advance online publication. https://dx.doi.org/10.1037/trm0000523

Motta, R. W. (2012). Secondary trauma in children and school personnel. *Journal of Applied School Psychology, 28*(3), 256–269. https://doi.org/10.1080/15377903.2012.695767

Ouzan, F. S. (2024) A strong Jewish identity in the face of anti-Semitism. *The Jerusalem Report*, March 25.

Pfefferbaum, B., Nixon, S., Tivis, R., Doughty, D., Pynoos, R., Gurwitch, R., and Foy, D. (2001). Television exposure in children after a terrorist incident. *Psychiatry, 64*, 202–211.

Propper, R. E., Stickgold, R., Keeley, R., and Christman, S. D. (2007). Is television traumatic? Dreams, stress, and media exposure in the aftermath of September 11, 2001. *Psychological Science, 18*(4), 334–340. https://doi.org/10.1111/j.1467-9280.2007.01900.x

Reingold, M., Reznik, S. (2024). Navigating crisis together: Canadian Jews, Israel, and October 7. *Contemporary Jewry, 44*(4), 885–902. https://doi.org/10.1007/s12397-024-09572-8

Saltzman, W. R., Layne, C. M., Steinberg, A. M., and Pynoos, R. S. (2006). Trauma/grief–focused group psychotherapy with adolescents. In L. A. Schein, H. I. Spitz, G. M. Burlingame, and P. R. Mushkin (Eds.), *Psychological effects of catastrophic disasters: Group approaches to treatment* (pp. 669–730). Haworth.

Singer, M. I., Flannery, D. J., Guo, S., Miller, D., and Leibbrandi, S. (2004). Exposure to violence, parental monitoring and television as contributors to children's psychological trauma. *Journal of Community Psychology, 32*, 489–504. https://doi.org/10.1002/jcop.20015

Smith, B. W., Pargament, K. I., Brant, C., and Oliver, J. M. (2000). Noah revisited: Religious coping by church members and the impact of the 1993 Midwest flood. *Journal of Community Psychology, 28*(2), 169–186. https://doi.org/10.1002/(SICI)1520-6629(200003)28:2%3C169::AID-JCOP5%3E3.0.CO;2-I

Worthington, E. L., Jr., Walter, S. L., Schultz, T., McConnell, J. M., Palmer, M. E., Cowden, R. G., and Hill, H. (2024). Treating traumas among Christians in Nigeria: A randomized controlled field study of the Healing the Wounds of Trauma program. *Spirituality in Clinical Practice, 11*(3), 269–283. https://doi.org/10.1037/scp0000368

Zerach, G., and Levi-Belz, Y. (2021). Letter to the editor: Moral injury: A new (old) challenge for world psychiatry. *Journal of Psychiatric Research, 143*, 599–601. https://doi.org/10.1016/j.jpsychires.2020.11.020

Tables

Table 3.1 *Percentage of Children Rated across the Grades by Parents and Teachers*

Source	Pre-K or Younger	K–5th	6th–8th	9th–12th
Parent	6		24	32
Teacher	6		87	84

Note. Teachers often taught multiple grades and were asked to rate the average child they taught.

Table 3.2 *Percentages for Parent and Teacher Ratings on Worry Items for their Children and Students*

Percentages for Each Question			
Rating	Worry about the events in Israel	Worried about the safety of individuals in Israel	Worry about their own safety or their family or local community
Parent Ratings			
(1) Completely disagree	8.4	6.2	13.5
(2) Somewhat disagree	6.7	4.0	16.9
(3) Neither agree nor disagree	10.7	10.2	18.5
(4) Somewhat agree	39.9	36.2	33.7
(5) Completely agree	34.3	43.5	17.4
$M\ (SD)$	3.85 (1.21)	4.07 (1.21)	3.25 (1.30)
Teacher Reports			
(1) None of my students	6.2	4.1	22.9
(2) Very few of my students	21.6	22.7	30.2
(3) Some of my students	38.1	34.0	34.4
(4) Many of my students	20.6	19.6	10.4
(5) Most of my students	13.4	19.6	2.1
$M\ (SD)$	3.13 (1.10)	3.28 (1.14)	2.39 (1.02)

Table 3.3 *Percentages for Parent and Teacher Ratings of Religion and Spiritual Impact on Children since October 7, 2023*

Items	Source	Percentages for Each Rating				
		Much less	Slightly less	No different	Slightly more	Much more
1. Asking questions about God's role in the world	P	.7	.7	69.7	24.3	4.6
	T	3.4	0	59.6	30.3	6.7
2. Sharing questions/concerns about bad things happening to good people	P	.7	.7	61.2	28.9	8.6
	T	3.3	0	58.9	32.2	5.6
3. Expressing prayer is not helpful	P	3.3	2.0	86.8	6.6	1.3
	T	4.5	6.8	72.7	14.8	1.1
4. Expressing anger about or towards God	P	.7	1.3	92.1	5.3	.7
	T	2.2	3.4	82.0	12.4	0
5. Expressing prayer is helpful	P	.7	1.3	56.0	29.3	12.7
	T	2.2	0	46.1	40.4	11.2
6. Showing interest in or commitment to prayer	P	1.3	.7	46.4	39.1	12.6
	T	2.3	0	36.4	44.3	17.0
7. Showing commitment to religious practices (e.g., wearing tzitzit, saying blessings)	P	1.3	1.3	58.9	30.5	7.9
	T	1.1	0	39.3	43.8	15.7

Note. P = Parent, T = Teacher.

Table 3.4 *Percentages for Parent and Teacher Ratings of Jewish Identity and Connection to Israel for Children since October 7, 2023*

Items	Source	Percentages for Each Rating				
		Much less	Slightly less	No difference	Slightly more	Much more
1. Remarking or talking about antisemitism	P	0	0	36.8	44.1	19.1
	T	2.4	0	22.6	41.7	33.3
2. Indicated being fearful of identifying or being identified as Jewish	P	.7	1.5	59.9	29.2	8.8
	T	2.4	7.2	49.4	34.9	6.0
3. Expressing negative views of Israel	P	4.4	6.6	81.6	6.6	.7
	T	15.7	18.1	65.1	1.2	0
4. Expressing a fear about visiting Israel	P	.7	2.9	59.6	23.5	14.0
	T	2.4	6.0	45.8	42.2	3.6
5. Making written or oral statements of pride in their Jewish identity	P	.7	.7	56.6	30.1	11.8
	T	1.2	1.2	34.5	39.3	23.8
6. Expressing positive views of Israel	P	1.5	2.9	35.8	35.8	24.1
	T	0	1.2	24.1	31.3	43.4
7. Expressing a desire to visit Israel	P	11.0	5.9	43.4	22.1	17.6
	T	0	3.6	36.1	34.9	25.3

Note. P = Parent, T = Teacher.

Table 3.5 *Correlations of Teacher and Parent Reports of Impact and Exposure with Child Adjustment*

	Media Exposure	Home or School Activity	Trauma	Mental Health Symptoms	Negative Religiosity	Positive Religiosity	Negative Jewish Identity and Connection to Israel	Positive Jewish Identity and Connection to Israel
1. TR of number of students impacted	.55***	.25**	.59***	.20	.11	.19	.06	.29**
2. TR of degree of impact on students	.61***	.28**	.66***	.25*	.14	.23*	.08	.30**
3. PR of degree of impact on their child	.41***	.37***	.53***	.38***	.29***	.18*	.41***	.15
4. TR of media exposure	–	.27**	.73***	.33**	.32**	.39***	.34**	.37***
5. PR of media exposure	–	.21**	.52***	.23**	.19*	.23**	.38***	.26**

Note. TR = Teacher Reports, PR = Parent Reports. * $p < .05$. ** $p < .01$. *** $p < .001$.

Collective Trauma, Resilience, and Jewish Education: How German Jews Navigate Life after October 7

Maor Shani, Jana Gerber, and Marie Herb

The attacks in Israel on October 7, 2023, sent shock waves through Jewish communities worldwide, intensifying concerns about identity, security, and continuity (Bankier-Karp and Graham, 2024; Reingold and Reznik, 2024). Jewish communities' expectations for solidarity and support were, in many cases, met with unexpected animosity and intensified hostility, exacerbated by the ongoing war against Hamas in Gaza (Greenwood, 2024). In Germany, a country shaped by the Holocaust's legacy, these repercussions were especially severe. Although physically distant from the conflict, German Jews, who form Europe's third-largest Jewish community with approximately 120,000 members (DellaPergola, 2022), experienced a dramatic rise in antisemitic incidents and rhetoric linking them to the violence in Israel (Oboler et al., 2024; Fischer and Wetzels, 2024). For example, the Research and Information Centers on Antisemitism (RIAS) reported 4,782 antisemitic incidents in 2023, an 83% increase from the previous year. Notably, 2,787 of these incidents occurred after October 7, with 52% categorized as Israel-related antisemitism (Fischer and Wetzels, 2024). These acts ranged from verbal abuse to vandalism and explicit threats, fostering anxiety about openly displaying Jewish identity (Hersh, 2024).

Understanding how Jewish communities in Germany experienced the collective trauma of the October 7 attacks and the subsequent surge in antisemitism is critically important. Recent quantitative data highlight widespread exposure to antisemitism and its harmful effects on psychosocial health and daily life. For instance, a survey of the Jewish community in Hamburg, Germany's second-largest city, found that 77% of Jewish residents encountered antisemitism in the past year, with 18.4% reporting frequent occurrences (Groß et al., 2024). Chronic exposure to such incidents has also been linked to significant mental health challenges, even before October 7, with these stressors undermining well-being and social participation (Shani, Goldberg, et al., 2024). Many Jews in Germany report feelings of isolation and vulnerability, drawing historical parallels to the precariousness of Jewish life in the country (Chernivsky and Lorenz-Sinai, 2024).

Despite a growing body of research on antisemitism in Germany, relatively few studies prioritize Jewish voices, limiting a comprehensive understanding of their lived experiences. As Chernivsky et al. (2020) observe, much of the literature treats Jews as subjects "talked about" rather than "talked with." This gap is particularly acute following October 7, when Jewish communities worldwide faced heightened hostility alongside internal reconfigurations of identity, belonging, and community life. Preliminary data indicate a surge in Israel-related antisemitic incidents (Fischer and Wetzels, 2024; Groß et al., 2024; Hersh, 2024; Oboler et al., 2024), yet large-scale surveys and qualitative investigations have not fully captured how Jewish individuals in Germany navigate these challenges emotionally, socially, and behaviorally. Existing qualitative research often isolates single issues, such as psychological distress or communal resilience, neglecting the complex interplay of identity, socio-political context, and personal meaning-making shaping Jewish life in Germany.

To address these gaps, we conducted in-depth interviews with eighteen Jewish individuals from diverse backgrounds, including Israeli and non-Israeli, secular and observant, and those living in urban, rural, and semi-urban areas. Our core questions examine the emotional impact of October 7, changes in experiences of antisemitism, coping strategies, and evolving notions of Jewish identity. This chapter focuses specifically on education as a critical domain, exploring how the attacks and rising antisemitism have influenced family relationships, parenting, child-rearing, and Jewish education. Situating these themes within broader questions about identity and resilience, we analyze participants' narratives to understand how educational practices—both formal and informal—serve as practical and symbolic means of preserving Jewish identity, addressing safety concerns, and fostering resilience for future generations.

Coping with Collective Trauma: The Role of Social Identity

This study draws on the framework of collective trauma (Alexander, 2004; Eyerman, 2019), which posits that diaspora communities can experience vicarious victimization through events that occur far from their physical location. Even when individuals are not directly subjected to violence, threats to a central collective identity, such as a shared religious or national affiliation, can cause acute psychological distress. Because Jewish communities often possess deeply embedded collective memories of persecution (Hirschberger, 2018; Janoff-Bulman, 1992), contemporary hostilities may trigger dormant fears or reactions rooted in historical precedents. The result is a ripple effect: diaspora Jews in Germany, for instance, respond not only to the factual aspects of a conflict but also to the symbolic rupture in their group's sense of security and moral standing (Ben Rafael et al., 2011; Goldblum, 2024).

How do Jewish communities outside Israel experience the current collective trauma and cope with it? Social identity theory (Tajfel and Turner, 2004) provides a critical framework for understanding responses related to Jewish identity. This theory posits that individuals derive a significant portion of their self-definition from the groups to which they belong. In an environment of escalating antisemitism, social identity processes can strengthen in-group cohesion as a way to bolster members' sense of safety and belonging (Badea et al., 2011; Branscombe et al., 1999). Alongside increased identification, other coping strategies and resilience mechanisms emerge as vital elements in shaping how Jewish individuals and communities adapt to these pressures (Boyd, 2024; Lazarus and Folkman, 1984). On one hand, problem-focused responses might include organizing advocacy campaigns, disseminating factual information about the conflict, or pursuing legal action against hate speech (Bonanno and Burton, 2013; Delker et al., 2020). On the other hand, emotion-focused coping might manifest in seeking solace through religious rituals, communal prayers, or supportive networks where members can openly express anxiety and grief. These communal practices often act as bulwarks, enabling Jewish families and youth to navigate the emotional toll of being perceived as targets or scapegoats and reinforcing their collective identity in the face of external hostility (Eshel et al., 2025; Reingold and Reznik, 2024).

Closely related to resilience and aiming to understand its long-term effects, post-traumatic growth (Tedeschi and Calhoun, 2004) broadens the perspective by exploring how adversity can lead to transformative benefits. In the context of diaspora Jewry, crises may strengthen attachments to religious traditions and cultural heritage, inspire innovative communal initiatives, and foster more empathetic connections across generational lines (Eyerman, 2019; Marciano et al., 2024). While post-traumatic growth does not diminish the suffering involved, it suggests that experiencing collective fear and hostility can, under certain conditions, inspire renewed commitment to one's identity, deepen ethical reflection, and strengthen communal bonds (Eshel et al., 2025; Hirschberger, 2018; Muldoon, 2024).

Contemporary Jewish Education in Germany: Between Antisemitism and Resilience

The duality of trauma and growth is particularly evident in Germany, where the weight of Jewish history intersects with evolving diaspora realities (Chernivsky and Lorenz-Sinai, 2024). In recent decades, Jewish education in Germany has gained renewed importance, serving not only as a means of cultural or religious instruction but also as a protective resource and a locus for resilience building (Anusiewicz-Baer, 2024; Körber and Kunze, 2024). This trend reflects developments in other countries, where enrollment in Jewish schools has grown significantly following October 7. For instance, a recent poll in the United States found that sixty percent of Jewish day schools expect increased enrollment in the 2024–2025 academic year, with antisemitism in public schools cited as a primary motivator (Epstein et al., 2024).

Historically, Jewish life in Germany was widely believed to be on the verge of extinction after the Holocaust (Damm, 2008). However, major demographic shifts, particularly the influx of Russian-speaking Jews in the 1990s, followed by the emergence of Israeli expat communities now estimated at 25,000 (Zeeman, 2022), revitalized communal infrastructures, including an extensive network of Jewish schools and educational programs (Ben Rafael et al., 2011). Today, these institutions serve a critical dual function: fostering religious and cultural identity while providing an environment where children can feel relatively safe expressing that identity. Their role became even more significant after October 7, as families seeking both emotional and physical security for their children turned to Jewish day schools and informal educational frameworks (Chernivsky and Lorenz-Sinai, 2024; Fork, 2021).

Recent studies emphasize how effective Jewish schools and community-led programs can be in fostering robust social cohesion and psychological well-being, thereby mitigating the adverse effects of external hostility (Mahla, 2024; Sedoff et al., 2024). At the same time, these institutions face significant operational challenges, including shortages of qualified educators, financial pressures, and philosophical debates about how to integrate Jewish heritage within broader civic engagement (Körber and Kunze, 2024; Sinclair and Milner, 2005). Nonetheless, the events of October 7 have highlighted the critical role educational settings play in reinforcing both identity and coping mechanisms: teachers incorporate discussions of collective trauma, activism, and resilience into their curricula, linking students' personal histories to contemporary global crises (Anusiewicz-Baer, 2024).

Methods

Data Collection and Participants

Eighteen participants were recruited online through an opportunistic sampling process, ensuring diversity across key demographic and experiential dimensions. Efforts were made to include a roughly equal number of Israeli-born and non-Israeli Jewish respondents, who were expected to exhibit considerable differences in their experiences, along with variation in gender, age, length of residence in Germany, and geographic location. Table 4.1 presents participant characteristics, highlighting the diversity of backgrounds and potential experiences within the sample. Semi-structured, in-depth interviews typically lasted between sixty and ninety minutes, although some extended beyond two hours to allow participants sufficient time to share their personal narratives and reflections. All interviews were conducted virtually using the Big Blue Button platform, transcribed with the Transcriptor tool, and manually corrected for inaccuracies. Since participants spoke German, English, and Hebrew, transcripts were preserved in their original languages to retain linguistic attributes and cultural context.

Coding and Qualitative Network Analysis

Following transcription, we adopted a multi-stage coding process guided by a global theme list encompassing seven core domains: Background and Identity, Experiences and Reactions to the October 7 Events, Antisemitism and Societal Responses in Germany, Coping Strategies and Resilience, Jewish Identity Expression, Personal Growth and Community Development, and Future Perspectives and Concerns. This initial framework was refined through an iterative, open-coding approach, with two analysts independently labeling text segments and resolving discrepancies through discussion. As recommended by Miles et al. (2014), recurring ideas or repeated incidents were flagged and subsequently merged or redefined to enhance coding clarity. For instance, closely related nodes (e.g., "Interpersonal Relations" and "Interpersonal Conflict") were consolidated into a single category when their co-occurrence patterns indicated strong conceptual overlap.

To address calls for greater transparency in qualitative research and to provide a systematic approach, we incorporated a qualitative network analysis strategy (Attride-Stirling, 2001; Pokorny et al., 2018). Interviews were coded both manually and, as a supportive tool, with the assistance of advanced Large Language Models (LLMs, e.g., ChatGPT, Claude), which recent studies have demonstrated can aid in qualitative coding tasks (De Paoli, 2024; Rathje et al., 2024). All outputs generated by the LLMs were subsequently validated and refined manually. Coding outputs from each interview were reconciled and refined, enabling the creation of a comprehensive "edge list" that captured co-occurrences between codes: whenever two codes appeared within the same segment of text, they were considered connected by an edge. If two codes frequently appeared together across multiple interviews, the weight of the corresponding edge was incrementally increased. This weighted edge list was then converted into a one-mode (code-by-code) matrix, quantifying the frequency of co-occurrence between codes.

Using these data, we employed the *igraph* package in R (Csárdi et al., 2024) to analyze two network structures: the complete edge list representing the entire network and a sub-network specifically constructed for this chapter's analytical focus. The sub-network, termed the "family-education network," concentrated on themes related to education, Jewish education, family relationships, and childrearing, encompassing all edges connected to at least one code addressing these topics. This specialized network offered unique insights into how participants perceive Jewish continuity and foster resilience among younger generations. As a nested structure within the larger network, it provided a targeted perspective on how concerns about antisemitism shape parental decisions regarding Jewish educational settings and how children's experiences in Germany contribute to their evolving sense of identity.

For each network, we calculated a range of network measures and created a visual representation of the thematic structure. Each node represented a distinct code, and each weighted edge indicated how often that pair of codes was mentioned together in participants' discussions. A node's degree reflected the number of other codes it connected to, while its weighted degree revealed the total number of times it co-occurred with those connected codes. As the network was weighted, these measures accounted for both the presence and relative frequency of edges. Finally, we applied a community detection algorithm to identify clusters of codes that frequently co-occurred, revealing higher-level thematic groupings. We believe that this network-based approach facilitated a transparent and systematic examination of the overlap in participants' perspectives. By combining iterative coding with weighted network construction, we sought to preserve the depth of qualitative inquiry while visualizing and quantifying the relationships among key themes.[1]

Results

Qualitative Network Analysis

Figure 4.1 presents the network graph for the whole network of codes in the study. Centrality measures for this network are available in Table 4.2. The study's network comprises of 144 nodes (codes) connected by 526 edges. The visualization divides these codes into nine shape-coded communities: Active Engagement and Empowerment through Activism, Adaptive Coping Strategies and Emotional Support, Community Solidarity and Engagement, Concerns about Jews and Israel's Future, Emotional Turmoil and Trauma, Experiences of Antisemitism and Vigilance, Jewish Identity and Emotional Ties to Israel, Media Critique and Perceived Bias, and Social Strain and Isolation. The analysis highlighted two major clusters of themes: collective unity and fear and uncertainty. Jewish solidarity, pride in Jewish identity, and community support emerged as closely interconnected, underscoring the role of collective unity as a coping mechanism in times of uncertainty. However, this solidarity often coexisted with anxieties about public expressions of Jewish identity, reflecting fears of antisemitism and potential targeting. The second cluster revealed deep concerns about the sustainability of Jewish life in Germany, with fears of rising antisemitism and public visibility contributing to doubts about societal acceptance. Participants also described various coping strategies, including political advocacy and personal identity reflection, to navigate the emotional toll and strained social ties resulting from the crisis. Together, these findings illustrate a community grappling with external threats while seeking to preserve identity and foster resilience.[2]

A parallel analysis of the Family-Education Network (Figure 4.2) examined themes related to family, children, and education. This sub-network

---

[1] Further information on our research methodology and procedure is available in the full research report (Shani, Jana, et al., 2024).

[2] Additional results from the main analysis on the whole network are available in the full research report (Shani, Jana, et al., 2024).

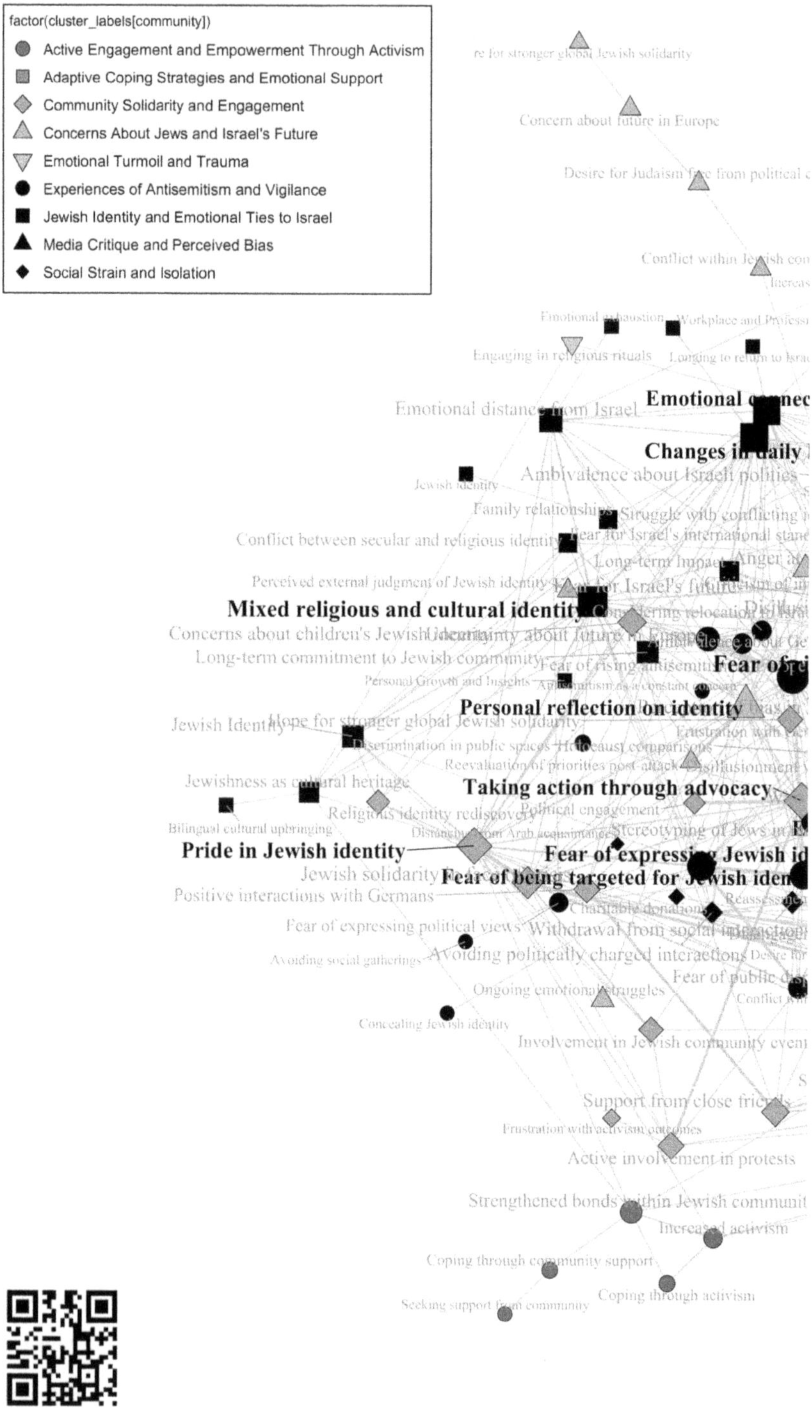
factor(cluster_labels[community])
Active Engagement and Empowerment Through Activism
Adaptive Coping Strategies and Emotional Support
Community Solidarity and Engagement
Concerns About Jews and Israel's Future
Emotional Turmoil and Trauma
Experiences of Antisemitism and Vigilance
Jewish Identity and Emotional Ties to Israel
Media Critique and Perceived Bias
Social Strain and Isolation
Concern about future in Europe
Engaging in religious rituals
Emotional distance from Israel
Jewish identity
Family relationships
Conflict between secular and religious identity
Perceived external judgment of Jewish identity
Mixed religious and cultural identity
Concerns about children's Jewish identity
Long-term commitment to Jewish community
Personal Growth and Insights
Personal reflection on identity
Hope for stronger global Jewish solidarity
Jewish Identity
Discrimination in public spaces
Holocaust comparisons
Reevaluation of priorities post-attack
Jewishness as cultural heritage
Taking action through advocacy
Religious identity rediscovery
Political engagement
Bilingual cultural upbringing
Distancing from Arab acquaintances
Pride in Jewish identity
Jewish solidarity
Fear of being targeted for Jewish identity
Positive interactions with Germans
Charitable donations
Fear of expressing political views
Withdrawal from social interactions
Avoiding social gatherings
Avoiding politically charged interactions
Ongoing emotional struggles
Concealing Jewish identity
Involvement in Jewish community events
Support from close friends
Frustration with activism outcomes
Active involvement in protests
Strengthened bonds within Jewish community
Increased activism
Coping through community support
Coping through activism
Seeking support from community

Collective Trauma, Resilience, and Jewish Education | 71

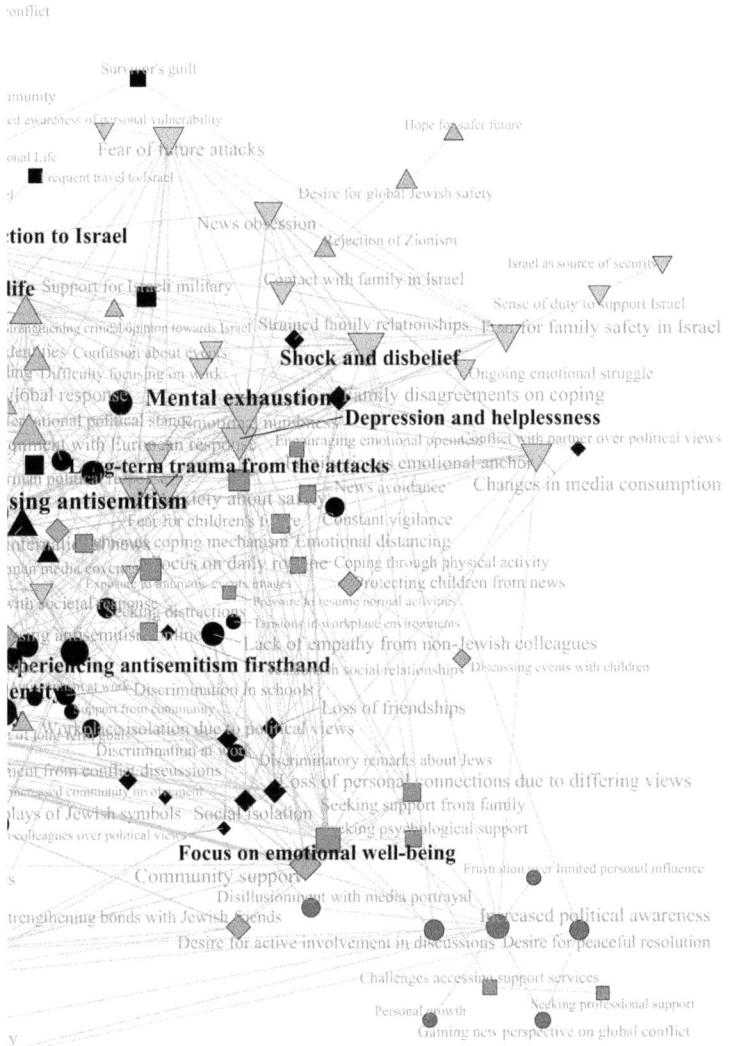

Network representation of thematic codes (nodes) and connections (edges) in the whole network
Note. The network graph includes 144 codes (nodes) connected by 526 weighted edges. Node size corresponds to degree (number of connections), while edge thickness reflects edge weight (frequency of co-occurrence). Shapes indicate distinct community clusters.

factor(cluster_labels[community])
- ● Social ruptures and isolation
- ■ Adjustments and dynamics in daily lives
- ◆ Child protection and heightened vigilance
- △ Confronting antisemitism through advocacy
- ▽ Emotional and social support networks
- ● Emotional reactions and safety concerns
- ■ Internal conflicts and identity tensions
- ▲ Jewish education as a protective resource
- ◆ Jewish identity and visibility
- ● Maintaining normalcy and daily routines

Collective Trauma, Resilience, and Jewish Education | 73

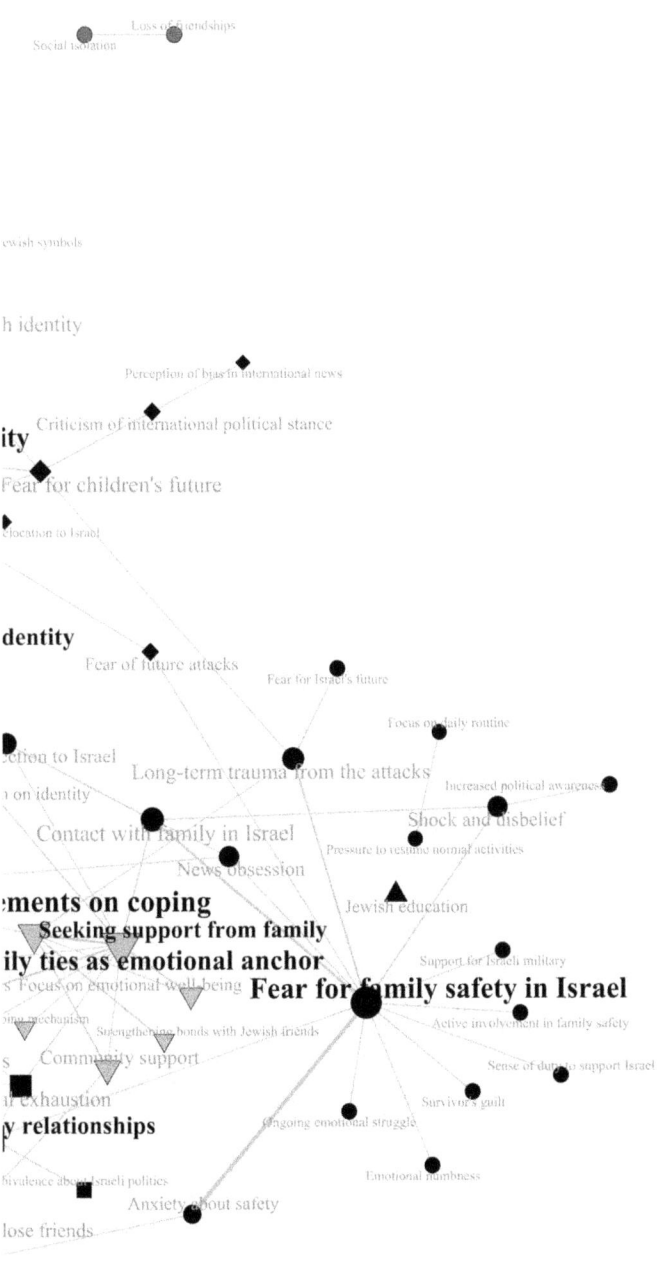

Network representation of thematic codes (nodes) and connections (edges) in the family-education network

Note. The network graph includes 71 codes (nodes) connected by 102 weighted edges. Node size corresponds to degree (number of connections), while edge thickness reflects edge weight (frequency of co-occurrence). Shapes indicate distinct community clusters.

contained 71 nodes and 102 edges, representing about half the nodes and one-fifth of the edges in the full network. These proportions suggest that issues related to family, children, and education were strongly connected to other themes and not isolated or marginal within participants' narratives. The visualization divides this network into ten communities, including social and cultural isolation, adjustments in daily lives, child protection and heightened vigilance, emotional support, advocacy, identity tensions, and Jewish education as protective resources.

A prominent cluster in the Family-Education Network (see Table 4.3) centered on emotional responses and family dynamics. The strongest thematic relationship linked anxiety about safety with fear for family safety in Israel, highlighting participants' heightened concerns for loved ones during the crisis. Similarly, family ties as emotional anchors were closely tied to seeking support from family, demonstrating the stabilizing role of familial relationships during periods of uncertainty. However, family dynamics also revealed tensions, with themes such as family disagreements on coping and loss of personal connections due to differing views reflecting the interpersonal strain caused by differing responses to the crisis.

Educational concerns formed the second most prominent cluster in this sub-network, particularly regarding children's safety and identity. The relationship between concerns about children's Jewish identity and pride in Jewish identity underscores participants' emphasis on fostering a strong cultural foundation for their children. At the same time, discrimination in schools emerged as a recurring theme, connecting with experiencing antisemitism firsthand and fear of being targeted for Jewish identity. These connections illustrate how broader societal prejudices infiltrate educational environments and contribute to participants' vulnerability.

Coping strategies intersected with interpersonal and familial strains. Themes such as contact with family in Israel connected strongly with fear for family safety in Israel and emotional connection to Israel, emphasizing the enduring role of familial ties in reinforcing cultural identity and emotional support. However, these ties also introduced additional stress as participants grappled with long-term fears tied to the crisis. Themes like encouraging emotional openness further underscored the importance of family cohesion and communication as mechanisms for coping with trauma.

Narrative Analysis

Although our interview guide did not explicitly address education, themes related to Jewish schooling, childrearing, and identity transmission emerged naturally in many participants' accounts. These discussions often arose when participants reflected on their long-term future in Germany, highlighting both the realities of diaspora life and the effects of the October 7 attacks. Parents and young adults, in particular, expressed concerns about Jewish education and identity formation as they evaluated their prospects in Germany. Younger participants also shared their thoughts on raising children, emphasizing the importance of Jewish community and educational frameworks as sources of reassurance. While these educational themes were not a primary focus of our network analysis, they underscore how a traumatic event like October 7 can influence educational decisions and practices within the German-Jewish community. These findings reveal evolving trends in contemporary Jewish education, highlighting both challenges and opportunities for strengthening these frameworks.

A central theme, identity expression versus concealment, frequently surfaced in discussions about children and educational contexts. Some parents described instructing their children to hide signs of Jewish identity for safety. Talia recounted a poignant moment when her daughter made an Israeli flag at kindergarten: "She happily waved the flag and said, 'Look, Mom, what I made!' I quickly told her, 'Let's put it in your bag and keep it at home.'" Similarly, Laura observed that her older child "avoids any expression of Jewish identity in school, which wasn't the case a year ago." Jessica admitted that she no longer wears her Star of David publicly: "I used to sometimes wear a Jewish star necklace. I haven't worn it anymore because people put Jews and Israel in one boat." These examples illustrate the disappointment, and sometimes heartbreak, parents feel as they balance pride in Jewish identity with the desire to protect their children from potential harm. Sophia described it as a "daily moral quandary," fearing that her child might perceive concealment as shame rather than caution.

Several parents perceived non-Jewish schools as failing to address antisemitism, prompting them to explore alternatives. Laura expressed disappointment with her children's private school, noting the contrast between its supportive response to the war in Ukraine and its silence on Israel: "The school of our children totally failed at that point, from a Jewish perspective... There is perhaps above all the contrast to how they reacted to the attack on

Ukraine and how they reacted now to the attack on Israel." Similarly, Ruth highlighted the need to correct narratives her children encountered: "It's hard for them because at school they hear a lot about how miserable the children in Gaza are. I have to explain to my kids what really happened and why." She emphasized that she was not against empathy, but that schools should provide greater balance and attention to Jewish safety concerns. These gaps in school practices effectively turned parents into at-home educators, using mealtime conversations to discuss current conflicts, historical traumas, and moral complexities.

Negative experiences in non-Jewish schools, coupled with an overall climate of insecurity, led some participants to consider Jewish education or voice support for these frameworks. However, not all families did so solely to shield their children from antisemitism. Rivka, who grew up in a "traditional, observant Yemeni family," contrasted her rigorous religious upbringing with her children's "almost nonexistent" participation in Jewish life in Germany. She added, "After October 7, this distance in their Jewish identity feels even more pronounced."

Rivka's remarks illustrate how hostility and diaspora pressures push families toward reinforcing or reclaiming Jewish identity, particularly for younger generations. Some participants responded to external threats by intensifying home-based educational and religious practices. Ruth noted, "We now do more Jewish holidays and Shabbat gatherings. Since October 7, everything has become more intense for us." Talia continued traditions even in the absence of formal Jewish institutions nearby: "I even arranged for a mohel to come from Bavaria for my son's circumcision. It was important to me to do this the traditional way." Language emerged as another important factor in preserving heritage. Ruth highlighted the significance of Hebrew in maintaining cultural ties: "Both of my children speak Hebrew because I make an effort to speak with them in Hebrew. They have a connection to my parents, to my sister, and to the family in Israel."

In such moments, the local Jewish community emerged as a crucial haven during uncertain times. Avi, who runs youth programs in his local Jewish community, explained, "In the community, we have shared prayers and discuss specific topics. It's one of the few places where I feel I can truly express myself without restrictions." Hans underscored the importance of stable community structures "from kindergarten through school, the youth center, and university," emphasizing the significance of educational continuity in shaping a family's sense of belonging.

Still, not all families can afford or access Jewish schools. Ruth, for instance, noted that "another 200 euros a month" for synagogue or community fees was beyond her budget, so she instead opted to celebrate holidays at home. Other families fostered community ties through creative solutions. Laura mentioned her son's Bar Mitzvah project: producing educational holiday videos for their synagogue's new YouTube channel. Additionally, some interviewees highlighted non-formal Jewish activities, such as youth camps or music programs. Avi organizes summer camps for Jewish children aged eight to eighteen, describing them as "safe spaces" where youth can explore identity without fear. Eitan, a Jewish music teacher, shared how cultural arts programs allow him to pass on Jewish heritage in an emotionally supportive way: "The greatest help for me was building events like concerts . . . it's not just art, it's also about passing on stories, words, and traditions to the kids."

Some participants, however, felt that Jewish education in Germany might not suffice given the current environment. Laura acknowledged preparing her children to relocate if necessary: "We have equipped our children from an early age with the resources that they can actually find a home anywhere in the world, and we also support that with multilingualism, education, and the like." Similarly, Sophia described a concrete plan to move: "We've decided to move to Israel when my son turns five. We feel it's no longer safe to raise him here in Germany."

Beneath the surface, generational mismatches emerged in how children approached Judaism compared to their parents. Rivka explained, "My connection to Judaism is strong, but my children's connection is almost nonexistent. After October 7, this distance in their Jewish identity feels even more pronounced." Shani and Jessica both described emotional confrontations with younger relatives or children who resisted hearing the graphic details of conflicts, illustrating how external traumas can spill over into internal family dialogues. Lena captured the challenge: "It's not about being silent; it's about not traumatizing them. But they have to know something."

Overall, these educational themes illustrate how Jewish families in Germany are adapting childrearing and schooling practices in response to concerns about antisemitism, obstacles to proper Jewish education within the state system, and intergenerational differences. Approaches ranged from reinforcing Jewish instruction at home to pursuing alternative schooling or intensifying community programs. Collectively, these findings underscore both the challenges and the resilience involved in sustaining Jewish education in contemporary Germany.

Conclusion

Despite growing public concern about antisemitic incidents, relatively few studies have centered the voices of Jews themselves (Chernivsky et al., 2020). This gap became particularly evident in the aftermath of October 7, when global tensions elicited heightened external hostility and profound questions about the viability of Jewish life in Europe. By foregrounding in-depth interviews with Jewish individuals in Germany, the present study addresses this gap and provides a preliminary, yet in-depth exploration of how collective trauma, identity negotiation, and educational choices intersect in the current sociopolitical context. Through qualitative network analysis, we mapped themes of fear, safety, and resilience, as well as the intricate relationships among these themes, particularly concerning Jewish education and parenting practices.

Facing mounting antisemitism and emotional strain, interviewees described various coping strategies, many of which revolved around social identity processes (Badea et al., 2011; Branscombe et al., 1999; Tajfel and Turner, 2004), strengthening ties with Jewish communities or intensifying religious and cultural practices. Others engaged in activism, organizing solidarity rallies, writing op-eds, or countering hateful speech online, reflecting the idea that direct action can buffer against feelings of helplessness (Delker et al., 2020). These sources of resilience, in turn, manifested through communal rituals and community education. Families described intensifying holiday observances and teaching Hebrew at home to preserve identity and reassure children that Jewish life endures, even in times of crisis. Parents reported forging closer relationships with Jewish schools or after-school programs, while educators incorporated discussions of identity, activism, and coping into their activities, reflecting similar trends documented elsewhere (Anusiewicz-Baer, 2024; Körber and Kunze, 2024). Participants described the difficult balance between fostering pride in Jewish identity and protecting their children from potential harm. Stories of advising children to avoid overt displays of Jewish identity, such as waving Israeli flags or speaking Hebrew in public, underscore the emotional toll parents face in reconciling cultural pride with vigilance. At the same time, intensified home-based practices, ranging from observing religious holidays to teaching Hebrew, highlight how adversity has spurred efforts to preserve Jewish traditions and foster resilience within families. Collectively, these findings align with the concept of post-traumatic growth (Tedeschi and Calhoun, 2004), applied here at the collective level, where adversity fosters greater communal engagement, deeper cultural and identity commitments, and moral reflection, despite the persistence of stress and fatigue as challenges.

When asked about future prospects, participants expressed a mix of pessimism and cautious optimism. Many questioned whether Germany remained viable for Jewish families, citing an environment they perceived as increasingly hostile or indifferent, Accordingly, a significant theme that emerged was dissatisfaction with how general (non-Jewish) schools addressed—or failed to address—antisemitism. Efforts to engage school administrators, correct biased narratives, and advocate for greater awareness of antisemitism in public schools were frequently discussed. These accounts aligned with findings from recent empirical studies on school-based antisemitism (Bernstein and Diddens, 2021; Chernivsky et al., 2020), which highlight that schools often lack the tools or willingness to address antisemitic bullying or correct misinformation about Jewish life and Israel. Consequently, several parents planned to enroll their children in Jewish day schools or considered relocating (e.g., to Israel) if conditions deteriorated further. For many, Jewish educational spaces provided both safety and a sense of shared identity, offering children the opportunity to learn Hebrew, celebrate traditions, and engage with complex global events without feeling singled out. Parents emphasized the importance of these institutions in providing both cultural continuity and emotional security. However, some acknowledged that Jewish communities in Germany have faced significant challenges before, and a spirit of resilience was evident. Participants called for greater public and political acknowledgment of antisemitism, urging local authorities and educational institutions to take stronger action. This included adopting clearer policies, implementing teacher training, and issuing unequivocal condemnations of antisemitic incidents, reflecting similar recommendations by Bernstein and Diddens (2021) for proactive institutional responses. Others stressed the importance of constructive engagement with non-Jewish society, rather than retreating into Jewish "bubbles," as a way to counter emotional coldness and foster empathy.

Our study has limitations that warrant acknowledgment. Although diverse in age and background, the sample does not fully capture the breadth of Jewish experiences in Germany, particularly given the underrepresentation of Russian-speaking Jews, who comprise a significant portion of the population. Additionally, data were collected within months of October 7, providing a snapshot of early reactions rather than a longitudinal view of how these experiences evolve over time. The reliance on self-reported narratives introduces potential recall bias, a common challenge in qualitative research. Furthermore, the relationships among codes in the network structure, derived from co-occurrences, do not necessarily indicate direct cause-and-effect linkages. A longitudinal approach could provide insights into how Jewish communities' emotional states and coping mechanisms develop as the immediate crisis recedes from public attention. Comparative research across different diaspora contexts (e.g., the United States versus Germany) could also reveal whether the intensification of group identity, activism, and Jewish education follows similar or divergent trajectories. Future studies might also explore how digital platforms influence coping strategies, especially in the face of rising online hate speech.

Based on our results, particularly those concerning Jewish education, we propose several general recommendations to enhance resilience, well-being, and flourishing of Jewish communities. Strengthening anti-antisemitism policies and teacher training is crucial, as participants frequently criticized schools for failing to address hate incidents. In line with Bernstein and Diddens (2021), public schools could collaborate with Jewish communities or NGOs to develop curricula and professional development sessions that address both historical antisemitism and contemporary tensions surrounding Israel. Equally important is expanding Jewish education in a way that fosters integration rather than isolation. While parents praised Jewish day schools, youth programs, and extracurricular frameworks, they also expressed concerns about further marginalization from broader German society. To address this, Jewish schools could organize joint initiatives with neighboring non-Jewish institutions, such as cross-school visits or interfaith workshops, to promote mutual understanding. These efforts could complement similar activities focused on Holocaust memory and historical reconciliation. Politicians and local councils also have a role to play. By funding intercultural programs and publicly affirming Jewish educational rights, they can counter the "emotional coldness" described by participants and strengthen feelings of belonging. Collaborative advocacy platforms within schools, or partnerships among Jewish, interfaith, and civic organizations, can further empower communities to respond proactively to antisemitism. Finally, promoting viewpoint pluralism within Jewish communities through moderated forums or dialogue groups would enable individuals to express diverse perspectives on Israeli policies in a respectful environment, reducing opportunities for outside groups to exploit dissent while preserving internal unity against antisemitic threats.

In conclusion, this qualitative study, grounded in interviews and qualitative network analysis, examined the critical role of education as both a practical and a symbolic site where Jewish identity is fostered, contested, and defended in the face of trauma and rising antisemitism. Participants' reflections revealed how educational choices were deeply intertwined with concerns about safety, identity preservation, and resilience-building in younger generations. By situating these findings within Germany's broader sociopolitical context, this chapter provided empirical insights and practical pathways for strengthening Jewish resilience, while encouraging educators, policymakers, and communal organizations, Jewish and non-Jewish alike, to better address the emotional and cultural needs of Jewish learners during times of crisis.

References

Alexander, J. C. (Ed.) (2004). *Cultural trauma and collective identity*. University of California Press.

Anusiewicz-Baer, S. (2024). Jüdischer Religionsunterricht in Deutschland— Eine Bestandsaufnahme jüdischer Erziehung im Spannungsfeld von Religion, Säkularisierung und Verstaatlichung. *Zeitschrift für Religion, Gesellschaft und Politik*. https://doi.org/10.1007/s41682-024-00193-4

Attride-Stirling, J. (2001). Thematic networks: An analytic tool for qualitative research. *Qualitative Research*, 1(3), 385–405. https://doi.org/10.1177/146879410100100307

Badea, C., Jetten, J., Iyer, A., and Er-rafiy, A. (2011). Negotiating dual identities: The impact of group-based rejection on identification and acculturation. *European Journal of Social Psychology*, 41(5), 586–595. https://doi.org/10.1002/ejsp.786

Bankier-Karp, A. L., and Graham, D. (2024). Surrounded by darkness, enfolded in light: Factors influencing the mental health of Australian Jews in the October 7 aftermath. *Contemporary Jewry*. https://doi.org/10.1007/s12397-024-09584-4

Ben Rafael, E., Glöckner, O., and Sternberg, Y. (2011). *Jews and Jewish education in Germany today*. Brill. https://doi.org/10.1163/ej.9789004201170.i-326

Bernstein, J., and Diddens, F. (2021). Antisemitismus an Schulen. Empirische Befunde. *Zeitschrift Für Pädagogik Und Theologie*, 73(2), 151–165. https://doi.org/10.1515/zpt-2021-0019

Bonanno, G. A., and Burton, C. L. (2013). Regulatory flexibility: An individual differences perspective on coping and emotion regulation. *Perspectives on Psychological Science*, 8(6), 591–612. https://doi.org/10.1177/1745691613504116

Boyd, J. (2024). Antisemitism in the aftermath of October 7: What do the data tell us, and what more do we still need to know?. *JPR*, October 1. https://www.jpr.org.uk/reports/antisemitism-aftermath-october-7-what-do-data-tell-us-and-what-more-do-we-still-need-know

Branscombe, N. R., Schmitt, M. T., and Harvey, R. D. (1999). Perceiving pervasive discrimination among African Americans: Implications for group identification and well-being. *Journal of Personality and Social Psychology*, 77(1), 135–149. https://doi.org/10.1037/0022-3514.77.1.135

Chernivsky, M., Lorenz, F., and Schweitzer, J. (2020). *Antisemitismus im (Schul-)Alltag.* https://zwst-kompetenzzentrum.de/wp-content/uploads/2021/04/Forschungsbericht_Familienstudie_2020.pdf

Chernivsky, M., and Lorenz-Sinai, F. (2024). *Institutioneller Antisemitismus in der Schule* (1st ed.). Aktion Courage e.V.

Csárdi, G., Nepusz, T., Müller, K., Horvát, S., Traag, V., Zanini, F., and Noom, D. (2024). *igraph for R: R interface of the igraph library for graph theory and network analysis* (version v2.1.2) [Computer software]. Zenodo. https://doi.org/10.5281/ZENODO.7682609

Damm, K. (2008). Wiederaufbau, Neubeginn, Neuorientierung–Jüdische Pädagogik im Nachkriegsdeutschland. *Medaon: Magazin Für Jüdisches Leben in Forschung Und Bildung*, 2.

DellaPergola, S. (2020). World Jewish population. In A. Dashefsky and I. M. Sheskin (Eds.), *American Jewish Year Book* (pp. 273–370). Springer. https://doi.org/10.1007/978-3-030-78706-6_7

De Paoli, S. (2024). Performing an inductive thematic analysis of semi-structured interviews with a large language model: An exploration and provocation on the limits of the approach. *Social Science Computer Review*, 42(4), 997–1019. https://doi.org/10.1177/08944393231220483

Delker, B. C., Salton, R., and McLean, K. C. (2020). Giving voice to silence: Empowerment and disempowerment in the developmental shift from trauma 'victim' to 'survivor-advocate.' *Journal of Trauma and Dissociation*, 21(2), 242–263. https://doi.org/10.1080/15299732.2019.1678212

Epstein, O., Rivkind, B., and Adler, A. (2024). *Enrolment trend report: Families turn to Jewish day school post 10/7*. PRIZMAH: Center for Jewish Day Schools. https://prizmah.org/knowledge/resource/enrollment-trend-report-families-turn-jewish-day-school-post-107

Eshel, Y., Marciano, H., Kimhi, S., Kaim, A., Tov, M. S., and Adini, B. (2025). National resilience rise following the Hamas invasion of southern Israel as an indicator of collective post-traumatic growth. *International Journal of Intercultural Relations*, 105, 102–130. https://doi.org/10.1016/j.ijintrel.2024.102130

Eyerman, R. (2019). *Memory, trauma, and identity*. Springer. https://doi.org/10.1007/978-3-030-13507-2

Fischer, J. M. K., and Wetzels, P. (2024). Die Verbreitung antisemitischer Einstellungen in Deutschland: Befunde aktueller repräsentativer Befragungen zu Trends seit 2021 und den Einflüssen von Migrationshintergrund, Religionszugehörigkeit und Religiosität. *Zeitschrift für Religion, Gesellschaft und Politik*. https://doi.org/10.1007/s41682-024-00167-6

Fork, S. (2021). On becoming a 'real' Jew: An ethnography of adolescents' identity formation in a Jewish community in Germany. *Culture and Psychology*, 27(1), 52–66. https://doi.org/10.1177/1354067X20922515

Goldblum, S. (2024). Kulturjudentum in der Geschichte der Juden in Deutschland: Von der Bildung zur Erinnerungskultur. *Symposium Culture@Culture*. https://doi.org/10.2478/sck-2024-0004

Greenwood, H. (2024). Jewish communities worldwide brace for rising hatred. *Israel Hayom*. https://www.israelhayom.com/2024/09/16/jewish-communities-worldwide-brace-against-rising-hatred/

Groß, E., Häfele, J., Bertram, F. E., and Kliem, S. (2024). *Jüdisches Leben und Alltag in Hamburg—LeAH*. Research report. Hochschule der Akademie der Polizei Hamburg and Polizeiakademie Niedersachsen.

Gruber, J., Loy, B., and Poensgen, D. (2024). Antisemitic reactions to October 7: The Germany case. In R. Freedman and D. Hirsh (Eds.), *Responses to October 7: Law and society* (pp. 91–100). Routledge.

Hersh, E. (2024). *A survey portrait of Jewish life on campus in the midst of the Israel-Hamas war: 7 key findings*. Jim Joseph Foundation Reports. https://jimjosephfoundation.org/wp-content/uploads/2024/03/part-2-A-Survey-Portrait-of-Jewish-Life-on-Campus-in-the-Midst-of-the-Israel-Hamas-War-7-Key-Findings_2024.pdf

Hirschberger, G. (2018). Collective trauma and the social construction of meaning. *Frontiers in Psychology*, 9, 1441. https://doi.org/10.3389/fpsyg.2018.01441

Janoff-Bulman, R. (1992). *Shattered assumptions: Towards a new psychology of trauma* (4th print ed.). Free Press.

Körber, K., and Kunze, S. (2024). Jüdische Schulbildung im 21. Jahrhundert—Neue Perspektiven auf Frankfurt am Main und Hamburg. *Zeitschrift für Religion, Gesellschaft und Politik*. https://doi.org/10.1007/s41682-024-00196-1

Lazarus, R., and Folkman, S. (1984). *Stress, appraisal, and coping*. Springer.

Mahla, D. (2024). Reclaiming agency through conversation: Life narrative interviews of German-speaking Jews in Israel. *German Studies Review*, 47(3), 497–516. https://doi.org/10.1353/gsr.2024.a940193

Marciano, H., Kimhi, S., Eshel, Y., and Adini, B. (2024). Resilience and coping during protracted conflict: A comparative analysis of general and evacuees populations. In review with *Israel Journal of Health Policy Research*. https://doi.org/10.21203/rs.3.rs-4371516/v1

Miles, M. B., Huberman, A. M., and Saldaña, J. (2014). *Qualitative data analysis: A methods sourcebook* (Third edition). Sage.

Muldoon, O. T. (2024). *The social psychology of trauma: Connecting the personal and the political* (1st ed.). Cambridge University Press. https://doi.org/10.1017/9781009306997

Oboler, A., Roth, E., Beinart, J.., and Beinart, J. (2024). *Online antisemitism after 7 October 2023*. Online Hate Prevention Institute. https://ohpi.org.au/wp-content/uploads/2024/03/Online_Antisemitism_After_October_7.pdf.

Pokorny, J. J., Norman, A., Zanesco, A. P., Bauer-Wu, S., Sahdra, B. K., and Saron, C. D. (2018). Network analysis for the visualization and analysis of qualitative data. *Psychological Methods*, 23(1), 169–183. https://doi.org/10.1037/met0000129

Rathje, S., Mirea, D.-M., Sucholutsky, I., Marjieh, R., Robertson, C. E., and Van Bavel, J. J. (2024). GPT is an effective tool for multilingual psychological text analysis. *Proceedings of the National Academy of Sciences*, 121(34), e2308950121. https://doi.org/10.1073/pnas.2308950121

Reingold, M., and Reznik, S. (2024). Navigating crisis together: Canadian Jews, Israel, and October 7. *Contemporary Jewry*. https://doi.org/10.1007/s12397-024-09572-8

Sedoff, O., Feingold, D., and Tzur Bitan, D. (2024). Social support as resilience factor in the aftermath of October 7th attack. *Journal of Loss and Trauma*, 1–14. https://doi.org/10.1080/15325024.2024.2441177

Shani, M., Goldberg, D., and Van Zalk, M. (2024). "If you prick us, do we not bleed"? Antisemitism and psychosocial health among Jews in Germany. *Frontiers in Psychology, 15*. https://doi.org/10.3389/fpsyg.2024.1499295

Shani, M., Jana, G., and Marie, H. (2024). *October 7, one year later: Resilience and coping among Jews in Germany amid rising antisemitism and collective trauma*. Open Science Framework. https://doi.org/10.31219/osf.io/dtgrb

Sinclair, J., and Milner, D. (2005). On being Jewish: A qualitative study of identity among British Jews in emerging adulthood. *Journal of Adolescent Research, 20*(1), 91–117. https://doi.org/10.1177/0743558404271132

Tajfel, H., and Turner, J. C. (2004). The Social Identity Theory of intergroup behavior. In J. T. Jost and J. Sidanius (Eds.), *Political Psychology* (pp. 276–293). Psychology Press. https://doi.org/10.4324/9780203505984-16

Tedeschi, R. G., and Calhoun, L. G. (2004). Target article: "Posttraumatic growth: Conceptual foundations and empirical evidence." *Psychological Inquiry, 15*(1), 1–18. https://doi.org/10.1207/s15327965pli1501_01

Wayment, H. A. (2004). It could have been me: Vicarious victims and disaster-focused distress. *Personality and Social Psychology Bulletin, 30*(4), 515–528. https://doi.org/10.1177/0146167203261892

Weisskirch, R. S., Kim, S. Y., Schwartz, S. J., and Whitbourne, S. K. (2016). The complexity of ethnic identity among Jewish American emerging adults. *Identity, 16*(3), 127–141. https://doi.org/10.1080/15283488.2016.1190724

Zeeman, R. (2022) Young Israeli study in Berlin; and stay there for love. *Christian Network Europe*. https://cne.news/article/529-young-israelis-study-in-berlin-and-stay-there-for-love

Tables

Table 4.1 *Participant Demographics*

Name	Age	Gender	Nationality	Year in Germany
Eitan	24	Male	Israeli	3
Ido	41	Male	German	11
Ruth	46	Female	Israeli + Austrian	19
Talia	39	Female	Israeli	8
Maya	43	Female	Israeli + German	16.5
Noam	30	Male	Israeli	2.5
Uriel	43	Male	German	12
Ben	30	Male	Israeli + German	6.5
Shani	55	Female	German	23
Rivka	57	Female	Israeli	5
Jessica	30	Female	American	5
Hans	68	Male	German	64
Sophia	30	Female	German	30
Laura	39	Female	German	30
Miriam	66	Female	Israeli	4
Avi	23	Male	Israeli + German	17
Anna	31	Female	German	7
Lena	24	Female	German	24

Table 4.2 *Network Metrics and Centrality Measures*

Metric	Entire Network	Family-Education Network
Nodes	144	71
Edges	526	102
Degree (M ± SE)	7.31 ± 0.6	2.87 ± 0.34
Weighted Degree (M ± SE)	21.75 ± 2.39	4.96 ± 0.73
Diameter	38	13
Density	0.05	0.04
Modularity	0.56	0.64
Communities	9	10

(Continued)

Table 4.2 *Network Metrics and Centrality Measures* **(Continued)**

Path Length (M)	4.53	4.80
PageRank (M ± SE)	0.007 ± 0.000	0.014 ± 0.002
Eigenvector (M ± SE)	0.09 ± 0.01	0.07 ± 0.02
Closeness (M ± SE)	0.25 ± 0.004	--
Betweenness (M ± SE)	0.02 ± 0.002	0.04 ± 0.008
Transitivity	0.22	0.09

Table 4.3 *Strongest Thematic Relationships in the Family-Education Network: Analysis of High-Weight Network Edges*

Node A	Node B	Weight	Number of Interviewees
Anxiety about safety	Fear for family safety in Israel	11	8
Family disagreements on coping	Loss of personal connections due to differing views	7	2
Concerns about children's Jewish identity	Pride in Jewish identity	6	3
Contact with family in Israel	Fear for family safety in Israel	6	5
Family disagreements on coping	Mixed religious and cultural identity	5	2
Family ties as emotional anchor	Seeking support from family	5	4
Encouraging emotional openness	Family ties as emotional anchor	4	4
Family disagreements on coping	Strained family relationships	4	2
Fear for family safety in Israel	Long-term trauma from the attacks	4	4
Community support	Seeking support from family	3	3
Concerns about children's Jewish identity	Fear for children's future	3	3

(Continued)

Table 4.3 *Strongest Thematic Relationships in the Family-Education Network: Analysis of High-Weight Network Edges* **(Continued)**

Contact with family in Israel	Emotional connection to Israel	3	3
Discrimination in schools	Experiencing anti-semitism firsthand	3	3
Discrimination in schools	Fear of being targeted for Jewish identity	3	2
Family ties as emotional anchor	Focus on emotional well-being	3	2
Fear of expressing Jewish identity	Fear of public displays of Jewish symbols	3	2
Jewish solidarity in face of crisis	Pride in Jewish identity	3	2
Political engagement	Taking action through advocacy	3	3
Seeking support from family	Strengthening bonds with Jewish friends	3	1

Note. Edge weights represent the frequency of thematic co-occurrence across all interviews, calculated through qualitative network analysis. Weight values indicate the total number of times two themes (nodes) were connected in the analysis across all interviews. The "Number of Interviewees" column indicates how many individual participants' narratives contained this thematic connection, providing context for the breadth versus depth of these relationships in the data. Maximum possible weight value is determined by the number of times a connection could appear across all interviews, while maximum number of interviewees is 18 (total sample size).

Section Two

PEDAGOGICAL INNOVATIONS: TEACHING ANEW AFTER OCTOBER 7

Rethinking Innocence and Building Resilience: Early Childhood Jewish Educators' Responses to October 7

Meir Muller, Lyndall Miller, and Alana Rifkin Gelnick

The October 7 Hamas attack on Israel sent shockwaves through Jewish communities worldwide, evoking profound existential fears (Anti-Defamation League, 2023). In the days following the attack, early childhood Jewish educators in North America returned to their classrooms. These educators faced the daunting task of responding to their students' emotional reactions and questions in the wake of this traumatic event.

This amplified the already significant emotional and professional demands placed on early childhood educators. Their roles are so multifaceted that "describing a professional ECEC [early childhood education and care] teacher is complex and difficult" (Arndt et al., 2021, p. 407). These professionals are tasked with promoting children's social, emotional, and academic well-being; monitoring their progress; and cultivating strong connections with families (Shelton, 2024). In Jewish preschools, these educators' responsibilities extend further to include nurturing spiritual and religious development, leading engagement with rituals and holiday celebrations, fostering connections to Israel, and serving as a gateway for families into Jewish communal life (Vogelstein et al., 2023).

One particularly complex challenge early childhood Jewish educators faced after the attack was balancing the desire to protect childhood innocence with the concern of how to recognize the children's understanding and agency alongside promoting resilience in the children. The concept of innocence, which traditionally advocates shielding children from distressing realities (Nguyen, 2021), has long shaped educational practices (Change-Kredl and Kozak, 2018). However, the staff of one Modern Orthodox early childhood program in a major US city found themselves carefully examining this approach in the wake of October 7. They observed their students' natural perceptiveness and resilience and, rather than fully shielding the children from information about the attack, weighed how and when to introduce difficult but vital conversations in age-appropriate ways.

By balancing emotional protection with opportunities for growth, these educators sought to safeguard the children's well-being while promoting their resilience—an essential capacity for managing emotions and supporting positive development in challenging circumstances. Despite lacking formal training in trauma response, these educators used their deep understanding of children's emotional and psychological needs to guide their practices. Teachers reported that familiar classroom routines and relationships provided immediate comfort, while structured discussions and creative outlets helped the children process and make sense of challenging realities. These resilience-building strategies fostered an environment where emotional safety and adaptive growth coexisted.

Two and a half months after October 7, 2023, we interviewed eight teachers from the school using a semi-clinical format with responses analyzed through qualitative coding. The strategies that emerged reflected a deliberate balancing act of responses along a continuum of approaches to childhood innocence. On one end was the traditional stance of shielding children entirely from distressing realities and on the other was embracing complete openness to any topic a child raised, even those involving painful details like children being taken hostage. In examining positions along this continuum as reported by these educators, this research highlights educational strategies that protect young children while empowering them to adapt and grow during times of crisis.

Literature Review

Conceptualization of the Innocence of Childhood

The concept of childhood innocence is deeply embedded in educational philosophies, particularly those dealing with children before the onset of puberty (Buhler-Niederberger, 2007). Challenging this construct can provoke discomfort or even be seen as uncaring. Woodrow and Brennan (2001) argue that the images associated with childhood innocence have become "so naturalized, so taken-for-granted, that questioning them often makes us uncomfortable" (p. 25). Similarly, Chang-Kredl and Kozak (2018) emphasize that the notion of the innocent child remains the most prominent image in educational settings, often perceived as the inherent condition of childhood, a perspective echoed by Woodrow (1999, p. 3). This idea also manifests in official curricula and instructional decisions, where potentially controversial topics are frequently avoided (Garlen, 2019, p. 64), underscoring how deeply ingrained the concept is within educational practices.

However, the widespread acceptance of childhood innocence in education and society does not mean that it is without issues or necessarily beneficial. Research has shown that adhering to this construct can lead to outcomes that perpetuate racist and sexist biases (Ben-Moshe et al., 2021; Egan and Hawkes, 2012; Maza, 2020). For example, policies and practices rooted in maintaining childhood innocence may overlook the diverse realities of children's experiences, leading to exclusionary or inequitable educational practices. In the same vein, it is important to note that not all groups of children have been granted the status of innocence, for example, Black children and immigrant children (Gilliam et al., 2016; Thomas, 2019). Duschinsky (2013) further contends that childhood innocence is often granted "unimpeachable moral status" (p. 764), which can hinder necessary inquiry and critical engagement with complex topics.

Adding to this critique, Faulkner (2011) explores how the construct of innocence shapes societal and educational perceptions of children. She argues that the idealization of childhood innocence can create unrealistic expectations, potentially limiting children's agency and their ability to navigate and respond to real-world challenges. This perspective suggests that prioritizing an unchallenged view of childhood innocence may ultimately constrain children's development by overlooking their capacity for resilience and complex understanding. These complexities are significant for understanding how educators navigate their roles during times of crisis.

Theories of Resilience

Resilience, often described as the capacity to adapt successfully to adversity, plays a central role in helping children navigate life's challenges (Masten and

Barnes, 2018). While the concept is multifaceted and complex, research has identified several key dimensions that can guide educators in fostering resilience in early childhood settings (American Psychological Association, 2020). These include cultivating supportive relationships and predictable routines, promoting emotion regulation, encouraging agency and problem-solving, grounding experiences in meaningful contexts, and leveraging cultural and community resources. Together, these interconnected facets create a holistic framework for supporting children's growth in the face of adversity.

At the heart of resilience is the importance of relationships and routines (Masten, 2018). Secure connections with caregivers and peers provide children with a sense of emotional safety, forming the foundation for their ability to adapt and thrive (Pfefferbaum et al., 2015). Predictable routines reinforce this stability by offering children a sense of structure and consistency amid uncertainty and disruption (Center on the Developing Child at Harvard University, 2016). A supportive environment grounded in consistent, predictable care from educators is essential for fostering resilience in children

Building on this foundation, teachers also need to nurture children's emotional awareness and emotion regulation. Learning to recognize, express, and manage emotions equips children with tools to navigate stress and maintain equilibrium in difficult situations (Berger and Martin, 2021). Educators play a critical role in modeling as well as offering opportunities to work these skills. They foster self-awareness and demonstrate constructive coping strategies and create spaces where children's emotions are acknowledged and validated (Sun et al., 2024).

Another key aspect of resilience is children's ability to take an active role in their own learning and problem-solving. Adults need to encourage children to make decisions, take risks, and tackle challenges that build self-efficacy—the belief in their own capabilities (Wassell and Daniel, 2002). A sense of agency is further strengthened by fostering a growth mindset that reframes obstacles as opportunities for learning and development (Yeager and Dweck, 2020). Together, these practices empower children to approach difficulties with confidence and perseverance.

Ultimately, there is a connection between resilience and identity. When children see their experiences reflected in cultural practices, storytelling, and community engagement, they develop a cohesive sense of self that helps them understand their place in the world (Bethell et al., 2019). When adults ground children's experiences in meaningful contexts, they not only support the children's identity formation but also offer a framework for processing adversity, enabling them to draw on their personal and collective strengths (Ungar, 2021).

Methodology

A study to explore educators' use and understanding of the concepts of innocence and resilience through the responses of early childhood Jewish educators in their classrooms following the October 7 attack was conducted at a Jewish early learning center within a Modern Orthodox school in a major US city over the two and a half months following October 7, 2023. This school was chosen because of relevant conversations that had emerged between the researchers and several of the educators at the school. Two of the researchers had been conducting professional development sessions for the school and noted that issues of how to deal with the Israel-Hamas war kept coming up for many of the teachers. The third researcher was the principal of the early learning center and provided background as well as co-conducted interviews.

The center serves 270 children, aged two to five, across sixteen classes, and requires its teachers to hold degrees in early childhood education and demonstrate knowledge of Jewish traditions. The school emphasizes fostering student confidence, curiosity, and achievement through respectful relationships and collaborative practices. Teachers are united by a shared commitment to Jewish values, Hebrew language proficiency, and a strong connection to Israel, as reflected in the school's curriculum.

Each classroom in the program includes a lead teacher, an assistant, and a native Hebrew-speaking teacher. Eight teachers across seven classes volunteered to participate in the study, including two Israeli-born educators and another with immediate family in Israel. Participants had teaching experience ranging from four to forty-one years, held bachelor's or master's degrees, and represented various Jewish denominations.

The participants were assigned pseudonyms, and no identifying information about the teachers, classrooms, or school was included in the study's findings. Although the teachers were known to the interviewers—two of whom had previously worked with the school on professional development and one of whom was the principal of the school—the study was designed to lessen the possibility that the positionality of the researchers would affect the validity of the study's findings. Teachers were briefed on the voluntary nature of their participation and informed that they could withdraw from the study at any time and openly share their experiences without fear of negative repercussions. Further, the third researcher, the principal, did not engage in independent data interpretation in order to minimize potential bias.

The study included educators from two preschool classrooms for three-year-olds (twenty-six students), referred to as 3A and 3B; one preschool classroom for four-year-olds (sixteen students), referred to as 4A; and four kindergarten classrooms for five-year-olds (eighty-five students), referred to as K1, K1A, K2, K3, and K4. All the children came from Jewish backgrounds, with most of their families following Modern Orthodox practices, a denomination that emphasizes observance of Jewish law, a focus on educational achievement, and a strong connection to Israel.

Data were collected using semi-clinical interviews with teachers. The semi-clinical interview approach provided a conversational framework, allowing for an in-depth exploration of the educators' experiences and insights (Bradshaw et al., 2021). Teachers were briefed on the study's focus on classroom dynamics after October 7, encouraged to ask clarifying questions, and invited to share examples from their own classrooms. Seven one-hour interviews were conducted via Zoom in December 2023, with one session including two co-teachers, K1 and K1A (who were the classroom's lead teacher and the Hebrew immersion teacher). Interviews were recorded, transcribed, and supplemented by interviewer observation notes. Teachers also contributed classroom newsletters, photos, and videos to enrich the context of their responses.

Data analysis was conducted using Spradley's (1980) domain analysis method to identify themes and patterns, which were categorized based on semantic relationships. The coding process began with identifying instances related to attitudes of childhood innocence and concepts of resilience. A consistent codebook was developed from the first four interviews to apply to the remaining transcripts. One researcher conducted the initial coding for all interviews, while two additional researchers coded at least two classrooms each to ensure thoroughness. Cross-referencing was conducted between themes and interview notes to validate findings. Researchers reviewed each other's coding for consistency, and member-checking with participants was performed to align findings with their perspectives.

Findings

The findings demonstrate the nuanced experiences of these eight educators as they navigated the tension between preserving childhood innocence and acknowledging the horrible reality of the conflict. They reveal the expectations the teachers carried into their first day back after the holiday break (October

9), juxtaposed against the realities they encountered in their classrooms. The unexpected depth of the children's knowledge made it clear to the participants that guarding the children entirely from discussions about the war was not possible. This recognition prompted the educators to consider how to balance emotional protection with opportunities for the children to process the realities they already knew. Some participants leaned toward shielding the children from distressing realities to maintain their emotional well-being. Others acknowledged the need for openness, responding to the children's questions and conversations about difficult topics like war and conflict.

The findings highlight how these educators moved along a spectrum of approaches to childhood innocence, adjusting them to protect children while also empowering them to process the complex realities they encountered. To preserve the innocence of childhood, the educators employed strategies such as carefully framing language, emphasizing positive narratives, and consistently reassuring children of their safety. At the same time, they challenged traditional notions of childhood innocence by creating spaces where children could openly explore complex topics through play and engage in meaningful conversations. They also asked guided questions, recognizing that shielding children or avoiding difficult subjects entirely would deny their natural ability—and right—to process complex realities.

The interviews also revealed how the strategies employed by the educators, partially guided by the children themselves, aimed to empower the children to handle the reality of the situation. Additionally, these strategies were well-suited to foster resilience in their young students as they dealt with the terrible attack and its aftermath. The components of the strategies most directly related to fostering resilience were nurturing supportive relationships, providing predictable routines, promoting emotional awareness and emotion regulation, encouraging agency and problem-solving, and grounding experiences in meaningful contexts.

Teachers' Expectations versus Reality

The reports of the initial moments of return set the stage for understanding how the educators recalibrated their approaches in response to the children's unexpected knowledge and questions about the war. The children's knowledge of the war was evident the very first day back to school after the holiday break for Simchat Torah. Teachers reported that children mentioned "men with masks coming into Israel" and said, "Israel was attacked." Rachel, the 4A teacher, noted, "Some children knew that people died, and some knew that a lot of people died." Leah, the K2 teacher, noted that four children in her class asked if she had heard about the war and said, "All the children in my class knew something." The K1 teacher, Deborah, encapsulated the teachers' responses, stating, "I was surprised that children . . . had so much knowledge about Israel [referring to the attack]."

Protecting Childhood Innocence

Careful Framing of Language. To uphold the notion of childhood innocence, all the participants used simplified and controlled language when discussing the events. For instance, the term "bad guys" was consistently employed in place of Hamas. Dina responded strongly when asked if her K1 children mentioned Hamas during play, exclaiming, "Oh my God! Who's talking about Hamas? We're in kindergarten. We don't talk about Hamas here; the children are too young." Sarah, the 3A teacher, described intervening when a child began to mention Hamas during lunch, sharing that she stopped the conversation between the children by saying, "Wait a second. How about telling me first about Hamas?" and having a one-on-one conversation, as she did not feel that it was age appropriate for the children to discuss Hamas.

Deborah summed up the position taken by all the participants:

> I think all teachers agree that it's okay to share facts that children discussed. It's okay to say "bad guys." It's not okay for a kindergarten teacher to say "Hamas." If a child brings up the word "Hamas," we can say "bad guys." You know, we need to be age appropriate.

Such language choices illustrate how these teachers sought to maintain a protective barrier around the children's understanding, aligning with the belief that difficult realities should be softened for young learners (Garlen, 2019). By reframing discussions in ways that preserved innocence, the teachers in these instances created a controlled environment that prioritized emotional protection.

Emphasizing Positive Narratives. To further shield the children from distress, the participants incorporated primarily positive imagery and narratives about Israel into their teaching. They chose emphasize joyful celebrations to preserve the children's innocence. Rosie, the K3 teacher, shared how she showed her students pictures of Israeli soldiers celebrating weddings and lighting Chanukah candles, explaining, "I've committed for years, long before this war, to try to bring only positive images so that children do not associate Israel with being scary." The 3B teacher, Esther, described highlighting a photograph of soldiers dancing at a wedding: "I told them how nice it was that all his friends came to the wedding, and I showed them the picture of the soldiers dancing. I'm showing them the positive piece of our amazing soldiers." Rosie and Esther both showed pictures of Israeli preschool children having routine and happy experiences in their schools. These strategies were aimed at reinforcing a sense of pride and cultural connection while preventing children from internalizing fear or anxiety about Israel.

Providing Consistent Reassurances of Safety. Another cornerstone of preserving childhood innocence during this time involved the participants offering concrete reassurances of safety. Teachers worked to provide children with a sense of protection for both themselves in the United States and for those living amidst the conflict in Israel. Deborah explained,

> We told them about the Iron Dome and how it is amazing in protecting people and also the Israeli soldiers protect people in the air, in the desert, and now in the entire country. We concluded with, "We're also safe here [in the United States]."

The teachers expressed that they found this type of framing essential for maintaining the emotional well-being of the children, who often relied on literal and tangible explanations for comfort.

The participants acknowledged the emotional complexity of providing such assurances. Rachel shared her struggle when speaking to a child whose father was serving in the Israeli Defense Forces: "You can try and reassure them, but I didn't know if his father was coming back. You must be overly optimistic because they need to feel safe." These moments underscored the educators' emphasis on presenting a secure world to the children even when the teachers recognized that this was far from assured.

Challenging Traditional Notions of Childhood Innocence

While the educators often adhered to the construct of childhood innocence to secure emotional well-being, there were moments when they found it beneficial to counter it to engage with children's awareness and cognitive understandings.

Allowing Complex Play. One such arena where innocence was challenged was with pretend play. Rachel described situations where the children's play mirrored real-world conflict, with children portraying themselves as "the good guys" (Israeli soldiers) confronting "the bad guys." In Rosie's K3 and Miriam's K4 classrooms, children independently constructed army bases in the block corners. Miriam recounted how the children in her class added elements such as lasers, security fences and gates, cameras, and vehicles to the base, along with a zipline that they made from tape, so that the soldiers could zipline into the army base. One of her students pointed out a block that represented an army plane, explaining that she had seen one in the sky in Israel. Miriam explained that, as the children came to understand more about the war, these block structures became more elaborate, and the block play lasted for a long time:

> Generally, we keep our block structure up for the week, and then on Fridays they clean up the blocks, but, with the army base, they always want to add to it, and we just would clean up the loose blocks and leave everything else. I think it stayed up until [winter] break.

Both classes allowed this freedom, viewing the block structures as an outlet for children to explore and express their ideas about the war.

The challenge to traditional views of childhood innocence also extended to the realm of gunplay. Although the preschool did not have explicit rules against gunplay, teachers generally discouraged such activities in their classes. After the attack, however, participants noted a significant rise in children incorporating guns into their imaginative play. Miriam described the dilemma she faced:

> I grew up in a household where there were no guns, like no water guns or toy guns. Similarly, my husband and our family have never had guns in our house. The topic has never even come up with my own kids. This narrative feels uncomfortable to me, as it goes against my values. However, as an educator, I understand that children need to explore and work through things. So, when they played with toy guns, I allowed it, sensing they were processing something.

These examples illustrate how the participants allowed the children to express their knowledge through play and conversation, even when the topic was war and weapons, which would have been discouraged prior to the war.

Offering Guided Questions. Another way that teachers encouraged children to explore their thoughts on the war was by asking them guided questions. Referring to the army base, Esther asked her class, "What do you think they do in an army base?" Children responded with, "They eat, sleep, play, and do things that we do," with one child adding, "They also do something we don't do, like battle. If someone attacks them, they attack back and defend themselves, and, if a country attacks us, then we must defend our country." The teacher, who never imagined she would be prompting children about war, shared that she asked her students questions of a similar nature over the two months following the attack.

A second example comes from Leah and occurred when her class was talking about the war. She asked if the students would like to make cards for Israeli soldiers. She prompted the children to draw pictures and write words. She then asked what types of pictures they wanted to draw. After prompting numerous children with guided questions, Leah estimated that ninety percent of the children took part in the activity. She added it was hard as they asked children: What should we draw for the Israeli soldiers? What message would make them feel good? And what would make them happy? She further reported that, while most children drew symbols like a Star of David or smiley faces, hearts, and rainbows, there were some who drew "something darker like with a little bit of blood, and like soldiers and guns." While these topics might not have been what teachers would have chosen to explore in the past, the need to meet the children where they were in their knowledge of the war led educators to adapt their approach. These examples highlight how the participants introduced difficult topics regarding the war, tailoring them to the children's maturity level but allowing the children to begin to process the complex reality.

Fostering Resilience

Providing Supportive Relationships and Predictable Routines. Leah described her approach to her relationship with her students, saying, "My way of support for some of the children is to hug and physically help them... sometimes with breathing to calm their bodies. Also important is my tone of voice and smile." This combination of physical and emotional reassurance was an attempt to facilitate children feeling secure and connected during moments of distress. This is an example of the type of relationship that could provide a foundation for the children developing the ability to adapt to difficult situations in the future.

The teachers maintained classroom rituals and kept routines such as morning circles and group activities in place because doing so provided the students with structure. As Rachel said, "We need to help the children with regulation by maintaining routines, taking a few minutes for quiet time. These really help to support the children now." They also ensured that celebrations, such as birthdays, continued uninterrupted. Deborah shared, "We made sure every child's birthday was celebrated with the same excitement and focus as always. It was important for the children to feel like their special day was just as meaningful during this time." Sarah added, "The children need their routines. It's not just about the celebration—it's about showing them that life continues, and we are here for them." In fact, during one birthday party, Sarah observed, "The children sang and clapped with such joy—it was like a moment of pure normalcy for them, and that's exactly what they needed." Deborah added, "Even with everything going on, seeing their excitement about birthdays reminded me how much they rely on these traditions to feel safe and happy." These familiar practices were designed to offer comfort and assure the students there could be predictability amid uncertainty. Esther noted a striking transformation during moments like singing "Hatikvah" (Israel's national anthem), when children shifted from chaotic behavior to silent and serious participation, exemplifying resilience through structured routines.

Promoting Emotional Awareness and Emotion Regulation. Like the teachers' guided questions previously discussed, classroom activities also afforded children the opportunity to articulate their feelings. These activities encouraged emotional awareness and regulation, two skills that are crucial to fostering resilience. Miriam described how they used the Zones of Regulation framework, a social-emotional learning curriculum created to teach children self-regulation and emotional control by organizing feelings, energy, and emotions around four colored descriptive "zones" (Kuypers, 2011). She explained:

> We often used the zones of regulation as a way to help children identify their feelings. I remember one day during our go-around share, the question was, "What zone are you in, and would you like to share why?" A few children responded by expressing two emotions at once. One child said, "I'm happy and I'm sad. I'm sad because there's the war happening in Israel, and I'm happy because I'm here and playing with my infant."

Participants reported that this framework helped the children recognize and express the complexity of their feelings about the situation, which arose even when the war was not the explicit focus in the classroom. Dina stated:

> Even when the war isn't the first thing we're talking about—like we're not making cards for *chayalim* [Israeli soldiers] every day—complex feelings still come up about the safety of Israel and here [United States]. For certain children, it's very much there, even when it seems like it's not.

Other examples of fostering resilience in the areas of emotional awareness and emotion regulation included validating students' feelings and creating routines that encouraged calm reflection. For example, Miriam explained how she validated children's emotions, by saying, "Yeah, it's really sad," when children expressed sadness over deaths during the war. This approach acknowledged their feelings without overwhelming them, fostering a safe emotional space where they could process their emotions. Similarly, Esther explained how activities like *davening* (praying) for specific people, such as soldiers or parents in Israel, provided children with a calm, ritualized practice. These moments of structured reflection reinforced the children's personal and emotional connections to Israel while helping them maintain their composure by channeling their emotions into meaningful, reassuring actions.

These practices underscore the value of creating intentional spaces for emotional exploration and employing strategies that nurture resilience, enabling children to process complex experiences while strengthening their emotional growth.

Encouraging Agency and Problem-Solving. The creative play that the participants encouraged in their classes when they challenged traditional notions of childhood innocence also appeared to foster children's agency, allowing them to take ownership of their actions and decisions in the classroom in a way that would be meaningful to them. In classroom 4A, children incorporated their understanding of real-world events into imaginative play. Rachel explained: "Their play has definitely been like, 'Oh, we're the good guys, and we're going to fight the bad guys in Israel.'" But the children could choose to shift their play, such as after significant events, like when Israeli soldiers returned safely. Rachel noted that then "they didn't want to play the game anymore because they're like, 'Oh, this is real life. It's not just pretend.'"

This ability to reinterpret and adapt their play shows how children can be empowered to take ownership of their narratives.

In classroom 3A, agency was encouraged by letting discussions extend beyond planned lessons or guided questions. Sarah stated that in a discussion about community helpers, "the children came up with some of them on their own . . . They said policemen and firemen are here to protect us, just like soldiers in Israel." This activity allowed the children to draw on their own knowledge and make meaningful connections.

Creative play also provided examples of how the children were encouraged to engage in problem-solving, an activity that promotes resilience by enhancing children's belief in their own capabilities. Regarding the previously described block play when children built army bases, Miriam noted how the structures evolved daily. Reflecting on this, she remarked, "It felt like they were working something through." Problem-solving was also evident in the teachers' descriptions of how the children brainstormed ways to bring joy to soldiers during art activities. Leah shared, "They were really thinking, 'What should we draw? What would they like? What would make them happy?'"

It also appeared in one classroom discussion that children were using problem-solving to make sense of their world using historical parallels. Deborah reported that, during a lesson about Chanukah, many of the children connected the story of a small army defeating a larger one to the current situation in Israel. One child said, "I hope that's now, I hope it is the same thing." Deborah noted, "That was his way of saying, 'I hope that we [Israel] win.'" Another child expressed that he hoped that the war in Israel would have the same outcome as the Chanukah story and "that we all get presents."

Across these examples, teachers created environments where children could exercise agency and engage in problem-solving, whether through play, creative expression, or meaningful discussions. Based on the students' responses reported by the teachers, these activities appeared to empower the children to process complex ideas and take ownership of their learning experiences in those instances.

Grounding Experiences in Meaningful Contexts. The setting of the Jewish early learning center ensured that all of the activities and discussions about the war were interwoven with lessons and activities involving Jewish identity and traditions, allowing the children to draw on their personal and collective strengths. For example, the children in the K1 classroom requested that their Thanksgiving celebration include both an Israeli and an American flag. This led to a child-led exploration of the Macy's Thanksgiving Day

Parade, where children created floats with both American and Israeli symbols. In another example, Sarah noted how, during a lesson on the creation of the sun, moon, and stars, the children in her class made connections between the stars in the classroom and the star on the Israeli flag. She explained, "The children realized that the star on the flag is a Magen David [Star of David], and they associated it with Israel, saying things like, 'It has six corners and points to the sky where Hashem [God] is,' and 'It's a special star.'"

Teachers particularly emphasized three aspects of Jewish culture: prayer, storytelling, and action. The singing of "Hatikvah," in addition to serving as a structured, became a profound expression of prayer and connection in the classrooms. Rosie shared, "When we sing 'Hatikvah,' the children stand with intention, often closing their eyes as if they are part of something much larger than themselves." Esther noted, "It's amazing to hear them sing 'Hatikvah' even during playtime—it shows how deeply it has resonated with them."

Storytelling, an essential part of Jewish culture, provided another avenue for grounding the children's understanding. Teachers connected current events to weekly Torah portions. For instance, the story of Abraham and Lot's conflict in the book of Genesis was used to help children draw parallels to modern events, fostering a deeper understanding of community and resilience. This was a strategy to enable the children to see their heritage as a source of strength and guidance.

Teachers also integrated the Jewish tradition of tzedakah, or charity, into their classroom practices. For example, children collected tzedakah money to support Israeli soldiers. Rosie explained, "The children know I'm going to bring goodies to the soldiers using their tzedakah money, and they're excited about that." The teacher utilized the Jewish value of giving back to the community to foster a sense of connection and purpose that could help the children see their place in the world, an essential component of resilience.

As part of the school experience, teachers routinely encouraged the children to recognize their role within a larger collective. During this challenging time, particularly when adults related or known to the children were directly involved in the war in Israel, teachers did things like creating a "soldier wall" showcasing soldiers connected to the school community. "Each soldier on the wall was meaningful to the kids. It helped them see themselves as part of a bigger story, offering both pride and comfort," Rosie shared. This reinforcement of identity and community was a strategy to not only provide a sense of stability in the present but also to ground the children's experience in a meaningful context, which could enhance their resilience and ability to cope with future adversity.

Discussion

This study describes how eight teachers at a Jewish early childhood learning center met the task of teaching their students in the aftermath of the October 7, 2023, terrorist attack on Israel. They attempted both to preserve the childhood innocence of their students and to challenge the traditional notions of childhood innocence by acknowledging the children's awareness of and need to process the tragic situation. The experiences shared by these teachers align with research suggesting that shielding children from difficult realities is not the most effective pedagogical approach (Baines et al., 2018; Ladson-Billings, 2017; Muller, 2022). While innocence has traditionally been framed as a shield (Nguyen, 2021), this study underscores the importance of treating it as a continuum—one that balances emotional protection with opportunities for growth and understanding. The educators interviewed for this study believe that their young students, when supported by thoughtful pedagogy, were capable of processing complex realities without compromising their emotional well-being and that doing so was of great importance. The study provides examples of strategies that were used by the teachers which can be utilized or modified for use by other early educators in times of national or communal crisis.

This study also highlights the potential for Jewish early childhood education to foster deep and meaningful connections to Israel within the framework of resilience-building and balanced innocence. Building on the work of Applebaum and Zakai (2020), who emphasize young children's capacity to conceptualize Israel as a distinctly Jewish place, the findings here suggest that intentional, age-appropriate pedagogy can extend these connections beyond cultural symbols. The teachers in this study reported that the children in their classes demonstrated clear ties to Israel, rooted in familial and communal experiences, which supported their resilience in processing difficult realities. This interplay between cultural identity and emotional well-being illustrates how early childhood Jewish educators can use discussions about Israel not only to deepen their students' cultural awareness but also to provide a stable, hopeful framework for them in navigating adversity.

The study also explains how strategies used by the educators to offer comfort to the students and help them understand and process what was happening were also well-suited to promote resilience in the students that could aid them in facing adversity in the future. An interesting finding was that it was often the nature and context of early childhood Jewish education itself that provided major components of teaching resilience to young children in a time of crisis—grounding their experience in a meaningful context; helping the children understand their place in the world; supporting their identity formation; enabling the children to see their experiences reflected in cultural practices, storytelling, and community engagement; and offering the children a framework for processing adversity, enabling them to draw on their personal and collective strengths. Therefore, it appears that in early childhood Jewish education, resilience-building strategies are readily available and take on additional depth through the integration of cultural and community resources. Jewish traditions—such as storytelling, rituals, and communal gatherings—naturally promote resilience by fostering belonging, continuity, and hope. Rituals that emphasize renewal and growth provide children with tools to process difficult experiences within a framework of stability and optimism.

This study provides a model for what early childhood education can look like in times of crisis by balancing the need to protect childhood innocence with an acknowledgment of and a desire to respect and nurture young children's understanding and agency. It also shows how the culture and traditions of early childhood Jewish education may promote resilience in students in facing crises—how its practices can transcend historical narratives, addressing contemporary crises and offering a blueprint for early childhood education that honors children's capacities while grounding them in meaning and purpose.

Limitations and Future Research

While this study provides valuable insights, it is limited by its small and culturally specific sample population, its reliance on self-reported data, and the personal involvement in the school by the researchers. All three of these factors may have introduced bias or influenced the interviewees. The short time frame captures only the immediate aftermath of the crisis, leaving long-term impacts and evolving strategies unexplored. Future research should include children's and families' perspectives to gain a holistic understanding of these educational approaches. Exploring how children experience trauma-informed teaching can illuminate its impact on their well-being, while family insights can reveal the broader ecosystem of support. Additionally, studying the role of the wider school community can provide a systemic view of resilience-building during crises.

Conclusion

The experiences of these early childhood Jewish educators offer a compelling model for rethinking childhood innocence and resilience. By drawing on Jewish narratives and practices, they demonstrated how to balance emotional protection with empowerment in their attempts to equip children for navigating a complex world with adaptability and hope. As Rabbi Kook (1963) wrote, "The purest light is that which emerges from the greatest darkness." By attempting to foster resilience and nurture hope in their young students, these educators provided examples of how to transform challenges into opportunities for growth. The findings contribute to calls for a shift in early childhood education away from focusing solely on protection towards actively fostering resilience and thriving. These educators provided a roadmap for how to use culturally meaningful practices in early childhood Jewish education to navigate crises while promoting growth. However, these insights are applicable not only to Jewish education but also to broader contexts, where cultural resources can be leveraged to build resilience and adaptability in young children, ensuring a brighter future for themselves and their communities.

References

American Psychological Association (2020). Building your resilience. https://www.apa.org/topics/resilience/building-your-resilience

Anti-Defamation League (2023). *Audit of antisemitic incidents 2023.* https://www.adl.org/audit2023

Applebaum, L., and Zakai, S. (2020). "I'm going to Israel and all I need to pack is my imagination": Pretend trips to Israel in Jewish early childhood education. *Journal of Jewish Education, 86*(1), 94–119. https://doi.org/10.1080/15244113.2019.1696659

Arndt, S., Smith, K., Urban, M., Ellegaard, T., Blue Swadener, B., and Murray, C. (2021). Reconceptualising and (re)forming early childhood professional identities: Ongoing transnational policy discussions. *Policy Futures in Education, 19*(4), 406–423. https://doi.org/10.1177/1478210320976015

Baines, J., Tisdale, C., and Long, S. (2018). *"We've been doing it your way long enough": Choosing the culturally relevant classroom.* Teachers College Press.

Ben-Moshe, L., Erevelles, N., and Meiners, E. R. (2021). Abolishing innocence: Disrupting the racist/ableist pathologies of childhood. In M. J. Smith and P. K. Lee (Eds.), *Building abolition* (pp. 58–67). Routledge.

Berger, E., and Martin, K. (2021). Embedding trauma-informed practice within the education sector. *Journal of Community and Applied Social Psychology, 31*(2), 223–227. https://doi.org/10.1002/casp.2494

Bethell, C., Jones, J., Gombojav, N., Linkenbach, J., and Sege, R. (2019). Positive childhood experiences and adult mental and relational health in a statewide sample: Associations across adverse childhood experiences levels. *JAMA Pediatrics, 173*(11), e193007. https://doi.org/10.1001/jamapediatrics.2019.3007

Bradshaw, E. L., Sahdra, B. K., Ciarrochi, J., Parker, P. D., Martos, T., and Ryan, R. M. (2021). A configural approach to aspirations: The social breadth of aspiration profiles predicts well-being over and above the intrinsic and extrinsic aspirations that comprise the profiles. *Journal of Personality and Social Psychology, 120*(1), 226–256.

Buhler-Niederberger, D. (2007). *The power of innocence: Social politics for children between separation and participation.* Children's Well-being International Documentation Centre.

Center on the Developing Child at Harvard University (2016). *Building core capabilities for life: The science behind the skills adults need to succeed in parenting and in the workplace.* Harvard University. https://developingchild.harvard.edu/resources/building-core-capabilities-for-life/

Chang-Kredl, S., and Kozak, S. (2018). Children using Facebook: Teachers' discursive constructions of childhood. *Learning, Media and Technology, 43*(2), 211–215.

Duschinsky, R. (2013). Childhood innocence: essence, education, and performativity. *Textual Practice, 27*(5), 763–781. https://doi.org/10.1080/0950236X.2012.751441

Egan, R. D., and Hawkes, G. L. (2012). Sexuality, youth and the perils of endangered innocence: How history can help us get past the panic. *Gender and Education, 24*(3), 269–284.

Faulkner, J. (2011). *The importance of being innocent: Why we worry about children*. Cambridge University Press.

Garlen, J. C. (2019). Interrogating innocence: "Childhood" as exclusionary social practice. *Childhood, 26*(1), 54–67. https://doi.org/10.1177/0907568218811484

Gilliam, W. S., Maupin, A. N., Reyes, C. R., Accavitti, M., and Shic, F. (2016). Do early educators' implicit biases regarding sex and race relate to behavior expectations and recommendations of preschool expulsions and suspensions. *Yale University Child Study Center, 9*(28), 1–16.

Kook, A. I. (1963). *Orot ha-teshuva* [The lights of repentance]. World Zionist Organization. (Original work published 1925.)

Kuypers, L. M. (2011). *The zones of regulation: A curriculum designed to foster self-regulation and emotional control*. Think Social Publishing, Incorporated.

Ladson-Billings, G. (2017). The (r)evolution will not be standardized: Teacher education, hip hop pedagogy, and culturally relevant pedagogy 2.0. In D. Paris and S. Alim (Eds.), *Culturally sustaining pedagogies: Teaching and learning for justice in a changing world* (pp. 141–156). Teachers College Press.

Masten, A. S. (2018). Resilience theory and research on children and families: Past, present, and promise. *Journal of Family Theory and Review, 10*(1), 12–31.

Masten, A. S., and Barnes, A. J. (2018). Resilience in children: Developmental perspectives. *Children, 5*(7), 98. https://doi.org/10.3390/children5070098

Maza, S. (2020). The kids aren't all right: Historians and the problem of childhood. *American Historical Review, 125*(4), 1261–1285.

Muller, M. (2022). Pre-service teachers engage young children in equity work. *Journal of Early Childhood Teacher Education, 43*(3), 347–362. https://doi.org/10.1080/10901027.2020.1832632

Nguyen, A. (2021). Childhood innocence and the racialized child in a white space. *NEOS, 13*(1). https://acyig.americananthro.org/nguyen/

Pfefferbaum, B., Jacobs, A. K., Houston, J. B., and Griffin, N. (2015). Children's disaster reactions: The influence of family and social factors. *Current Psychiatry Reports, 17*, 57.

Shelton, A. (2024). If I could turn back time: An educator's reflective journey into trauma-informed care. *Childhood Education, 100*(2), 36–41.

Spradley, J. (1980). *Participant observation*. Holt, Rinehart and Winston.

Sun, Y., Skouteris, H., Bowden, M., Cameron, L., and Blewitt, C. (2024). "It takes reflection at all different levels, not just people on the floor": A qualitative exploration of early childhood professionals' experiences and perspectives towards trauma-informed early childhood organisations. *School Mental Health*, 16(6), 959–972. https://doi.org/10.1007/s12310-024-09674-6

Thomas, E. E. (2019). *The dark fantastic: Race and the imagination from Harry Potter to the Hunger Games*. New York University Press.

Ungar, M. (2021). *Multisystemic resilience: Adaptation and transformation in contexts of change*. Oxford University Press.

Vogelstein, I., Goodman, R., and Alexander, S. (2023). Early childhood Jewish education in the United States. In S. Achituv, M. Muller, S. T. Alexander, and H. Alexander (Eds.), *Early childhood Jewish education: Multicultural, gender, and constructivist perspectives* (pp. 69–82). Bloomsbury Publishing.

Wassell, S., and Daniel, B. (2002). *The early years: Assessing and promoting resilience in vulnerable children*. Jessica Kingsley Publishers.

Woodrow, C. (1999). Revisiting images of the child in early childhood education: Reflections and considerations. *Australian Journal of Early Childhood*, 24(4), 7–12.

Woodrow, C., and Brennan, M. (2001). Interrupting dominant images: Critical and ethical issues. CQUniversity. Chapter. https://hdl.handle.net/10018/922439

Yeager, D. S., and Dweck, C. S. (2020). What can be learned from growth mindset controversies? *American Psychologist*, 75(9), 1269.

Teaching Palestinian Perspectives and the Pedagogy of "Historical Empathy"

Benji Davis

Introduction

Since the introduction of the phrase "Hugging and Wrestling with Israel" to describe what the vision and pedagogy of Israel education should embody (Gringras, 2008), the field has come to embrace "Israel in all its complexity" (Mapping the Landscape, 2012, p. 29). Israel educators describe their curriculum, pedagogy, experiences, and visions within the framing of complexity (Davis and Alexander, 2023). Given this communal and professional consensus to the "complexity hypothesis" to Israel education (Backenroth and Sinclair, 2014), how do Israel education teachers continue to teach Israel as a complex educational subject, even during times of existential war? How do Israel education teachers teach about Palestinians and their perspectives on Zionism and Israel in the aftermath of the Hamas massacre on October 7 and Israel's subsequent war against Palestinian terror groups? How do Israel educators teach about the history of the Israeli-Palestinian Conflict when that history is playing out in the present? How do they embrace the "complexity hypothesis" with increasing antisemitism directly tied to pro-Palestinian activists in their communities and on many of the campuses their students will attend upon graduation? How did the October 7 War's impact on their personal orientations to the subject matter influence their teaching in the classroom?

This qualitative study is about how Israel education teachers teach about Palestinian perspectives of Zionism and Israel after October 7. It contributes to a burgeoning body of research on Israel education as a subfield of Jewish education (Davis and Alexander, 2023; Reingold, 2017; Zakai, 2014), with a focus on teaching (Davis and Alexander, 2024, 2025; Zakai and Reingold, 2024). It also supplements emerging educational research after October 7 on North American Jewish educators (Kopelowitz et al., 2024), high school students (Reingold, 2024), college students (*Boundless Israel,* 2024), and participants on Israel programs (Wright et al., 2024).

This study also contributes to educational scholarship on teaching history with "historical empathy" (Barton and Levstik, 2004). Similarly to teaching "morally complex narratives" (Reingold, 2017) in Israel education, history teachers embrace the pedagogy of "historical empathy" from a "multiperspectivity" approach, which treats history as "interpretational and subjective with multiple coexisting narratives about particular historical events rather than being objectively represented by one closed narrative" (Bartelds et al., 2020, p. 531). Just as this study contributes to the body of literature on teaching of Israel education, with its focus on the pedagogy for teaching about Palestinian perspectives, it supplements the scholarship on teaching with "historical empathy" by investigating teaching conflicting history during a time of war.

The findings of this study demonstrate how teachers continued teaching Palestinian perspectives with a pedagogy of "historical empathy" after October 7. This study reveals how Israel education teachers navigate their personal orientation to the subject matter to continue teaching "morally complex narratives" with "historical empathy" about Palestinian perspectives about Zionism and Israel after October 7. In contrast with many of their Israeli counterparts, the teachers of Israel education in Jewish high schools interviewed in this study continued with the curriculum of their courses subsequently in the aftermath October 7 because of their educational goals to teach "morally complex narratives", as opposed to their Israeli counterparts who made pedagogical choices on whether to continue their curricula based on an "ethics of care" (Hassenfeld, 2024). But similarly to educators in Israel, October 7 deeply impacted North American Israel education teachers' epistemological understandings and political beliefs, which influenced how they pedagogically approached their teaching material. For Israel education teachers, the impact of October 7 and the subsequent war impacted whether and how they adjusted content pieces, lessons, and pedagogies in their classroom to teach about Palestinian perspectives. This was most apparent in teachers' pedagogy regarding humanizing Palestinians in their classroom in the shadows of the October 7 massacre as the war was being fought on multiple fronts. This ranged from continuing the same pedagogical approach as before October 7 to cultivate empathy amongst their students to grappling with how to humanize Palestinians during a war in which their personal beliefs shifted to decreasing or lacking feeling empathy or sympathy for Palestinians.

This chapter suggests two educational implications, one for history education and the second for those concerned with Israel education. Firstly, it presents pedagogical insights into how teachers reconcile epistemological and political shifts in their personal orientations to the subject matter while continuing to teach conflicted history with a pedagogy of "historical empathy". Secondly, it supports previous scholarship on the relevance of emphasizing teaching Israel as a civic and political issue, otherwise known as the Jewish Civic Education approach to Israel education (Davis and Alexander, 2023). However, the evidence-based examples in this study emphasize the need to philosophically address the weakness of the ethical liberalism embraced by North American Jewish educators to ensure Jewish civic engagement continues when Israel is no longer a pressing controversial issue. These pedagogic insights emphasize how embracing the Mature Zionism approach to Israel education (Alexander, 2015a; Davis and Alexander, 2023) teaches students to consider what it means to have a nuanced commitment to Israel as they define their own ethical Jewish identities.

Data Collection and Analysis

Utilizing snowball sampling (Noy, 2008), this study utilized a phenomenological approach to qualitative research (Eddles-Hirsch, 2015). The phenomenon investigated was the teaching of Palestinian perspectives of Zionism and Israel after October 7 in Israel education. Utilizing semi-structured interviews, I interviewed ten teachers of Israel education in ten North American Jewish high schools across the religious denominational spectrum. I interviewed each teacher for 60-90 minutes. The interviews were conducted, recorded, and transcribed through the Zoom platform. Teachers described their experience in teaching about Palestinian perspectives in their courses on Modern Israeli history in their Jewish high schools. Following phenomenological approaches to qualitative research, I analyzed each interview as a single phenomenon (Cilesiz, 2011). Utilizing what Moustakas (1994) describes as horizons, I then synthesized the themes embodied in each teachers' experience to understand interviewees shared phenomenon of teaching Palestinian perspectives after October 7 in their Israel education courses.

Research Field

The Israel education teachers I interviewed taught courses in Community Pluralistic, Independent, Community Modern Orthodox, and Modern Orthodox Jewish High Schools. The Israel education courses teachers taught were either required history, required elective, or optional elective courses for students in tenth, eleventh, or twelfth grade. The length of each course ranged from a quarter, semester, or year long. Each course's curriculum spent a significant time on the Israeli-Palestinian conflict and perspectives of Palestinians.

Ethics of Research and Positioning

This study was approved by the institutional review board of George Mason University's Humanities Faculty. All interviewees gave their consent to participate in the study. I gave pseudonyms to each research participant to anonymize their identities. Where relevant, their institutions also gave permission for the teachers to participate in this study.

Similarly to the teachers interviewed, I'm also an "Israel educator." In addition to teaching Israel studies on a North American campus, I have worked professionally in the Israel education space as a teacher, director, and experiential educator. Like the interviewees, I'm also a North American Jew. Many of the teachers in this study have lived or spent significant time in Israel. I made *aliyah* at age twenty-two and lived in Israel for fifteen years. Like the teachers, I also have been living through the October 7 War, with all its personal and professional challenges. My cultural familiarity with the personal and professional references teachers made gave me a broader understanding of the context of the phenomenon in question, which enriched this study's insights.

Findings

Commitment to teaching with "Historical Empathy" after October 7

Jewish communal researchers and professionals call the increased interest in Israel and Jewish life after October 7 as "the surge" (Kravetz, Eisenman, and Manchester, 2024). Similarly, Israel education teachers commented on an increased interest in their work by parents, administrators, and their community at large. As Marissa reflected on this point and the "greater responsibility" she feels after October 7, "my class is the most important class in the school which I felt before, anyway. But now I really feel it." But the massacre and subsequent war also emphasized the importance of continuing to teach with complexity.

> Having a solid grounding in a sophisticated, nuanced understanding of the history of the modern State of Israel is not really a luxury, it's a necessity. So, it wasn't so much content needed to change as much as like we got to get this to as many students as possible. (Ariel)

Teachers described the increased importance of teaching Israel from a historical approach after October 7. Isaac explained his approach, "the shock of October 7 also necessitated paying more attention to how history impacted the conflict" (Isaac). Ariel emphasized that "the impact of October 7 is much more a doubling down on the need for kids to understand the history."

Similarly to before October 7, teachers utilize different types of primary sources to teach about the complexity of Zionism and Israel, which includes considering Palestinian perspectives on historical events. They employed documentaries and podcasts by non-Palestinian content creators, and Palestinian poetry and intellectual histories by Palestinian scholars like Rashid Khalidi and Edward Said. They had students critically examine international documents and treaties, which included "McMahon-Hussein to the British Mandate to Balfour to [the] Peel commission, etc., [to analyze] what the documents say and how it impacted history and how it impacts where we are today" (Isaac). Teachers asked students to grapple with early twentieth-century Zionist texts that consider how the Arabs of Palestine should react to Zionism, like Yitzhak Epstein's *The Hidden Question*. Ariel explains the utility of this text in teaching "historical empathy" because it shows how early Zionists considered Palestinian perspectives about their mission to settle the land of Israel: "It's great that we are Zionists, and it's great that we're forming this connection with our homeland . . . but have we really considered about what's going to happen when we buy land legally you know that the *falachin* [Arab Palestinians] are living on, and they can no longer live on the land?" Israel educators utilize Palestinian primary sources such as the PLO

(Palestinian Liberation Organization) charter to teach about Palestinian rejectionism of Zionism. One teacher describes utilizing this text reflecting Palestinian perspectives to help her students understand the concept of Jewish nationhood: "Part of the PLO charter is that the Jews are not actually a nation. How does this relate back to previous conversations we have had about Jewish nationhood and the way it has been conceived over the course of the nineteenth to twentieth century?" (Talia).

Teachers described continuing this emphasis on teaching Palestinian perspectives of and experiences with Zionism even after October 7 because it is an essential approach to Israel education. David comments that he continued teaching Palestinian perspectives after October 7 because "it's part of the approach of Israel education to bring in multiple narratives and to help cultivate empathy, which doesn't necessarily mean that you agree with the other side." Teachers believe in an increased importance for teaching Palestinian perspectives after October 7 because it best prepares students for "campus." Evan summarized this sentiment, "I think, especially again after October 7, I think back to my own experience when I was a graduate student. These moments, where it becomes very obvious that you are the Jew who's in the room, and you're expected to have some kind of thought about this." Teachers describe teaching conflicted history about Palestinian perspectives helps students better understand current events. Marissa explains this approach to her curriculum: "I plowed on because I really felt, if I only focused on the modern stuff, or, like, answered their [students'] questions in the now, then they would lose the history piece of it, which I think obviously builds up to where we are." Just like before October 7, Israel educators continued to believe teaching conflicted history about Israel, including Palestinian perspectives, requires embracing complexity.

> The purpose is, we teach history in a complex way... When I teach US history, I teach about all the horrible things that we did, and the trail of tears and slavery, and the Jim Crow South and lynching.... I want my students to walk out patriotic Americans and proud citizens of this country. Why would I teach Israel any differently? (Leah)

Teachers encourage students to grapple with the ethical dilemma of Palestinians not having their own state and what it means for Israel to historically, whether partially or fully, rule over them. One teacher describes their pedagogy for teaching this Palestinian perspective by showing a picture of an Israeli soldier bending down on one knee to speak at the eye level of a Palestinian child:

> So, they're [students] going to say, well, we see an Israeli soldier who's like going down to the level of a kid . . . And I said, "Okay, where is this picture taken?" They look, and they're like, "Well, we don't know 100%." I said, "Okay, but like, take a guess. Where do you think it's taken?" And they then realize that they see the barbed wire behind in the back [that] it's possible that this girl is a Palestinian girl as opposed to a Jewish girl. It's possible that they could go down that road. They then realize that they're probably at a checkpoint. And then we talk about, "Okay, so now you're only focusing on the soldier. Could you see why this could make someone uncomfortable?" And they will turn around and say, "Yeah, I got it. That little girl now has to see life around this soldier." (Brad)

Teachers emphasized the rootedness of Palestinians in their homeland and the lived experience of Palestinians. Jason described how he teaches students to understand that "Palestinians exist, they're a people. They have an authentic and deep and long-lasting connection to the land in the same way that we do." Another teacher echoed this sentiment for enriching students' complex understandings of the Palestinian experience.

> I think it's fundamental to say they're a legitimate people who have claims. I think it's fundamental to help [students] understand Palestinians' lived lives in the West Bank and East Jerusalem today, and for it not to be sort of this, "Well, we had to put up this barrier because of the Second Intifada, and whatever, it's kept Israel safe. So, you know, that's it." (Leah)

Teachers framed teaching Palestinian historical perspectives as crucial for their students to understand their Jewish identities. David describes this pedagogical approach: "You don't just teach Israel as if we're teaching another country. We're teaching it specifically, not just so that they end up being supporters of Israel, but that it becomes part of their Jewish identity." Israel educators teach about Palestinian perspectives of Israel because it helps students understand what it means to be a Zionist.

> It really just comes back to like the core questions, "Does Israel have the right to exist as a country?" That is actually the great challenge. And for that, you have to know your history, and to know your history, you also have to understand Palestinian history because it's inextricably linked. (Ariel)

Navigating Personal Orientations to Humanizing Palestinians

As before October 7, teachers emphasized the importance of pedagogically humanizing Palestinians.

> I would just say that another big goal for me, too, is just to find a way to humanize Palestinians... These students will actually read the voices of Palestinians. [How do they] understand, to some small degree, at the very least, what is the Palestinian experience? How are Palestinians viewing this conflict, past and present? (Evan)

While teachers mentioned the importance of humanizing Palestinians because of their commitment to teaching complex Israel education, they also described how they navigated the impact of October 7 and the subsequent war on their personal orientation regarding the subject matter to continue teaching with "historical empathy."

No Political or Epistemological Change in Orientation. As October 7 confirmed Ariel's previous epistemological understanding, he did not change what or how he taught, except with adding a "selection of eulogies from post October 7... to the back of the reader." He explains why the contemporary reality solidified his previous understanding of Palestinian rejectionism.

> While October 7 is the worst possible representation of Hamas's desires against the State of Israel since its founding, it is still representative of those desires. Since its founding, they've never done this [massacre] before. But Israel in their eyes does not have the right to exist. Jews everywhere do not have the right to live. That's, for better or for worse, in their charter. The kids already had been exposed to their charter or would have been even if it wasn't 2023. (Ariel)

Teachers who continued to exhibit personal empathy for Palestinians after October 7 connected their personal orientations to the subject matter to their "historical empathy" pedagogy in the classroom.

> I gotta recognize their humanity. You gotta recognize their humanity, and I try to keep my politics outside of the classroom. I would say that I really hope that my students come away from this class feeling it's much harder to say "no" in regards to this question of whether or not Palestinians deserve civil and human rights. (Evan)

Such teachers' pedagogy emphasized the importance of students distinguishing enmity for Hamas and sympathy for innocent Palestinians. They attempt to help students reconcile two conflicting truths about a controversial issue, a historically pedagogic point of contention amongst scholars of education (Piaget, 2007; Vygotsky, 1978).

> One of the things that I've sort of taught all along about the war in Gaza is we can both say that Hamas is evil and needs to be defeated, and also have empathy and articulate, and, like, feel bad about the suffering of the Palestinians on the ground there. Like I think that's a notion that, like I don't know is sometimes hard for students to have those two things together which seems like pretty basic. (Jason)

However, even if their political and epistemological understandings were not transformed by the war, teachers still grappled with how to humanize Palestinians because of their personal, student, and communal connections to the Israeli side in the war. David explains, "So yeah, it's difficult. How are you meant to cultivate empathy for the other side when you're actually in a war?" Pedagogically, David adjusted his unit on religious peace building to teach students how "Arabs are not the enemy. Islam is not the enemy. Nothing is inevitable." Reframing religious peace building to distancing individual people from the violent and hateful actions of ideological Arab or Islamist groups embodied his attempt to humanize Palestinians. However, he grappled with his pedagogic impulse to humanize Palestinians when the context of the war enters his classroom.

> How am I meant to tell a student who told me that his older brother is in the IDF, is in *Tzanchanim* [paratroopers], and they're serving in Gaza, and, just the other day, they were inside some building, a sniper shot his commander, who was standing a few meters away from his brother. How am I meant to respond to that? How am I meant to go from that tenth-grade lesson where that tenth grader told me that to an eleventh-grade course on Israel and teaching that there's multiple perspectives? It's not so simple. And yeah, not all Arabs are the enemy. (David)

Continued Pedagogical Commitment to Complexity despite Decreased Personal Empathy. Teachers who were no longer empathetic towards Palestinian perspectives because of October 7 continued teaching with the same commitment to "complexity." They grappled with how to continue teaching such a controversial issue with "historical empathy" given their new personal orientation. Donna reflects on this challenge: "I think, as I feel less sympathy, I make less of an effort to engender empathy, which is not great." Leah frames teaching Palestinian perspectives as a cognitive rather than moral exercise after October 7.

> I found myself saying, "It's important to understand," and I sort of eschewed the word "empathy" . . . I don't know that anyone picked up on that. I didn't announce to them. I used to say "empathy." And now I'm just going to say understanding, because that's how I'm feeling right now. (Leah)

She describes the challenge in teaching with "historical empathy" given her new personal orientation.

> It was more difficult for me personally than it's been in the past to say. "Well, you know, when the protesters say, 'from the river to the sea,' they're just saying there should be one State [for Israelis and Palestinians], and everybody should be free, and it's not necessarily antisemitic. And when Jews hear that, or Zionists, or Israelis who hear that, most of them hear it as a genocidal call to destroy the Jews in Israel. And for me personally it was very difficult. I did it, but much more

difficult than in the past to sort of give that, "Well, this is what they say, and this is what we say." (Leah)

Teachers identifying a change in their personal empathy for Palestinians describe how they continued teaching with "historical empathy" by preventing their personal beliefs from entering the classroom. Donna describes navigating this tension: "Even if I know myself to be personally hardened, I don't think it's appropriate for teachers to entirely teach from their own perspectives. Right? What use is that?" Talia echoes this sentiment and describes her continued commitment to teaching towards having students grapple with the complexity of the subject matter.

> Something in me hardened for sure. At the same time, we're dealing with like millions of people. I think that, post October 7, I don't think that things necessarily have to be different in terms of the way we teach certain things. It just strengthens the need to when you're analyzing anything that people are saying, posting public statements, "What's the motivation? And how do you know what you know? What is the proof for any assertion?" I think that existing questions probably just got strengthened. (Talia)

Teachers whose epistemological and political orientations to the subject matter led to decreased sympathy for Palestinians describe how their changed orientations influenced their pedagogic decisions in humanizing Palestinians by returning to Jewish historical narratives. Brad reflects on his teaching: "I will always end it with 'But remember, we've been there for 3,400 years.' Whereas maybe then [before October 7], I may not have added that last little bit. I recognize it's, like, in my head. It's because I don't want to leave that doubt anymore." These educators also emphasize teaching this controversial content from an objective history perspective. Donna explains she includes "more content on the Palestinian perspective than there used to be. But it used to be more from a sympathetic position. And I think now it's more from a historical position where I'm not nearly as sympathetic as I used to be." To navigate this personal change in beliefs, teachers employ content reflecting the complexity of the content they no longer believe in themselves.

> I would emotionally have a tough time being objective about it on a personal level because I'm just so disgusted post-October 7. I am so unbelievably disgusted and angry... It's best for me to use the historical sources, and then probably best for me to use stuff from Unpacked,[1] which has already gone through the process of being approached with nuance and compassion and complexity. (Talia)

Donna summarizes navigating this tension between her personal cynicism with her pedagogical commitment to "historical empathy":

> Like there's no moderation. I guess everything is extremism now. And I guess, really, how it's changed is that I'm attempting to teach moderation, even if it's moderation I don't always feel myself. (Donna)

Discussion

This study highlights two key implications for educational scholars and practitioners. One pertains to teaching Palestinian perspectives in Jewish education classrooms, while the other concerns addressing controversial issues in history and Israel education.

Firstly, teachers' navigation of their epistemological and political changes in their personal orientation to the subject matter while upholding their pedagogical principles in the history classroom highlights the connection between high school teacher beliefs and pedagogical content knowledge (Cess-Newsome, 1999). For teachers to teach with "historical empathy", they must be able to navigate potential transformations in their political identities that may distance themselves from personally believing in the empathy their professional obligations require of them as teachers. Otherwise, their teaching may no longer embody education and slide toward indoctrination (Alexander, 2015b).

Secondly, this study underscores Israel as a "rich case" (Zakai, 2022) for teaching civic and political issues in Jewish education, but only if such teaching cultivates students to conceive of their ethical Jewish identities (Davis and

---

1   Unpacked for Educators, https://unpacked.education/.

Alexander, 2023). Otherwise, Israel education as Jewish civic education may in fact only be another example of civic education if Israel is not understood as being integral to something particularly Jewish.

Navigating Cynical Personal Orientations to Teach with "Historical Empathy"

This study's findings demonstrate how teachers address changes in their personal orientations to the subject matter to continue their pedagogical, curricular, and vision towards teaching conflicted history with "historical empathy." When teachers had new epistemological understandings, they continued to find additional sources or pedagogies to teach about Palestinian perspectives and experiences. When teachers' political transformations regarding Palestinians decreased their capacity for sympathy or empathy, they found other ways to frame or teach about the subject matter. Teachers' professional commitment to educating conflicting history with "historical empathy" did not erode even as they no longer believed in the empathy they were teaching their students to embrace. As Donna emphasized, "I'm attempting to teach moderation, even if it's moderation I don't always feel myself." Teachers' commitment to teaching with "historical empathy" about an ongoing existential war in the homeland as a diaspora community presents a rich case for teaching controversial issues in the history classroom. It shows how teachers can continue to teach controversial issues when they are personally affected by events, occurring abroad or at home, that impact them personally and transform their beliefs.

This case confirms educational literature on the connection between teacher orientations to their subject matter and how that integrates with their pedagogical content knowledge (Cess-Newsome, 1999). It solidifies the importance that teacher educators emphasize teaching conflicted history with "historical empathy" during transformative moments in the present, even if doing so challenges teachers' sense of empathy to the "multiperspectivity" of their subject matter (Colby, 2008). These pedagogic insights counter a trend in educational scholarship embracing critical social theory in the social studies classroom that teaches students to accept teachers' political and epistemological beliefs regarding the subject matter as the embodiment of ethical beliefs without acknowledging their own agency to define their own beliefs beyond group identity (Alexander, 2018). This contrasts with an ethical educational approach to embrace the human agency of learners to empower students to cultivate autonomous orientations (Alexander, 1997;

Davis and Alexander, 2025; Taylor, 1992). Such commitments are a necessity for liberal education and a society that sees history education as foundational to preparing students to be engaged citizens in a democracy.

Teaching Israel as a Jewish Civic and Political Issue by Embracing Mature Zionism

This research confirms previous scholarship's findings that Israel is a rich case for Jewish civic education (Levisohn, 2020; Pomson and Held, 2012; Reingold, 2022; Zakai, 2022; Zakai and Reingold, 2024). This study's findings support previous empirical insights on why and how Jewish educators should teach Israel as a political and civic issue, especially since that is how their students and communities engage with it (Zakai, 2022). It confirms both teachers' (Davis and Alexander, 2024, 2025; Zakai and Reingold, 2024) and students' (Applebaum and Zakai, 2024; Zakai, 2022) interest and capacity to grapple with Israel as a controversial issue in the classroom (Hess and Gatti, 2010) not just during times of peace, but during an existential war.

However, for Israel to be a case for Jewish civic engagement, teachers must grapple with the particularity of Israel's meaning to Jewish students beyond its richness as a civic and political issue. Teachers emphasized how they embraced teaching controversial issues with "historical empathy"; however, they felt a "greater responsibility" (Leah; Talia) and "huge obligation" (Marissa) when it came to Israel. This acknowledges the increased Jewish civic engagement amongst teachers to teach Israel. This follows trends regarding transformative Jewish moments of pain and crisis catalyzing increased civic and political knowledge and engagement, such as when Jews organized to free Soviet Jews (Friedman, 1999), demonstrated during the Second Intifada (Kane, 2010), or came out in record numbers following the October 7 massacre in November 2023 for the March on Washington (*New York Times*, 2023). But just a year later in November 2024, a fraction of Jews came out to demonstrate (Jewish News Syndicate, 2024).

October 7 and the subsequent war and increased antisemitism in North America led to what many have called "the surge" in Jewish life. But when that ends, how will Israel as a civic and political issue continue to catalyze Jewish civic engagement if North American Jewish Education continues to frame Israel as part of a liberal religious identity that does not preference any vision of what it means to be Jewish over the right to choose whatever one wants to be (Davis and Alexander, 2023, 2024, 2025)? Therefore, when Israel recedes as a captive civic or political issue, so will Jewish civic engagement.

Israel education teachers in this study implement a "historical empathy" pedagogy for teaching Palestinian perspectives to help cultivate their students' ethical Jewish identities. As one teacher explained that, for Jewish students to know their own story, they must "understand Palestinian history because it's inextricably linked" (Ariel). Teachers of Israel education courses teach their subject matter not only for "complexity's" sake, but because teaching towards the cultivation of their students' Jewish identities requires contrasting their students' rootedness in the Jewish, Israeli, and Zionist story with the perspectives and experiences of Palestinians, even during an ongoing war between the sides. This study's findings demonstrate that for Israel education to effectively achieve its Jewish civic engagement aims, students should be given the opportunity to understand how Israel as a civic and political issue integrates with their ethical Jewishness beyond the richness of Israel as a controversial topic in the classroom. This may help them conceptualize what it means for them to live a meaningful Jewish life.

This pedagogy for teaching Palestinian perspectives with "historical empathy" in the shadows of October 7 embodies what Hanan Alexander and I describe as the Mature Zionism approach to Israel education (Alexander, 2015a; Davis and Alexander, 2023, 2024). Teachers interviewed in this study demonstrate how to implement a "pedagogy of difference" for teaching Israel and controversial issues in the classroom, which contends that to educate within a particular community's values, heritage, and tradition, teachers must also teach about perspectives that challenge that sacred position (Alexander, 2001). Even in a time of war, Israel educators teach the "other side." They grapple with how to humanize Palestinians. But they do so from their own community's particular position as Jews. They teach Palestinian perspectives for students not to just have a cognitive understanding of the conflicting history, but how students can learn about their Jewish rootedness in their story, land, and culture by contrasting it with that of Palestinians' sense of connection and meaning to their own stories. Israel education teachers demonstrate how to teach "multiperspectivity" regarding their subject matter, Israel, not only for "complexity's" sake, but because it represents an essential educational outlet to empower their students to conceive of their ethical Jewish identities in conversation with alternative visions of the good.

Conclusion

By navigating epistemological and political shifts in their personal beliefs, the Israel education teachers interviewed for this study all model some form of a pedagogy of "historical empathy" in their approach to teaching Palestinian perspectives. Their work offers valuable insights not only for Israel education but also for broader discussions on history education and identity formation in contexts of conflict. This study's findings underscore the transformative potential of teachers to foster ethical identity development through the teaching of conflicting histories, regardless of their political positions. In an era of intensifying illiberalism in democratic societies, the case of Israel educators teaching Palestinian perspectives—against the backdrop of the worst massacre of Jews since the Holocaust and during an existential war in Israel—provides a foundation for education scholars to further investigate pedagogies for teaching controversial issues that cultivate learners' rootedness in their civic and political identities while respecting the humanity of others.

References

Alexander, H. A. (1997). Jewish education and the search for authenticity: A study of Jewish identity. In D. Zisenwine & D. Schers (Eds.), *Making a difference: Jewish identity and education*, 37–65. Kelman Center for Jewish Education.

Alexander, H. A. (2001). *Reclaiming goodness: Education and the spiritual quest.* University of Notre Dame Press.

Alexander, H. A. (2015a). Mature Zionism: Education and the scholarly study of Israel. *Journal of Jewish Education, 81*(2), 136–161. https://doi.org/10.1080/15244113.2015.1035979.

Alexander, H. A. (2015b). *Reimaging liberal education: Affiliation and inquiry in democratic schooling.* New York: Bloomsbury.

Alexander, H. A. (2018). What is critical about critical pedagogy? Conflicting conceptions of criticism in the curriculum. *Educational Philosophy and Theory, 50*(10), 903–916. https://doi.org/10.1080/00131857.2016.1228519

Applebaum, L., & Zakai, S. (2024). Learning from children's ideas about October 7th and the Israel-Hamas war. Jewish Educational Leadership, Fall 2024. https://www.lookstein.org/journal-article/f_24/learning-from-childrens-ideas-about-october-7th-and-the-israel-hamas-war/

Backenroth, O., and Sinclair, A. (2014). Vision, Curriculum, and pedagogical content knowledge in the preparation of Israel educators.

Journal of Jewish Education, 80(2), 121–147. https://doi.org/10.1080/15244113.2014.907013

Bartelds, H., Savenije, G. M., and Van Boxtel, C. (2020). Students' and teachers' beliefs about historical empathy in secondary history education. *Theory and Research in Social Education, 48*(4), 529–551. https://doi.org/10.1080/00933104.2020.1808131

Barton, K. C., and Levstik, L. S. (2004). *Teaching history for the common good.* Lawrence Erlbaum Associates.

Boundless Israel (2024). Examining views on Israel and Jewish identity. *Boundless Israel*, August. https://boundlessisrael.org/August%202024%20Examining%20Views%20on%20Israel%20and%20Jewish%20Identity.pdf

Cess-Newsome, J. (1999). Secondary teachers' knowledge and beliefs about subject matter and their impact on instruction. In J. Gess-Newsome and N. G. Lederman (Eds.), *Examining pedagogical content knowledge: The construct and its implications for science education* (pp. 51–94). Springer.

Cilesiz, S. (2011). A phenomenological approach to experiences with technology: Current state, promise, and future directions for research. *Educational Technology Research and Development, 59*(4), 487–510. https://doi.org/10.1007/s11423-010-9173-2

Colby, S. R. (2008). Energizing the history classroom: Historical narrative inquiry and historical empathy. *Social Studies Research and Practice, 3*(3), 60–79. https://doi.org/10.1108/SSRP-03-2008-B0005

Davis, B., and Alexander, H.A. (2023). Israel education: A philosophical analysis. *Journal of Jewish Education, 89*(1), 6–33. https://doi.org/10.1080/15244113.2023.2169213

Davis, B., and Alexander, H.A. (2024). "You never told me": The pedagogical content knowledge (PCK) of Israel education. *Contemporary Jewry, 44*(2), 369–395. https://doi.org/10.1007/s12397-024-09562-w

Davis, B., & Alexander, H.A. (2025). Liberal Jewish identity and the pedagogy of Israel education. *Journal of Religious Education, 73*, 207–230. https://doi.org/10.1007/s40839-025-00261-8

Eddles-Hirsch, K. (2015). Phenomenology and educational research. *International Journal of Advanced Research, 3*(8).

Friedman, M. (1999). *A second exodus: The American movement to free Soviet Jews.* UPNE.

Gringras, R. (2008). Jewish World / We should stop hugging Israel and start wrestling. *Haaretz*, August 17.

Hassenfeld, Z. R. (2024). Curriculum on the front line: An ethics of care during war. *Contemporary Jewry*. https://doi.org/10.1007/s12397-024-09614-1

Hess, D., and Gatti, L. (2010). Putting politics where it belongs: In the classroom. *New Directions for Higher Education*, 2010(152), 19–26.

Jewish News Syndicate (2024). Organizers play down low turnout for Jewish pro-Israel rally in Washington. November 11. https://www.jns.org/organizers-play-down-low-turnout-for-jewish-pro-israel-rally-in-washington/

Levisohn, J. A. (2020). Mature love, nuanced loyalty, and redemptive vision: Conceptualizing the desired outcomes of Israel education. In J. Ariel (Ed.), *Israel education: The next edge* (pp. 37–56). The Israel Education Lab.

Kane, M. G. (2010). *From throwing stones to gathering stones: The impact of the second intifada on American Jewish identity.* Doctoral dissertation, Hebrew Union College-Jewish Institute of Religion, New York.

Kopelowitz, E., Ravid, S., Posklinsky, I., Golden, J., and Gillis, J. (2024). Responding to the fallout from October 7th: From crisis to opportunity. The Jewish Education Project, November 13. https://educator.jewishedproject.org/sites/default/files/2024-12/Educators%20Responding%20to%20post-October%207th.pdf

Kravetz, M., Eisenman, S., and Manchester, D. (2024). 'The surge,' 'the core' and more: What you need to know about the explosion of interest in Jewish life. *eJewishPhilanthropy*, May 9. https://ejewishphilanthropy.com/what-you-need-to-know-about-the-surge-of-interest-in-jewish-life/

Mapping the Landscape: The emergence of Israel education. (2012). The iCenter for Israel education.https://theicenter.org/wp-content/uploads/2021/03/Mapping-the-Field-of-Israel-Education-February-2012.pdf

Moustakas, C. (1994). *Phenomenological research methods*. Sage Publications.

New York Times (2023). March for Israel draws tens of thousands to Washington, D.C. rally. November 14. https://www.nytimes.com/2023/11/14/us/march-for-israel-washington-dc-rally.html

Noy, C. (2008). Sampling knowledge: The hermeneutics of snowball sampling in qualitative research. *International Journal of Social Research Methodology, 11*(4), 327–344. https://doi.org/10.1080/13645570701401305

Piaget, J. (2007). *The psychology of the child* (B. Weiss, Trans.). Basic Books.

Pomson, A., and Held, D. (2012). Why Israel? Reviewing Israel education through the lenses of civic and political engagement. *Journal of Jewish Education, 78*(2), 97–113. https://doi.org/10.1080/15244113.2012.682338

Reingold, M. (2017). Not the Israel of my elementary school: An exploration of Jewish-Canadian secondary students' attempts to process morally complex Israeli narratives. *The Social Studies, 108*(3), 87–98. https://doi.org/10.1080/00377996.2017.1324392

Reingold, M. (2024). Look What you made me do: Jewish Swifties and a fundraiser for Gaza. *Journal of Jewish Identities, 17*(2), 161–184. https://doi.org/10.1353/jji.2024.a936747

Taylor, C. (1992). *The ethics of authenticity.* Harvard University Press.

Vygotsky, L. S. (1978). *Mind in society: The development of higher psychological processes* (M. Cole, V. John-Steiner, S. Scribner, and E. Souberman, Eds.). Harvard University Press.

Wright, G., Hecht, S., Volodarsky, S., and Saxe, L. (2024). Birthright Israel's impact in the shadow of the Israel-Hamas war: Findings from the summer 2023 cohort. *Brandeis University Maurice and Marilyn Cohen Center for Modern Jewish Studies*, March.

Zakai, S. (2022). *My second favorite country.* NYU Press.

Zakai, S. (2014). "My Heart Is in the East and I Am in the West": Enduring Questions of Israel Education in North America. *Journal of Jewish Education, 80*(3), 287–318. https://doi.org/10.1080/15244113.2014.937192

Zakai, S., and Reingold, M. (Eds.) (2024). *Teaching Israel: Studies of Pedagogy from the Field.* Brandeis University Press.

Teachers' Identities in Transition: Hebrew Education in Light of October 7 and the Aftermath

*Vardit Ringvald and
Sharon Schoenfeld*[1]

"התלמידים מחפשים את זה, את הקשר. הם שמחים שאנחנו באות משם... הם באים לכיתה שלי ואומרים שהם רואים אותי. . . הם רואים את ישראל."

"The students are looking for it, for the connection. They're happy that we come from there . . . They come to my classroom and say that when they see me . . . They see Israel."[1]

—Aya, study participant[2]

For Hebrew language educators teaching outside of Israel, the events of October 7 marked a defining moment and a critical test of their roles and responsibilities. These educators experienced a significant shift, transforming from providers of Hebrew language education in an Israeli cultural context to professionals focused on interpreting and conveying Israel's new and complex reality to learners and their communities. Language education has undergone numerous transformations over the years, but our research brings

---

1 We are deeply grateful to our research assistant, Rosie Fellig, for her invaluable support in identifying and reviewing the literature for this article.
2 All names of interviewees mentioned in this article are pseudonyms to protect interviewees' privacy and ensure confidentiality.

to the surface the importance of the shift toward the integration of Israeli cultural instruction as a core component of Hebrew language teaching.

The Big Shift

In the late 1960s, second-language teaching underwent a pivotal transformation. Educators shifted their focus from teaching linguistic structures and grammar primarily for written translation to fostering communicative proficiency (Manoliu, 2012; Brown, 1997). This shift emphasized the need for language learners to master cultural nuances, enabling effective communication with native speakers in the target language (Hall, 1959; Hymes, 1964). However, while educators recognized the importance of integrating cultural elements, they often lacked the knowledge and tools to do so effectively. This challenge sparked debates around which cultural elements to teach, who should teach them, and how to balance cultural instruction with language acquisition goals (Kramsch, 2006).

Our observations from many years in the field working with Hebrew educators is that their expertise in language did not prepare them to teach the broad range of cultural knowledge necessary for contextualizing the target language. Two primary solutions emerged to address this challenge.

The first solution involved providing lessons on the target language's culture, often delivered by experts in the learners' native language and *outside* the language classroom. The second solution embedded cultural instruction *within* language lessons by including information about cultural elements that appeared in the teaching materials. This latter approach gained popularity, especially with the introduction of the concept authentic texts or materials[3] in the teaching of foreign languages (Rahman, 2014).

First released in 1986, the ACTFL Proficiency Guidelines remain a global standard for assessing learners' ability to communicate effectively in speaking, listening, writing, and reading (ACTFL, 1986). These guidelines set clear goals for language learners, emphasizing the ability to function in authentic

---

3   ACTFL authentic materials provide real-life examples of language used in everyday situations. They can be used to add more interest for the learner. They can serve as a reminder to learners that there is an entire population who use the target language in their everyday lives. Authentic materials can provide information about the target culture and provide that culture's perspective on an issue or event. The rich language found in authentic materials provides a source of input language learners need for acquisition.

contexts reflective of native speakers' communication styles. Successful language use, therefore, requires language skills that align with native speakers' cultural perspectives—shaped by historical events, beliefs, geography, and current realities.

This idea resonated with Hebrew language instructors in the early 1990s, especially following the publication of the Hebrew Functional Proficiency Guidelines (Gollan et al., 1990). It found a receptive audience in Jewish educational institutions, which used them to strengthen Hebrew teaching programs. The guidelines indicated that Hebrew language educators must undergo formal academic training, which would equip them to design curricula, develop teaching materials, and integrate cultural elements into their instruction effectively. The ACTFL's *Standards for Foreign Language Learning in the 21st Century* (1996), a further development of the Proficiency Guidelines, were designed to address all expectations of language learners, including cultural competency. These standards emphasized that "language is the primary vehicle for expressing cultural perspectives and participating in social practices" (ACTFL, 1996).

Despite broad consensus on the importance of cultural integration in language learning, its implementation remains uneven. Many programs continue to separate cultural lessons from language instruction or include cultural elements sporadically.

As stated above, since as early as the 1960s, experts and researchers have emphasized the importance of integrating cultural elements into language teaching in order to understand the perspectives of the native speaker of the target language. While the field of Hebrew language teaching has also embraced these ideas, the need to include the perspective shaped by the complexities of Israeli history and the Palestinian-Israeli conflict have presented unique challenges.

The events surrounding October 7 revealed even more and also profound challenges that underscore the indispensability of the Hebrew language educator, how they are perceived and how they see their role. This relates not just to Hebrew instruction, but also to the role of the language as it relates to connections with Israel and its people.

For Hebrew language educators, the close connection between the Hebrew language and Israel's realities posed unique difficulties. The Hebrew educators' role in facilitating real-life language acquisition was profoundly affected, reshaping their professional identity and approach to teaching.

This study explores the experiences and perspectives of Hebrew language educators in the aftermath of October 7. It examines how these events have influenced their professional roles and considers the broader implications for language educators in complex cultural and historical contexts, similar to past periods in which language educators were faced with similar challenges (Girard, 1943). The findings aim to inform the development of future training programs for Hebrew educators, ensuring they are equipped to meet the evolving demands of their profession.

Methods

To address the challenges facing Hebrew teachers following October 7, we collected data through a series of focus group meetings held via Zoom. This approach allowed participants not only to respond to the questions posed but also to engage with the perspectives and experiences shared by their peers. The focus group method provided a more comprehensive and efficient means of gathering the nuanced data required for our study (Kreuger, 2002; Sim and Waterfield, 2019).

The focus groups were held in November 2024, allowing participants to reflect on the start of the new academic year and the implications for Hebrew language teaching one year after October 7. Interested educators completed an online form distributed via Qualtrics, which collected general information about their background, including place of work, years of experience teaching Hebrew, educational background, and professional development in the field.

To participate, educators needed to meet two criteria: they had to be actively teaching or involved in Hebrew education programs in North American institutions as of October 7, 2023, and they needed to remain engaged in the new school year beginning in 2024. A total of twenty-three individuals, twenty-two females and one male, participated in six focus group sessions, with most groups consisting of three to six participants.

The sessions were moderated by Vardit Ringvald, who guided the discussions, ensuring all participants had the opportunity to contribute while preventing any single individual from dominating the conversation. The questions used during the sessions were semi-structured, allowing for flexibility (see Appendix). Follow-up questions were tailored to participants' responses, and additional prompts were used to clarify statements and encourage deeper exploration of the topics discussed. The focus groups were conducted in Hebrew.

The final video recordings were downloaded from Zoom and transcribed using the Sonix program. A total of nine hours and fifteen minutes of data were transcribed. The research team subsequently reviewed the transcriptions to ensure accuracy, validating the material against the audio recordings. Once confirmed, the team coded and analyzed the data using thematic analysis, focusing on key themes, which are outlined in the findings section of this article.

The participants represented a wide range of teaching contexts and responsibilities. Specific roles included nine educators teaching or managing Hebrew programs for multiple age groups at their institutions. Four participants worked in early childhood education, eight in elementary school, nine in middle school, six in high school, and nine in university settings. Of the nine university-affiliated educators, six taught Hebrew exclusively at the university level. Six participants also taught Judaism or Jewish studies, two worked in Hebrew programs at summer camps, and two were employed in public schools (one in a high school and the other in a charter school). One participant additionally served as the director of education at a synagogue.

We were aware of the known limitations of the use of focus groups, which include the concept of groupthink, issues with confidentiality and the risk of dominant voices (Smithson, 2000). We made every effort to minimize these obstacles by employing a skilled moderator, establishing specific protocols at the beginning of each meeting, encouraging contributions from quieter participants, and keeping the groups small in size.

Findings

Most of the participants in this study are native Hebrew-speaking Israeli Americans engaged in teaching Hebrew across various educational settings. Before October 7, their roles could be broadly categorized as "service-oriented," encompassing two main responsibilities: serving as language providers and representing Israel. As native speakers, they were tasked with teaching Hebrew in the classroom. Additionally, due to their Israeli backgrounds, they often carried the responsibility of organizing events such as *Yom Ha'atzmaut* (Israeli Independence Day), Memorial Day for fallen Israeli soldiers and victims of terror, and Israel Day. They also contributed to enrichment and extracurricular activities related to Israeli culture. During school-wide Jewish events and ceremonies, their primary role was to provide support where

Hebrew was integral—be it through songs, readings, or plays. However, the events of October 7 transformed the nature of their role. Suddenly, their Israeli experience became the central essence of their work. Overnight, they found themselves acting, as several participants shared, intermediaries between two worlds—Israeli and American. This mediation extended beyond the classroom to interactions with fellow educators, school administrations, and, in many cases, parents.

Notably, this intermediary role was not explicitly assigned by school administrations. According to educators' accounts, they assumed this responsibility naturally. Sarah shared that "no one gave us this responsibility," they did it because they were Hebrew teachers. As Israelis, they became immediate and ongoing sources of information due to their access to Hebrew-language Israeli media, as Raya called it "source of Israeli news" as most of the students do not read or watch the news in Hebrew. The teachers also brought real-time updates they received from family and friends in Israel.

For most of these educators, the events of October 7 were deeply personal. Many, like Aya were directly impacted by their proximity to those affected: "My cousin's daughter was murdered." Others spoke of family members called up to the reserves or children serving in Gaza or elsewhere in the military. Despite their personal pain, as Sarah shared, they felt a profound sense of professional responsibility. They viewed their roles as more than just teaching Hebrew; to them, Hebrew education was inherently linked to Israel education. As Aya explained, "I come from the idea that language studies are Israeli studies." This perspective, they believed, was also shared by their students and their families. She added: "I know that, when they see me, they see Israel first and then the Hebrew language." Roni added that the need to connect knowledge of the country and society with the language became more critical" She felt it was a burden, "but it was also a privilege to be in that place, and it helped me to deal with the situation."

Michal perceives her professional role as the "information pipeline" for learners: "As a Hebrew language teacher, it is my responsibility to inform them about what is happening in Israel." She and the others saw this role that capitalized on their unique ability to convey a personal connection to Israel through their direct experiences and, as Avigail remarked, that it was like "open a door or window to Israeli society" for her students. Lilach shared that she "is not a Hebrew teacher, in fact, I feel like a *shlicha* (emissary) of Israel."

Pedagogical Approaches

The responsibility felt by the participants to convey the new Israeli reality to learners brought up dilemmas related to the fulfillment of their roles. These dilemmas involve choices about content, teaching methods and the role of the Hebrew language in the learning process. In the absence of direct guidance, each participant, alone or with their Hebrew-teacher colleagues, determined what should be taught and how. We identified four strategies employed by the participants of this study.

The reactive approach. This approach emerged primarily as a natural response to students' inquiries and the individual teacher's belief in child-centered education (Dewey, 1916, 1938; Rogers, 1969). It was common at the beginning of the war, during a period marked by chaos and pain, when teachers could only react. As Aya remarked, "At the beginning of the war I was like a robot, I wasn't a teacher, I was a mother and an Israeli." She felt that, although she was physically in the classroom, her mind was in Israel, and the discourse with the students revolved around responding to their questions.

Consensus-building. Many teachers operated with sensitivity regarding the information they provided to the learners. They wanted to teach "information that will not provoke an argument" (Maya) or "harsh reactions." They did so because of a perception that American culture tends to "avoid arguments". For example, as Michal shared, "there is no disagreement on the hostages"—and therefore it is "more comfortable to talk about it" or about things that are already being taught in school as part of Israel education—it is convenient to expand on it in the Hebrew language classes.

Following School Guidelines. Some of the participants pointed out that a tendency toward cancel culture or what Leah called "political correctness" created challenges even before October 7. Meaning, if the content about Israel did not fit in with the school's worldview, she avoided sharing it. This created dilemmas about which information to convey and left teachers like Leah feeling limited. Lilach said: "I'm operating in a very anemic or very lackluster culture. The school tries very hard to be balanced all the time to the point that it doesn't say *anything*."

Not all the participants agreed with their school's approach of filtering or excluding information. Orit said that "they want to protect the kids so much so that they don't see the difficult and horrible things," but protecting the students from exposure to horrors led to a distortion of authenticity. Some teachers didn't hesitate to confront their principals "without fear" as Maya noted, or as Ariella said, "I'm not afraid of these landmines," and express their opinion on the subject. This aligns with Lipsky's concept of street-level bureaucrats, who exercise discretion in response to organizational constraints and their own judgements (Lipsky, 1980). Mali chose to use after-school office hours to talk about some of the things she couldn't cover in class. Because of these cultural differences, Meital often found that she wrote letters to parents two or three times before she found wording that would not scare or offend them.

Freire (1970) emphasizes that education should not shield students from reality but instead engage them in critical thinking to confront and understand the world. Meier (1995) supports this notion, arguing that schools must provide students with tools to cope with real-world challenges rather than isolating them in a sanitized environment. Aviva echoed these sentiments, asserting that schools need to "stop living in their unrealistic alternative world" and instead help students develop coping mechanisms for difficult realities.

Being unable to express her own political opinions made Lilach think, "Am I being loyal to myself? Will this hurt my motivation to continue teaching?" In order to avoid dealing with these feelings, Ariela described how she adopted a "neutral" style of speech, using general sentences such as "some people think that...." For Leah, this also created a difficulty in starting a lesson, especially in the days after October 7 when children started the lesson with questions like "is it true that children are killed in Gaza?" In this case, she couldn't help but tell them that it was possible to support Israel—the state, the people—while also disagreeing with the government.

Decisions based on personal preference. The educators often felt that they are the source for learners' understanding of the "full picture," as Michal called it, or "the whole story" motivated them to provide it to them from their personal point of view. The justification for this approach comes from the recognition that they themselves are "the culture" and hence must bring themselves into the classroom. Penina shared that she should not only "know how to teach a second language, but also to come to it from a very personal approach." Although they emphasize their personal experience as a source of information, it still did not make the job easier for them—the commitment to present students with the full picture burdens them, especially because for them it is the necessary and important condition for dialogue with the learners because without it "it is impossible." Michal sees this dialogue as critical in this particular situation (Shor and Freire, 1987). In addition, the feeling that it was natural to "speak about myself in relation to the war," and that Israel was their "real" space and that it was "in their best interest" to share this with the students. Another participant described it as a sensitivity to their personal narrative and their perspectives, "I teach what I want to teach—what I see as right."

Becoming Israel Educators

The relationship that formed between the teachers, the learners, and the learning environment "suddenly" made it clear to them that they are, in fact, dealing with the "teaching of Israel." They understood that their intention in this instruction is not only to satisfy the students' curiosity about what is happening, but also, as Leah pointed out, to provide them with tools to stand up to "the haters and opposers" that question the right for the State of Israel to exist and give them ways to handle this knowledge.

The topics the teachers focused on included various aspects of current events as well as history and geopolitics of Israel and the region. Sigal shared that she reluctantly became the lecturer on Middle Eastern affairs, and the challenge was to give her students a complete picture of Israel. Ariela stated that "I made efforts to bridge gaps in the knowledge," both her own and the students'.

As time went on, some extended their teaching to include information about the history and current affairs of the wider Middle East conflict. The question was how much to delve into the complexities—mainly due to the fact that it is impossible to teach "everything." Leah, who has experience teaching history, found a way to explain the complexity of the Israel-Palestine conflict by making sure to present a range of opinions from across the political spectrum regarding the conflict—"not just right and left"—to show that not all Israelis are "on the right side of the political map."

The participants all felt that their "Israeliness" is an integral part of Hebrew language education, a fact underscored by the events of October 7 and their aftermath. For example, Michal sees herself as part of the "content" being taught, with her authenticity, behavior, and personal experiences serving as a means to convey information and connect students more deeply to the current situation.

Teaching their own "Israeliness" as content elicited mixed reactions. Some teachers objected to the implicit expectation that language instructors would also teach about Israel during this critical time. They viewed this not only because of the administration and faculty's reluctance to take on the challenge of explaining the situation themselves but also as a form of "exploitation." To these teachers, it felt like a cynical use of their Israeli identity and an insensitivity to their emotional state during this difficult period.

Moreover, the events of October 7 became a turning point in their understanding of the profound impact of the content they teach. Aya shared, "I suddenly realized that they [the students] are influenced by what I think, which led me to rethink what I should share . . . I decided to change direction." Before October 7, she focused on the internal conflicts within Israeli society, expressing her disgust and feelings of hopelessness: "There's no hope and no chance." However, after October 7, she realized that the students lacked sufficient knowledge about Israel to form their own critiques. Consequently, she decided to emphasize positive aspects of her own life, such as her experience growing up in a multicultural society in Jaffa—a mixed city. Her goal was "to show the side of hope," a topic she felt was rarely discussed. She found herself empowered by "the power to do so" and admitted, "I surprised myself."

Participants who were less inclined to actively address the obligation of being a direct source of information chose instead to share cultural products created in response to the war—products that reflect both the harsh reality and a sense of hope. Noah chose to show a video clip of the famous singer Netta Barzilai performing the song "Na'ari shuva elai" (My boy, return to me; originally performed by Dani Shoshan in 1986) in Hostages Square. He explained, "The whole story is there; it's such a big story. Just playing the song in class felt right. I didn't tell them how I was feeling or what I was thinking, but the music—the music says it all." He described how the elements in the clip—musicians stomping their feet, the yellow sign, the presence of the hostages' families, and the fact that one of the musicians' brothers is being held hostage in Gaza—conveyed the message without requiring further discussion in class.

Being Israel Educators

The events of October 7 placed the teachers in a dual role. First, they became a source of information for their students about a fateful and painful event that had deeply affected them personally. Second, they felt compelled to filter and adjust the content due to restrictions imposed by their educational institutions. This dynamic significantly influenced the teaching methods they used to convey information to their students. In some instances, teachers received guidance on how to approach discussions about October 7 and the war with their students.

From what was shared, it seems that this group of teachers adopted two pedagogical approaches to teaching Israel education. Following October 7, these approaches focused on two pedagogical approaches, characterized by experiential education and emotional engagement.

Experiential teaching had a number of applications. For instance, teachers involved their students in projects as Orli did with an "Anemone Planting Ceremony" in solidarity with residents of the Gaza border area. Additionally, some teacher-initiated projects connected students with Israeli peers, particularly those around the same age.

Inspired by their experimentation, the participants also believed that what was meaningful for them would also be meaningful for their students. Just as they had become activists—attending gatherings in the community and volunteering—they encouraged their students to be activists too, urging them to attend events outside of school and, in Meital's school, to "collect donations and belongings for the hostages' families."

Many participants emphasized the importance of integrating emotion into teaching and learning, describing it as a powerful method that benefits both teachers and students. Swain (2011) and Dewaele (2015) both argue that the emotional connection can have a lasting impact on language learners, influencing attitudes and behaviors long after the formal learning process. In this context, participants noted that emotion plays a critical role in supporting the learning process and fostering a connection to Israel. Beyond its immediate impact, they highlighted emotion's more profound value: its potential to establish a long-term bond with the country and its people. Meital, for example, articulated this by saying, "In twenty years, they will need to defend and protect Israel's existence—and only a deep sense of emotional connection will help them achieve that." Noga, likewise, emphasized the importance of emotional engagement in her classroom, hoping that her students would "enter my classroom happily," with the feeling "that they came and they learned something and they enjoyed it and they developed and something happened to them."

The participants also pointed out that, as individuals who have personally experienced the horrors of October 7—even from afar—they bring a unique perspective to their teaching. This perspective, they believe, allows students to "feel us and who we are." As Chana explained, "We are the link that connects to Israel before and still."

One recommendation for "increasing emotion" involved connecting with the families of hostages, which they described as an "emotional experience" that every student should undergo. Those participants, including Sarah, who had not visited Israel since October 7 expressed a sense of loss, particularly because some of their students had made such visits. In these instances, they encouraged students who had visited Israel to share their experiences with classmates, a step that further engaged students and fostered excitement about learning. According to the participants, these accounts offer "an encounter with the day-to-day life of Israelis" of all ages and as Orli said to allow students "to feel what a child or teenager of their age feels who had to leave his home and live somewhere else."

Some felt a sense of empathy from those around them. For example, Meital's daughter served in the army during the war, and both the students and the staff at the school expressed a great deal of empathy. This support made the her feel that emotions were legitimate and could be included in the teaching process, allowing them to invite students to share in the emotional experience. Despite this, some participants noted that even within the context of emotional expression, it was necessary to "obey" school rules about how much emotion could be expressed. They tried not to appear "negative" about the situation, as at times they were asked to remain, as Aya shared, "positive and optimistic."

The tension between handling the situation on a personal level and maintaining strength in front of their students led many teachers to take on a caregiver role. As Gal described, "That's how they feel confident and safe with us—and it is our duty to support them and unite everyone" in light of these events. As the war continued, the scenes became tougher, and in some cases, other voices began to be heard in academic institutions. To provide students with a safe space to express themselves without fear of judgment—to voice opinions and ask questions. Avigail shared that her students also "went experienced difficulties during this time and I find myself in a situation where I have to be very sensitive and give *them* support." One participant even created a WhatsApp group, allowing students to express their feelings in a more private space.

The aftermath of October 7 and the need to educate students about the situation in Israel served as major motivational drivers for the participants in this study. These educators are striving to become more informed about the conflict, understand its impact, and delve deeper into issues surrounding antisemitism and anti-Israel sentiment. Their motivation to learn about

Israeli culture has grown, driven by the recognition that many people lack sufficient knowledge about Israel. Avigail explained that her students had a "lack of knowledge and I am the one who brings them this knowledge and I am the source that they can come to without knowledge."

Remaining Hebrew Teachers while Teaching about Israel

In their new roles as Hebrew teachers teaching about Israel, the educators felt both challenged and empowered. As Ariella said: "I am more motivated to teach Hebrew in Jewish education, because it is actually teaching Israel, sometimes I feel that I represent the state—I am engaged in *hasbara*." Michal added to this and said that while she agrees, she believes that the role is actually the same, just 'plus,' and that it just has new branches.

Others, however, were less sure about their new role. Leah pointed out that she was hired to teach a language and nothing more, "and that's what the institution expects." Therefore, she did not give up the language lessons in favor of a discourse about Israel that would require her to switch to the students' mother tongue, which in this case is English, a practice for which there is much debate (Timor, 2012.) Other participants used different approaches to find a balance that worked for their students.

The first is to find suitable/appropriate learning opportunities where culture (the material) and the language can be integrated. Ariela shared how she uses current events, such as the weekly Saturday night rallies in Israel for the return of the hostages, to teach relevant vocabulary and expressions. This helped the students understand what was happening. "I describe the demonstrations; I play them songs about the hostages and that's my priority right now." The content of the lessons depends on the circumstances, and sometimes teachers chose to switch to English. For Noga, this approach addresses the need to engage and interest the learners. In classes where the students are more proficient in Hebrew, the language features much more prominently in the lessons.

In other cases, classes worked on projects that combined both languages. For younger learners, the content was taught primarily in English by the Hebrew teachers, and Hebrew was used only when possible, according to proficiency levels. Hebrew was still present most of the time. "It was impossible to give it up," Ariela remarked. The Hebrew content is often related to the events of October 7, with an emphasis on relevant language. For example, this was achieved using lyrics or articles with simpler words. The integration was typically gradual: "I let the students express themselves in their own language—it was important that they could express themselves." Leah had a different experience because of her mandate to only speak Hebrew in class: "I see the students for a very limited time and, in that time, I'm supposed to teach them a language . . . I can't speak to them in their language either and talking to them in Hebrew about October 7, because of the complex messages involved, I'm limited."

For some, the transition from English back to Hebrew occurred gradually. During the first weeks following October 7, Hebrew was secondary, and learning about Israel took center stage. Consequently, the discourse and teaching were primarily conducted in English. Ariela explained: "I want them to feel close to Israel, to care about Israel, and in order to care about something, you have to know that something. As a Hebrew teacher, I also felt the need to include the language in the process, but that was challenging, so the content took priority over the language." Noah further described the progression:

> At the beginning of the lesson, eighty percent of the time was devoted to conversation in English, with only ten minutes in Hebrew. Then, we transitioned to splitting the lesson evenly between the two languages. The content was always related to Israel, such as watching and discussing a show by Shlomo Artzi singing in Hostages Square, viewing daily news, or watching an interview with the parent of a hostage. These discussions lasted about twenty minutes.

It is worth noting that the use of English, although intended to make learning easier and foster identification with the material, was not always successful. In one instance, a teacher conducted a lesson in broken English, and one student left the class feeling less supportive of Israel. This led to an angry reaction from the student's parents, who felt the school had failed to uphold their values.

One Year After

More than a year after October 7, these sentiments have not faded. On the contrary, this shift in the significance of their professional responsibilities—emphasizing the study of Israel and "Israeliness"—has become a dominant and permanent aspect of their daily practice as Hebrew language educators.

The participants overwhelmingly feel that they are still living in the midst of October 7. With their families remaining in Israel and the war ongoing, they continue to share this experience with their loved ones. This sense of being in the midst of the crisis has been further intensified by the wave of antisemitism sweeping across North America, which Noga said was a major issue. However, that situation has also created a new sense of shared fate, which is further strengthening their connection to the students, the school, and the broader community.

The ongoing presence of October 7 in schools still prevents some of the participants from fully expressing their emotions and thoughts. However, the actions shown by most of them indicate that, a year later, they have learned to separate their professional duties from their emotions and personal politics. They have adopted a pragmatic approach of being "smart, but not right" in order to continue in their roles. They now feel "experienced in conveying messages" and have greater clarity about their school's policies, behaving accordingly—even when these policies do not align with their personal beliefs. For instance, when a first-grade teacher asked the children to name a word beginning with the letter "H," one child raised his hand and said "Hamas." The participant shared that she restrained herself from reacting, knowing that to do so could undermine the school's messaging and values.

There was a general feeling among the participants that educational topics have gained a deeper significance. Each topic now needs to carry meaning, as Roni shared:

> No more teaching casual aspects of culture, like how to order coffee. Instead, we focus on meaningful subjects that resonate in the current moment. For example, Hanukkah, a holiday symbolizing the battle between light and darkness, is directly linked to the issue of the hostages. Similarly, when discussing places in Israel, such as the Dead Sea, the conversation also includes information about the evacuees from that region.

For some, there is a sense of resentment towards the expectation that Hebrew teachers should be experts on cultural issues. In some cases, they lack the necessary expertise, and in others, there's simply no desire to address such topics in the classroom. Ariella shared that "I'm asked to discuss the conflict and history, but I don't have the facts—I'm learning as I go, because who else will do it? Here, I am only an expert in language teaching, but I really have no clue." She added, "I'm doing my best to learn and understand, mainly to interpret the meaning," and "We need to tell the school that it's not our role to be informants or commentators."

As families from Israel moved into their communities and schools, the role of Israeli Hebrew teachers as intermediaries became even more pronounced. They became the bridge between the families' origins and their new environments. Although this was outside the scope of their official duties, they performed this role with love and a sense of mission. They became a source of knowledge for these families on multiple occasions. Chana explained that she saw the Hebrew teachers as *shlichim*.

Conclusion

As a result of the events of October 7 and the aftermath, the teachers realized that their roles as Hebrew language educators are inextricably linked to teaching about Israel. This new role involves providing learners with in-depth knowledge about the culture of Hebrew and doing so reflects the diverse perspectives of its speakers.

As mentioned above, the expectation for a language educator is to incorporate cultural elements into language instruction. However, the events surrounding October 7 presented a particular challenge due to their shocking nature. These educators, deeply connected to Israel and its people, became involved in teaching these events. As a result, their roles as intermediaries changed and presented them with new challenges.

Many of the participants shared that the feeling of not performing professionally constantly lingered in the background. This sense of inadequacy sparked anger and frustration, as they were expected to handle work for which they had not been trained to address. Additionally, due to learners' linguistic limitations, much of the content had to be taught in English. This left the participants feeling that they were not fully fulfilling their role as language educators, further compounding their frustration.

Their training in teaching culture followed the accepted model—the sporadic inclusion of cultural elements alongside functional linguistic components. However, the experiences of these teachers in the wake of October 7 demonstrated that this model was inadequate in such unique and unparalleled circumstances. The situation required not only the skillful delivery of current information but also the ability to explain and interpret the fundamental assumptions, values, and beliefs they represented. They often felt unable to do so. Mali expressed that there is a need to develop "a pedagogy of how to teach cultural subjects . . . there's a deficiency in it and we need to strengthen it . . . a lot . . . and to build a course or something related to teaching language and culture in times of crisis. What tools do we have? What tools can we use? Or how can we adapt to an existing curriculum or goals we had so that they would fit in a time of crisis?"

The insights from this study emphasize a need for greater access to dynamic content and resources that can help these teachers prepare educational materials related to Israel and Israeli identity and reveal a lack of training and tools to effectively convey the multifaceted and complex realities of Israel. This included addressing complex historical and geopolitical questions, contextualizing the Israeli-Middle Eastern dynamic, and interpreting and explaining these matters for students and the broader community.

Hebrew language teachers are no longer solely language providers, sporadically allowing learners to "peek" into cultural elements, Hebrew educators are now central to fostering an understanding of Israel. This is a task that was sometimes explicitly, and more often implicitly, expected of them by learners, colleagues, and the administration.

The study participants, who are native speakers with diverse academic backgrounds, are representative of the average Hebrew language educator. While most have been trained in teaching Hebrew as an additional language, they identified a critical need for deeper knowledge of teaching Israeli culture and history to meet the growing expectations of their role. This gap stems from the traditional model of cultural instruction, which often integrates cultural elements sporadically alongside linguistic components. However, the unique circumstances they faced required not only linguistic expertise but also the ability to interpret and convey complex cultural, historical, and geopolitical realities

These evolving expectations requires redefining the role of Hebrew as a second language educators through the lens of Israel education. Achieving this integration is no simple task. While Israel education allows for diverse curricula and methods, second-language teaching—whether for Hebrew or other languages—relies on precise protocols to develop functional language skills. However, aligning these two disciplines can yield significant benefits. By fostering crossover expertise between language educators and Israel educators, we can establish a field of study that equips language educators with tools to provide nuanced, holistic perspectives, enhancing cross-cultural learning and deepening students' understanding of the Hebrew language, Israeli people, and culture.

To succeed in this hybrid role, Hebrew educators must receive training for making informed decisions about content and teaching methods that balance language acquisition with cultural understanding. In other words, they must become "autonomous curriculum designers" (Eddy, 2022). Developing innovative teaching methods that integrate these disciplines is essential. For instance, "comprehensible input" (Krashen, 1981; Van Patten, 1990) can be embedded within authentic Israeli cultural contexts relevant to learners, considering acquisition principles, learner variables, and linguistic goals. Importantly, these methods must ensure that materials portray Israeli culture realistically and authentically.

New learning materials will be vital, and authenticity should be a cornerstone of this hybrid approach to curriculum design in order to ensure cultural content engages learners comprehensively while aligning with their proficiency levels. According to the ACTFL Proficiency Guidelines, beginner learners might engage with authentic materials reflecting home, family, and community life in Israeli contexts. This allows learners to connect the material to their own lives, fostering meaningful cultural understanding and connections. Through this approach, learners encounter culture first, using it as a foundation to acquire and produce language.

October 7 served as a turning point that reinforced a long-held mantra in language education: **language is culture**, and that language teachers must go beyond teaching linguistic skills and assume the role of cultural educators. This connection, often acknowledged but rarely prioritized, became undeniable. Cutshall (2012) asserts that "culture can't wait," emphasizing that cultural engagement does not need to be reserved for students at higher proficiency levels. Rather than treating cultural instruction as supplementary, it must now become central to Hebrew language educators' pedagogy.

In the introduction to this essay, we outlined the professional expectations for language educators: to facilitate students' understanding of both the language and the culture it represents. This has been the subject of ongoing debates, criticisms, and evolving approaches in language education. However, October 7 not only confirmed the importance of integrating culture into language teaching—it highlighted the urgency of elevating cultural pedagogy as a critical component of the role of the language teacher.

References

American Council on the Teaching of Foreign Language (1986). *ACTFL proficiency guidelines.*

American Council on the Teaching of Foreign Language (1996). *Standards for foreign language learning: Preparing for the 21st century.* ERIC Clearinghouse.

Brown, H. D. (1997). English language teaching in the "post-method" era: Toward better diagnosis, treatment, and assessment. *PASAA, 27*(1), 1–11.

Clark, J. (2023). Rep. Noah Arbit statement on atrocities in Israel. *MI House Dems,* October 12. https://housedems.com/rep-noah-arbit-statement-on-atrocities-in-israel.

Cutshall, S. (2012). More than a decade of standards. *Language, 32.* https://www.actfl.org/uploads/files/general/Communities.pdf.

Dewaele, J. M. (2015). On emotions in foreign language learning and use. *The Language Teacher, 39*(3), 13–15. http://jalt-publications.org/tlt/articles/4467-jalt2015-conference-article-emotions-foreign-language-learning-and-use

Dewey, J. (1916). Nationalizing education. *Journal of Education, 84*(16), 425–428. https://doi.org/10.7312/dewe19894-025

Dewey, J. (1986). Experience and education. *The Educational Forum, 50*(3), 241–252. https://doi.org/10.1080/00131728609335764

Eddy, J. (2022). *Designing world language curriculum for intercultural communicative competence.* Bloomsbury.

Freire, P. (2020). Pedagogy of the oppressed. In J. Beck, C. Jenks, N. Keddie, M. F. D. Young (Eds.), *Toward a sociology of education* (pp. 374–386). Routledge.

Freire, P., and Shor, I. (1987). *A pedagogy for liberation: Dialogues on transforming education.* Praeger.

Girard, D. P. (1943). The teaching of foreign languages during and after the war. *The French Review, 17*(1), 23–29. http://www.jstor.org/stable/380477

Glisan, E. W., and Donato, R. (2017). *Enacting the work of language instruction: High-leverage teaching practices.* American Council on the Teaching of Foreign Languages.

Gollan, R., et al. (1990). *Hebrew proficiency guidelines.* Brandeis University, Waltham, MA. Prepared under NIH grant number PO17A80042.

Gottlieb, E. (2024). A year after Oct. 7, silence isn't an option for teachers (opinion). *Education Week*, October 7. https://www.edweek.org/teaching-learning/opinion-a-year-after-oct-7-silence-isnt-an-option-for-teachers/2024/10

Hall, E. T. (1959). *The silent language*. Doubleday.

Havens, G. R. (1941). The modern language teacher in a troubled world. *The Modern Language Journal*, 25(4), 306–313. https://doi.org/10.2307/317304

Hiver, P., Kim, T., and Kim, Y. (2018). Language teacher motivation. In S. Mercer and A. Kostoulas (Eds.), *Language teacher psychology* (pp. 18–33). Multilingual Matters. https://doi.org/10.21832/9781783099467-006

Hymes, D. (1964). Introduction: Toward ethnographies of communication 1. *American Anthropologist*, 66(6_PART2), 1–34.

Kopelowitz, E., Ravid, S., Posklinsky, I., Golden, J., and Gillis, J. (2024). *Responding to the fallout from October 7th: From crisis to opportunity*. Jim Joseph Foundation. https://jimjosephfoundation.org/learning-resources/responding-to-the-fallout-from-october-7th-from-crisis-to-opportunity-a-survey-of-jewish-educators-and-engagement-professionals/

Kramsch, C. (2006). From communicative competence to symbolic competence. *The modern Language Journal*, 90(2), 249–252. https://www.jstor.org/stable/3876875

Krashen, S. (1981). Second language acquisition. *Second Language Learning*, 3(7), 19–39.

Krueger, R. A., and Casey, M. A. (2002). *Designing and conducting focus group interviews*. https://www.eiu.edu/ihec/Krueger-FocusGroupInterviews.pdf

Lipsky, M. (2010). *Street-level bureaucracy: Dilemmas of the individual in public service*. Russell Sage Foundation.

Meier, D. (2002). *The power of their ideas: Lessons for America from a small school in Harlem*. Beacon Press.

Manoliu, M. N. (2012). A communicative approach to language teaching-origins and development. *International Journal of Communication Research*, 2(2), 138.

Rogers, C. R., and Freiberg, H. J. (1970). *Freedom to learn*. Charles Merrill.

Sim, J., and Waterfield, J. (2019). Focus group methodology: Some ethical challenges. *Quality and Quantity*, 53(6), 3003–3022. https://doi.org/10.1007/s11135-019-00914-5

Smithson, J. (2000). Using and analysing focus groups: Limitations and possibilities. *International Journal of Social Research Methodology*, 3(2), 103–119. https://doi.org/10.1080/136455700405172

Swain, M. (2013). The inseparability of cognition and emotion in second language learning. *Language Teaching*, 46(2), 195–207. https://doi.org/10.1017/S0261444811000486

Timor, T. (2012). Use of the mother tongue in teaching a foreign language. *Language Education in Asia*, 3(1), 7–17. http://dx.doi.org/10.5746/LEiA/12/V3/I1/A02/Timor

VanPatten, B. (1990). Attending to form and content in the input: An experiment in consciousness. *Studies in Second Language Acquisition*, 12(3), 287–301. https://www.jstor.org/stable/44488301

Zakai, S. (2022). *My second-favorite country: How American Jewish children think about Israel*. NYU Press.

Appendix

Teachers' Identities in Transition: Hebrew Education in Light of October 7 and the Aftermath

---

Guiding Questions for Focus Groups

- What role do you think the Hebrew language plays in connecting students to Israeli society, culture, and identity? How does this connection manifest in the classroom? Was this an expectation placed upon you, or something you chose to take on yourself?
- Were you viewed as a representative of the Israeli experience by your students and colleagues during this time?
- Did you need to balance your role as a Hebrew language instructor with the expectation to provide insights into the Israeli experience?
- How did you manage your own emotional responses while still fulfilling your teaching responsibilities? Explain.
- Were there moments when you felt conflicted between your personal feelings and professional responsibilities? If so, how did you handle them?
- How, if at all, did you adapt your teaching methods or content in response to the events?
- Did you need to address the political and humanitarian aspects of the situation in your classes? How did you approach these topics?

- What strategies did you find most effective in helping students understand and cope with the events of October 7? Give an example.
- Do you think that your approach influenced your students' perceptions of Israel and the ongoing conflict? Please explain.
- What challenges did you encounter when discussing complex or sensitive topics, and how did you address these challenges?
- What kinds of support (emotional, professional, or instructional) did you need and did you receive it from your supervisor/school or other organization or individual? What kinds of support do you wish you had during this time?
- What resources or training would have been helpful to better navigate your dual roles after the attacks?
- Has your understanding of your role as a Hebrew educator changed since October 7? If so, in what ways?
- How do you now see your role in shaping your students' understanding of Israeli culture, language, Jewish Identity?
- What advice would you give to other educators facing similar challenges in balancing their professional and personal identities?
- What changes, if any, would you recommend for future professional development programs to better prepare educators for such situations?

Section Three

TEACHING ABOUT HOME: ISRAELIS ABROAD

The Impact of the October 7 War on Emissary Teachers—Shlichim: A Study of Pedagogical Adaptations, Non-Formal Educational Initiatives, and Community Interactions in North American Jewish Schools in 2024–2025

Michal Shapira Junger

Introduction

On October 7, 2023, Hamas launched an attack against the State of Israel in the Gaza envelope region, resulting in the murder of over 1,000 Israeli civilians. This date marks the beginning of the longest war in Israel's history, which subsequently expanded to the country's northern front against Hezbollah in southern Lebanon.

The war's reverberations profoundly impacted Jewish communities worldwide, creating unprecedented challenges for Israeli teaching emissaries who were stationed in these communities. These educators, officially dispatched by the State of Israel to teach Hebrew and Jewish studies in Jewish schools around the world, found themselves in a uniquely complex position: while physically distant from the conflict, they were personally and professionally affected as Israeli citizens and teachers during a time of crisis in their homeland. Their role as official representatives of Israel in educational settings abroad placed them at the intersection of multiple responsibilities—as educators, as members of their host communities, and as Israelis connected to the ongoing conflict. This situation created distinctive challenges in their professional roles as they attempted to balance their pedagogical duties with their personal connections to the unfolding events in Israel.

Scholarly research examining the phenomenon of emissaries in general and teaching emissaries in particular is extremely limited. This gap is particularly evident in the study of their pedagogical practices, including their teaching methods, educational approaches, and classroom strategies. Within the broader field of wartime education research, the situation of teaching emissaries represents a unique case study that does not align with existing research categories. Current academic literature in this domain typically focuses on two distinct scenarios: either examining educational practices under active warfare conditions where both teachers and students are directly affected by conflict, or analyzing how educators in countries removed from conflict teach about distant wars. The case of teaching emissaries presents a novel research context, as it involves educators who are citizens of a nation actively engaged in warfare and who are teaching students in communities physically removed from the conflict yet emotionally connected to it through their Jewish identity.

The present study addresses this research gap by examining the complex pedagogical adaptations implemented by teaching emissaries in response to the profound social-emotional impacts of the October 7 events. Through detailed analysis, this research investigates several critical questions: What specific pedagogical modifications did teaching emissaries implement in response to the war in Israel? How did these changes manifest in their daily teaching practices? Were these adaptations temporary responses to immediate needs, or did they represent more fundamental, long-term shifts in teaching methodology? Additionally, the study explores how these educators navigated their dual role as both teachers and Israeli citizens during this period of crisis. This study reveals that teaching emissaries operate along two main axes: the first, "top-down" axis, is characterized by clear administrative guidelines regarding boundaries of discourse with students that lead to practical approaches with a shift to civilian heroism stories and community engagement; the second, "bottom-up" axis, reflects teaching emissaries' personal need to adapt their teaching methods through project-based learning, curated news content, and optimism-focused pedagogy in response to October 7 events.

Literature Review

Shlichut

Shlichut (emissary missions) is a practice that was established during the Second Temple period to maintain the connection between Jewish communities in the diaspora and the sacred site. The institution of *Shlichut* evolved through various transformations over the decades until its current form. Despite their historical significance, the phenomenon of emissaries has been remarkably underexplored in academic research to date (Shapira Junger, 2024). There are various categories of emissaries, such as *Shinshinim* (gap-year emissaries), campus emissaries, youth movement emissaries, community emissaries, and teaching emissaries (Aharonov, 2015). This study focuses on teaching emissaries. Since 1939, with the establishment of the Emissary Training Institute, thousands of educational emissaries have been sent by the World Zionist Organization to Jewish communities in the diaspora. Teaching emissaries are educators from the Israeli educational system who are deployed for extended mission periods, spanning from a single calendar year to four years. During their mission, these teachers are sent to teach Hebrew, Judaism, and Jewish history in Jewish schools worldwide by official Israeli state entities: national institutions and youth movements, with some directly dispatched by the Ministry of Education. These educators integrate into the local educational infrastructure and instruct according to the curricular standards of their destination country (Cohen, 2000). Annually, approximately one hundred teaching emissaries are deployed, with over sixty percent traveling to North American countries, primarily teaching in Jewish elementary and middle schools (Shapira Junger, 2024). Since 2010, a small group of teachers have been teaching Hebrew in US public schools with significant Jewish populations (World Zionist Organization, 2015).

Over time, the mission objectives defined by the State of Israel have evolved beyond the formal teaching role. Currently, the Jewish Agency's Education Department's vision, as presented on the organization's website, is: "Our educational purpose is to deepen Israel's unique and multidimensional significance by connecting the next generation to their Judaism, people, and homeland" (Morim Shlichim, 2024). In its vision, such a connection can be built through *tikkun olam* (repairing the world) and "disseminating Jewish values." This definition of the role is reflected in research that discovered a perception gap between the emissaries themselves and diaspora schools. While schools viewed the emissary as a full-fledged staff member, the emissary primarily saw themselves as an agent intended to influence the entire school broadly, and only secondarily as a professional educator (Aharonov, 2015; Shapira Junger, 2024). This perceptual disparity generates numerous professionals because it creates tension between institutional pedagogical expectations and emissaries' perceived broader cultural mission (Harlap, 2014).

Research highlights the professional and cultural alienation experience of the emissary teacher in their school and residing community (e.g., Aharonov, 2009, 2015; Cohen, 1996, 2000; Pomson and Gilis, 2010; Rosenfeld et al., 2023, Rosenfeld et al., 2022; Ta'ir and Dashevsky, 2009). This alienation stems from disconnection from their familiar environment and social isolation in their new residential and unfamiliar work settings (Aharonov, 2015; Rosenfeld et al., 2023). An additional dimension of alienation is the professional-cultural aspect. Samuels (1992) collected opinion articles written by various teaching emissaries in North America. Through analyzing recurring characteristics and themes, Samuels found that teaching emissaries repeatedly expressed feelings constrained in their actions. Moreover, research findings revealed that emissaries struggled with the fundamental differences between teaching in Israeli public schools (not parent-managed) and transitioning to private schools managed by a board composed of school parents. Ultimately, Samuels discovers that teaching emissaries perceive themselves as the last guardians of students' Jewish identity (Samuels, 1992). Teaching emissaries encounter professional challenges related to an unfamiliar teaching syllabus that differ significantly from their country of origin. Moreover, the subjects they teach—Judaism and Hebrew—often have syllabi that are relatively less structured compared to core subjects in North American schools (Rosenfeld et al., 2022, 2023).

The challenges described in existing research address the routine life of the emissary teacher, with current scholarship notably lacking examination of crisis periods involving warfare in Israel.

Teachers during Wartime

Research exploring teachers and warfare is extensive and multifaceted, addressing numerous dimensions of the subject. This scholarship ranges from teaching the history of wars (Alvén, 2024; Clark, 2006; Goldberg et al., 2019) to studies examining learning management during conflict, as well as the capacity to maintain an active learning environment over extended periods

(Davies, 2004; Sharifian and Kennedyl, 2019; Tal, 2021; Thomas et al., 2019). An additional research dimension focuses on psychological well-being and resilience development among teachers and students during wartime (Baum et al., 2013; Kello, 2016), alongside the creation of educational initiatives and pedagogical approaches specifically adapted to conflict contexts (Davies, 2004; Tal, 2021; Tal and Hoffman, 2021). Sommers (2002) suggests that the role of teachers during a crisis is even more critical than during peacetime. In addition to teaching and educating, teachers promote and foster the physical, social, and psychosocial development of children, helping them navigate the trauma and uncertainty that war brings. By creating a safe learning environment, teachers play a crucial role in instilling hope for a better future. In this way, educators not only facilitate academic learning but also serve as pillars of resilience, guiding students through the complexities of their experiences and encouraging them to envision a path forward despite adversity. Therefore, teachers must exhibit greater resilience to maintain quality teaching amidst the chaos of war. However, research on teacher resilience in war zones is limited compared to more stable environments (Baum et al., 2013).

In addition to research focusing on schools and teachers physically situated within warfare, other scholarly investigations examine teaching during wartime in countries not directly involved in the violent conflict. These studies primarily address the critical pedagogical challenges of how to teach about war and how to communicate with younger and older students about ongoing conflict (Durish, 2013; Mosley, 2009). As teaching about conflicts has become an integral aspect of school syllabi, research has increasingly focused on examining its impact on teacher perspectives, student achievement, and classroom interactions (Alvén, 2024; Berg and Persson, 2023; Goldberg et al., 2019; Larsson and Lindström, 2020). Research has also examined the pedagogical materials and curricular content employed in classrooms, evaluating both their relevance and cultural responsiveness to students' diverse backgrounds (Chaikovska, 2023; Durish, 2013; Kello, 2016; Oplatka, 2024; Thomas et al., 2019).

Wartime and trauma have influenced teaching methodologies as well. Educators are increasingly adopting strategies that recognize and address the emotional and psychological needs of students who have experienced trauma. This shift aims to create a more supportive learning environment (Thomas et al., 2019). Research has found various pedagogical tools used by teachers during wartime. For example, out-of-classroom learning, that is, learning that occurs outside the traditional sedentary classroom environment, such as off-campus site visits and engagement with communities beyond the school setting, significantly influences the educational development and the engagement of the students. This engagement allows learners to confront and reflect on collective suffering and loss (Tal, 2024). Other studies have found that in periods of strife and uncertainty, schools attempt to avoid conflict and to highlight unity. In most instances, schools seek to avoid dealing with conflictual questions, thus hindering conflict transformation, or even contributing to its perpetuation and aggravation (Davies, 2004). An additional strategy documented in research literature is the "pedagogy of optimism," which focuses on examining reality through an optimistic lens. Scholarly investigations in this domain have revealed that learning from such a perspective enhances students' identification with studied topics, particularly during periods of conflict. The pedagogy of optimism encompasses learning methodologies and coping strategies that include investigating emotional experiences, accepting situational contexts, engaging in critical thinking, and fostering creativity (Chaikovska et al., 2023; Oplatka, 2024).

The case study of teaching emissaries during wartime is unique and does not conform to existing research categories. On one hand, the students do not reside in a war zone, while the teaching emissaries are citizens of a country engaged in active warfare, with some even returning to active military reserve service during the conflict. This research is groundbreaking in that it is the first to examine teachers whose civilian identity is situated within a wartime context while their students are not. The study investigates the coping mechanisms of teaching emissaries at both pedagogical and socio-emotional levels in light of their distinctive situational context.

Methodology

A field study utilizing an ethnographic and qualitative approach was employed. I focused on content and narrative analysis to reveal individual and interpersonal processes within a specific population. These processes facilitate inference to broader, more generalized social dynamics (Bar-Shalom, 2011). This research approach is a holistic methodology dedicated to data collection within a cultural context to describe and interpret the studied culture or phenomenon (Pole and Morrison, 2003).

I conducted eight semi-structured in-depth interviews with middle school teaching emissaries across North America. Data collection was conducted between September and October 2024. The demographic characteristics of the interviewees were diverse and constituted a representative sample consistent with previous demographic research findings on the teaching emissary population (Shapira Junger, 2024). All teaching emissaries were educators in Israel prior to their North American mission. Furthermore, each participant was in their third year of teaching emissary roles, providing a teaching perspective preceding October 7.

Participants were recruited through multiple strategies. In the beginning, I used direct outreach via the World Zionist Organization, and then "snowball sampling" wherein each interviewee referred me to others in their own emissary networks. Further participant recruitment was conducted through emissaries' WhatsApp groups.

The interviews were analyzed using the "grounded theory" approach (Heath and Cowley, 2004). The data were analyzed using Dedoose qualitative analysis software based on "flexible coding" (Deterding and Waters, 2021), wherein the first stage involved indexing data according to the research protocol and research questions, and the second stage incorporated thematic, ground-up analysis. Themes were only identified if they were present in at least three different interviews.

Findings

The analysis of the eight interviews conducted with teaching emissaries across North America revealed two overarching themes from which teachers' practical approaches are derived.

The first theme is a "top-down" theme where school administrators established clear boundary lines regarding permissible and impermissible discussions with students and new expectations of teacher emissaries. Within this theme, practical approaches included: abandoning battlefield and death narratives in favor of civilian heroism stories, sharing anecdotal and personal teacher narratives, transitioning to community work beyond school boundaries and hours, and fundraising for civilian initiatives in Israel.

The second theme identified is a "bottom-up" theme, and it reveals that teaching emissaries had a personal need to implement pedagogical shifts and to create interruptions to standard learning sequences based on what happened in Israel on and after October 7. This theme encompassed practices such as transitioning to project-based learning, language instruction using carefully curated news from Israeli newspapers that aligned with the established boundaries, and adopting an optimism-based pedagogy.

Clear Boundary Lines

The first theme that emerged from the research findings is the establishment of clear boundaries by administrative teams and parent boards regarding discourse limitations and what content students should not be exposed to. Teaching emissaries discussed the complexities created by these boundaries. For instance, Shir described the situation at her school as follows:

> It was mainly at the beginning—you couldn't talk about anything. Because things were ongoing. They really wanted a moment to understand where this was going. And you couldn't talk. To anyone about anything. We would mostly gather among ourselves, with the Israeli teachers. And I'm the only *Shlicha* (emissary) here, which is also an important factor in this whole thing. And basically you weren't allowed to talk about anything. With time, they gradually loosened up. Of course it wasn't personal against us, or anything against Israel. It was about protecting the students and their well-being, but it was challenging.

The established guidelines arise not from questions of teacher credibility or capability but from the institutional need to monitor and understand how sensitive information of atrocities and wartime imagery is being conveyed to students. Findings indicate that teachers practiced significant self-censorship in their efforts to adhere to established discourse parameters. Hana noted the following:

> We're very restricted. It doesn't matter how much space we have or how much they respect us as professionals. Everything I bring to the classroom, I need to think about three times over. And also get approval. And make sure it's okay. At the ceremony for the war anniversary, we really had to cut down all kinds of quotes and video clips that we wanted to show.

The "top-down" theme of boundaries emerges as a persistent motif throughout the period, beginning on October 7, as evidenced in Shir's testimony, and extending into the subsequent academic year (2024–2025), as demonstrated through Hana's testimony regarding the preparation of the first memorial ceremony commemorating the war.

Teaching emissaries adopted four primary practices to address boundary-related challenges. The first practice involved teaching through personal narratives and individual encounters. As Adam recalled:

> At some point I realized that wherever there's a personal connection, that's where bonding happens. And then suddenly they [students] do see, and they're attentive. And when I tell them about our family that was evacuated from Kiryat Shmona,[4] or the friend who lives in Sderot, it gets a name and a face and that creates the connection. It's very different from the American ethos, where teachers don't share anything from their personal lives. And it creates closeness and allows us to open up even more complex topics related to the war. That is how they feel the connection. They come to ask me every day how my family in Kiryat Shmona is doing.

These personal stories served to reduce the intensity of the broader war context while enabling teaching emissaries to share specific and contained points of pain. This approach was designed to simultaneously facilitate student identification and engagement while maintaining appropriate exposure levels for young learners. Furthermore, the use of personal proximity narratives enabled teachers to share measured accounts of losses of their own loved ones during the war. For example, Shir shared:

> I started bringing some information, processed, of course, with the school's approval . . . I simply brought information in a more personal way, found opportunities to bring content that touches me personally. The school where I taught in Israel lost many students. Twelve of my students. At the beginning of the war, every time one of my students was killed, I couldn't even tell that I was going through

---

4 An Israeli city on the Lebanese border whose residents were evacuated to central Israel during the war.

something, tell that something happened. One time, when it was a student who was really close to me, I even thought about taking a day off, just to deal with it myself because I couldn't share ... With time, the changes were small, and I decided to only talk about my personal students whom I knew as a teacher.

The utilization of personal accounts enabled teachers to balance institutional boundaries designed to protect students with their own human need for expression. Through the selective sharing of personal experiences with grief, they established interface points between these competing needs, enabling necessary emotional articulation.

The second practice was the incorporation of civilian heroism narratives. These accounts, while not necessarily war stories, contained elements of patriotism and national pride. Tal shared:

> I told the kids about Rachel from Ofakim. How, thanks to her resourcefulness and hospitality, she survived. She managed to stall for time until soldiers came to help her. I didn't go into all the exact details. But we did talk about and emphasize the person that she was.

Hana added another point of view:

> It's all a very delicate game, between what you can and can't say. Like, in the October 7 anniversary ceremony, I put in the story about the hostage rescue in Operation Arnon. We talked about Arnon's character. And how special he was, and that he freed four hostages! We didn't tell that he was killed ... So yes, we said the word "hostages," but we didn't go into what that means and how they got into that situation ...

The findings indicate that the practice of incorporating civilian heroism narratives served as a delicate mediation between considering students' emotional well-being and being sensitive to their exposure to wartime events in Israel. Through highlighting inspirational stories, teaching emissaries established foundational narratives designed to enable students to construct a more complex understanding.

The third practice involved fundraising for various causes in Israel, thereby engaging students proactively in tangible action. Ben said: "Throughout the whole year, we did a lot of fundraising and gathering things for Israel. But we tried to connect it to our personal story—to my army unit. We even did a Zoom meeting for the students with my friends who were serving in the reserves." Dafna had a similar experience at her school, remarking: "We raised money for gifts for children who were evacuated from their homes before the holidays." Research findings revealed that numerous teaching emissaries employed fundraising practices as a complementary strategy to personal narratives and heroism accounts. They reported that through fundraising for specific causes, they were able to engage students with the Israeli experience while maintaining minimal exposure to sensitive content.

The fourth practice teachers used was community engagement. Shir shared:

> At some point I realized it would be simpler to share and teach outside of school. With adults. In the Jewish community. I felt that in every situation, I also tried more to reach out to the community, which I kind of avoided at first, tried more to attend community meetings, to get involved in community education. You also need to be very delicate and respectful in your mission. But at every social event, even if I found myself in the company of three, four adult American Jews who are with them, there are no restrictions, with them there's no censorship. And it was important to me to bring Israel to them. To share what's happening in the country.

Tal described the school-community collaboration that emerged during the past year:

> Several families from Israel who were evacuated from the north came to our community, and suddenly we found ourselves more involved in afternoon community activities, where we could speak more freely and not have to think about every word and step.

Teaching emissaries discovered that community engagement beyond formal school hours provided both an effective bridge between Israel and the United States and a platform for their own emotional expression. These community frameworks offered emissaries spaces for unrestricted dialogue about their experiences, uninhibited by the boundaries established within their educational institutions.

Personal Need for Pedagogical Transformation

The second theme that emerged from the research findings concerns teaching emissaries' need to modify their lesson structures and pedagogical approach that were in place prior to October 7. The practices within the clear boundaries theme are specific and relate to emotional discourse and actions; these can occur both during formal instruction and beyond it in informal teaching or even outside the school framework. In contrast, the pedagogical change theme addresses modifications made within formal lessons and teaching practices. These practices were designed to address both the emotional needs of teaching emissaries and their desire to teach about events in Israel. The interviews revealed distinct variations among different types of schools and in the degree of flexibility allowed for the pedagogical changes. Teaching emissaries report that upon returning to their classrooms in the immediate aftermath of October 7, they experienced an urgent imperative to modify their curricular approach. Their testimonies indicate a perceived impossibility of maintaining pre-existing instructional methodologies. The emissaries articulate that their lived experiences during this period necessitated their integration into their pedagogical practice and how they engaged students. Adi reflected on those feelings:

> On October 9 we went back to school. So, we said to ourselves—there's no way. How do we enter the classroom and like teach as if . . . how do we go in? How do we adapt the materials for students, especially when they're overprotected? They really shield students here even before October 7.

The emissaries' primary realization was that mediating their perspective to students required transitioning the classroom language from Hebrew to English. The emissaries adopted the practice of temporarily suspending Hebrew instruction to bridge language barriers. Adam said:

> In the end, when you speak their language, it gets through. And Hebrew isn't their language . . . So even at events, like,

when there were big events, I found myself saying, okay, now it's important to me that they understand, so I tell them really, like, it's important to me that you understand, English in class, whatever it took to make sure they really understand, whether it's some video clips in English.

A similar sentiment was shared by Gal:

> I wasn't available to teach Hebrew like before, I think in the first two months, it was, say, 50–50, Hebrew and English in classes. It was very much my own need. And then I think I found materials that were more divided by levels, and I could really incorporate it into Hebrew class. I could speak in Hebrew with appropriate materials related to the war . . . But it took time.

The findings indicate that teaching emissaries recognized the necessity of navigating a pedagogical trade-off: either maintaining Hebrew instruction at the students' existing proficiency level, which limited comprehensive communication and complex topic delivery, or temporarily suspending Hebrew instruction, either for a defined period or during specific lesson segments, to facilitate a deeper understanding and a clearer message transmission to students.

The second pedagogical practice adopted by the emissaries was to transition to project-based learning. Tal shared:

> In the first two months of the war, it was chaotic. It was really hard to teach. We found ourselves doing all kinds of projects that we mainly tried to do just to calm ourselves down—to feel like we're part of what's happening back in Israel.

Shir explained her approach to project development in this way:

> I really think that American pedagogy is so structured and framed, it's not . . . it was very hard to break out of it. So no, but we did small things. Projects inside the classroom. For example, we took stones and wrote wishes for Israel in Hebrew. Or we had a baking day throughout the school and sold cookies,

the money we collected we sent to Israel. More things that create optimism. Less war—more hope.

A similar sentiment was shared by Gal:

> My approach changed. More projects, less traditional teaching. We did a *hasbara* [public diplomacy] project. Students had to write a script, and they had several options relevant to their lives in the US—things they know from the news here: a conversation with someone who tears down hostage posters / campus protesters / responses to an anti-Israel YouTube video. And create some kind of video that they could post on social media.

The implementation of project-based learning addressed two distinct dimensions. First, it helped to stabilize classroom dynamics during chaotic periods through sustained and clearly defined long-term projects. Second, this learning practice also had a meaning-making aspect that enabled teaching emissaries to generate impact and facilitate deep emotional and pedagogical learning regarding the war in Israel through these projects.

What began as a practice that developed because of immediate wartime needs eventually evolved into being intentionally woven into formal pedagogy. The data indicates that most teachers integrated project-based learning into their regular instructional framework, and they reported that, approaching 2025, they had incorporated this methodology as a recurring component of their teaching practice. As Ben explained:

> The reality shaped itself and changed . . . and you don't look at it while you're in motion . . . acting from your gut, suddenly, nothing was consistent. And then slowly you realize that you've created a new framework. And the projects became a method. Today, once a week, I do a news lesson in Hebrew. And now it's already part of the methodology.

Hana added an additional perspective for her approach to the process:

> We were looking for a long-term project that could continue even after we leave. We connected with one of the *kibbutzim* in

> the Gaza envelope and started doing a twin school program. We send them videos in Hebrew and they send us videos in English. It started from our need to do something different and good, and then we realized we should formalize it and turn it into a long-term program. And then we expanded it into a program that includes the afternoon community as well.

As demonstrated in the findings, the success of project-based learning proved so significant that teaching emissaries adopted it as a core pedagogical methodology, even developing long-term projects designed to continue beyond their mission tenure.

A third new pedagogic practice involved the strategic integration of news media as an instructional bridge connecting Hebrew language acquisition with contemporary wartime developments in Israel. Dafna shared:

> I was looking for a simple method that would, on one hand, keep me in Hebrew class, and on the other hand, allow me to create discussion about what's happening in Israel. I found that reading news answers exactly this need. So yes, I spend quite a bit of time finding articles that fit the discourse limitations and what I'm allowed and not allowed to do in class. But using the news really brought my lessons to life.

The incorporation of multimedia news sources as pedagogical instruments in language instruction emerged as a consistent practice throughout the war period. In contrast to boundary-theme practices developed as responses to constraints, this news-based methodology was fundamentally pedagogical, with teaching emissaries actively modifying content to conform to administrative parameters.

The fourth practice identified was the implementation of optimism-based pedagogy. Teaching emissaries repeatedly expressed that they operated from a desire to create an optimistic outlook toward a better future. Adam shared:

> I felt a strong need to strengthen the connection to Israel specifically from a positive place. From a place of love. A bit more of the basics, physically knowing places in Israel. At first, I improvised. And then I realized this was a good direction, and I built a new program that deals with teaching Hebrew

through learning the map. What was good was that I built it based on the existing program, and it actually got administrative approval. And it's already entered the routine of a second year [the project began its second year in the 2024–2025 school year].

The final recurring pedagogical practice identified among teaching emissaries effectively provides resolution to the boundaries established by administrators for student protection. Through the deliberate choice to frame war-related instruction through optimism-based pedagogy, teaching emissaries created a bridge between pedagogical and emotional domains, reconciling their own needs with those of their students.

Discussion and Conclusion

The data collected for this study reveals a complex interplay between institutional constraints and personal pedagogical adaptations among Israeli teaching emissaries during the October 7 War period. These findings both align with and extend existing research on wartime education while highlighting unique aspects of the emissary experience. Furthermore, this study reveals novel findings previously unidentified in the literature.

All practices identified throughout the research operated along an emotional-pedagogical axis, addressing the needs of both students and teaching emissaries. This represents a significant finding in and of itself, as previous research has rarely addressed teachers' emotional aspects during wartime or their resilience building. The current study reveals that teaching emissaries actively operate to address their personal needs through their choice of practices.

Furthermore, these practices exist along two parallel axes: top-down practices implemented in response to administrative directives and established boundaries, and bottom-up practices comprising pedagogical initiatives originated by emissaries that subsequently evolved into sustainable pedagogical changes. The emergence of clear boundary lines as a primary theme reflects what Davies (2004) identified as schools' tendency to avoid conflict and highlight unity during periods of strife. However, the teaching emissaries' experience presents a unique case where educators themselves are citizens of a nation at war while teaching in communities physically removed from the conflict. This creates what could be termed a "dual consciousness"—simultaneously processing personal trauma while maintaining professional boundaries.

The shift toward personal narrative teaching aligns with Sommers's (2002) assertion that teachers' impact during crisis is even more critical than during peacetime. However, while Sommers focused on teachers promoting physical and psychosocial development in war zones, this study reveals how teaching emissaries utilized personal narratives as a bridge between their war-affected homeland and their physically distant but emotionally connected students. The transition to project-based learning and community engagement represents what Thomas et al. (2019) described as strategies that recognize and address the emotional and psychological needs of students who have experienced trauma. However, in this case, the trauma was not direct but rather experienced through cultural and communal connection. This finding extends our understanding of how trauma-informed teaching can be applied in contexts where the trauma is culturally rather than directly experienced. The emergence of optimism-based pedagogy among teaching emissaries aligns with recent research by Chaikovska et al. (2023) on the importance of fostering hope and resilience during wartime. However, this study reveals how such pedagogy can be effectively implemented even in communities physically removed from conflict, suggesting its potential broader applicability in diaspora education during homeland crises. The findings regarding language adaptation—specifically the temporary suspension of Hebrew instruction in favor of emotional connection—represents a significant departure from traditional emissary practice. This finding resonates with Rosenfeld et al.'s (2022) analysis of professional identity adaptation among mobile teachers; it further expands their framework to encompass crisis-driven scenarios. A particularly noteworthy finding is the evolution of crisis-response teaching methods into formalized pedagogical approaches. What began as improvisational responses to immediate needs developed into structured methodologies that teaching emissaries intended to maintain beyond the immediate crisis period. This suggests that crisis periods, while challenging, can serve as catalysts for pedagogical innovation.

The research also reveals an interesting tension between what Aharonov (2015) identified as the "perceptual disparity" between schools viewing emissaries as professional teachers and emissaries seeing themselves as broader community influencers. During the war period, this tension facilitated adaptation, as emissaries leveraged their dual role to create new spaces for engagement outside formal school hours.

The study's limitations include its focus on North American Jewish middle schools and its timing during an ongoing conflict. Future research might examine how these findings compare to teaching emissaries' experiences with other age groups. Additionally, longitudinal studies could investigate the long-term impact of these pedagogical adaptations on student learning and Jewish identity formation. Future research might explore how the pedagogical innovations developed during this period influence long-term teaching practices in diaspora Jewish education, and how these findings might inform preparation and support for teaching emissaries in future crisis situations.

In conclusion, this study makes significant contributions to understanding educational practices during crisis periods through its examination of teaching emissaries' unique position. The research illuminates a distinctive phenomenon of "dual consciousness," where educators navigate being citizens of a nation at war while teaching in physically removed communities. The findings extend existing frameworks in two key areas: expanding trauma-informed teaching to contexts where trauma is culturally experienced, and demonstrating how crisis-response methods can evolve into sustainable pedagogical innovations.

The study uniquely documents the parallel development of top-down and bottom-up practices along an emotional-pedagogical axis, addressing a significant gap in literature regarding teachers' emotional resilience during wartime. These insights advance both theoretical understanding of crisis education and practical approaches to pedagogical adaptation during periods of national crisis.

References

Aharonov, Y. (2009). *The educational expatriate in a diaspora community: The case of the Israeli Shaliach in Australia*. Doctoral dissertation, The University of Sydney, Australia.

Aharonov, Y. (2015). The educational mission of the Shaliach: A case study in Australia. *Journal of Jewish Education*, *81*(2), 189–211. https://doi.org/10.1080/15244113.2015.1027869

Alvén, F. (2024). Controversial issues in history teaching. *Journal of Curriculum Studies*, 56(5), 537–553. https://doi.org/10.1080/00220272.2024.2322502

Atef, A., Mahdi, M. (2017). A teacher and students' transformation at a time of war. In S. Baily, F. Shahrokhi, and T. Carsillo (Eds.), *Experiments in agency: A global partnership to transform teacher research*. SensePublishers. https://doi.org/10.1007/978-94-6300-944-7_5

Bar-Shalom, Y. (2011). Reflections on ethnographic research. *Research Paths, Annual Research Publication of the Research Authority at the Mofet Institute*, 17.

Baum, N. L., Cardozo, B. L., Pat-Horenczyk, R., Ziv, Y., Blanton, C., Reza, A., and Brom, D. (2013). Training teachers to build resilience in children in the aftermath of war: A cluster randomized trial. *Child and Youth Care Forum*, 42, 339–350.

Buchanan, T. K., Casbergue, R. M., and Baumgartner, J. J. (2010). Consequences for classroom environments and school personnel: Evaluating Katrina's effect on schools and system response. In R. P. Kilmer, V. Gil-Rivas, R. G. Tedeschi, and L. G. Calhoun (Eds.), *Helping families and communities recover from disaster: Lessons learned from hurricane Katrina and its aftermath* (pp. 117–139). American Psychological Association. https://doi.org/10.1037/12054-005

Catoto, J. (2022). Teachers in the war zone: A hermeneutics phenomenology. *SSRN*. http://dx.doi.org/10.2139/ssrn.4137839

Chaikovska, O., Palyliulko, O., Komarnitska, L., and Ikonnikova, M. (2023). Impact of mindset activities on psychological well-being and EFL skills of engineering students in wartime. *Proceedings of the International Scientific Conference Engineering for Rural Development*, 22, 282–288.

Clark, A. (2006). *Teaching the nation: Politics and pedagogy in Australian history*. Melbourne University Publishing.

Cohen, E. H. (1996). *Educational shlichim 1973–1993: Data-bank on sociodemographic and functioning*. Research and Evaluation.

Cohen, E. H. (2000). The Shlihim Training Institute: A contribution to the history and analysis of educational shlihut. In B. Bacon, D. Schers, and D. Zisenwine (Eds.), *New trends in research in Jewish education* (pp. 39–60). Tel Aviv University.

Davies, L. (2004). *Education and conflict: Complexity and chaos*. Routledge.

Deterding, N. M., and Waters, M. C. (2021). Flexible coding of in-depth interviews: A twenty-first-century approach. *Sociological Methods and Research, 50*(2), 708–739. https://doi.org/10.1177/0049124118799377

Durish, P. (2012). War, trauma, and learning: staying present in the classroom. In S. Mojab (Ed.), *Women, war, violence and learning*. Routledge.

Goldberg, T., Wagner, W., and Petrović, N. (2019). From sensitive historical issues to history teachers' sensibility: a look across and within countries. *Pedagogy, Culture and Society, 27*(1), 7–38. https://doi.org/10.1080/14681366.2019.1566165

Heath, H., and Cowley, S. (2004). Developing a grounded theory approach: A comparison of Glaser and Strauss. *International Journal of Nursing Studies, 41*(2), 141–150. https://doi.org/10.1016/S0020-7489(03)00113-5

Kello, K. (2016). Sensitive and controversial issues in the classroom: teaching history in a divided society. *Teachers and Teaching, 22*(1), 35–53. https://doi.org/10.1080/13540602.2015.1023027

Kennedy, R. (2014). *The Children's War: Britain, 1914–1918*. Palgrave Macmillan.

Morim Shlichim (2024). https://www.israelieducators.co.il/

Mosley, M. (2009). Talking about war in a second grade classroom. In R. Rogers, M. A. Kramer, M. Mosley, and The Literacy for Social Justice Teacher Research Group (Eds.). *Designing socially just learning communities: Critical literacy education across the lifespan* (1st ed.) (pp. 57–68). Routledge. https://doi.org/10.4324/9780203881675

Oplatka, I. (2024). A call to adopt pedagogies of optimism in times of armed conflicts: theoretical and practical insights. *Journal of Professional Capital and Community*. Advance online publication. https://doi.org/10.1108/JPCC-06-2024-0088

Pole, C., and Morrison, M. (2003). *Ethnography for education*. McGraw-Hill Education.

Pomson, A., and Gillis, M. (2010). The teacher-as-stranger as model and metaphor. *Teacher Development, 14*(1), 45–56. https://doi.org/10.1080/13664531003696576

Rosenfeld, I., and Yemini, M. (2023). Identity in the making: The influence of context on mobile teachers' construction of a professional identity. *International Journal of Educational Research, 120*, 102212. https://doi.org/10.1016/j.ijer.2023.102212

Rosenfeld, I., Yemini, M., and Mamlok, D. (2022). Agency and professional identity among mobile teachers: how does the experience of teaching abroad shape teachers' professional identity? *Teachers and Teaching, 28*(6), 668–689. https://doi.org/10.1080/13540602.2022.2097216

Samuels, A. R. (1992). *Israeli teachers in American Jewish day schools: The teachers' perspective.* The Jewish Theological Seminary of America.

Sharifian, M. S., and Kennedy, P. (2019). Teachers in war zone education: Literature review and implications. *International Journal of the Whole Child, 4*(2), 9–26.

Shapira Junger, M. (2024). *Returning educational shlichim as agents of change in the Israeli educational system.* Doctoral dissertation, Ariel University, Israel.

Sommers, M. (2002). *Children, education and war: Reaching education for all (EFA) objectives in countries affected by conflict.* Conflict Prevention and Reconstruction Unit. Working paper 1. World Bank. https://documents1.worldbank.org/curated/en/376921468762874069/pdf/multi0page.pdf

Tair, U., and Dashefsky, I. (2009). Mutual relations between *shelihim* and local teachers at Jewish schools in the former Soviet Union. In A. Pomson and H. Deitcher (Eds.), *Jewish day schools, Jewish communities: A reconsideration* (pp. 155–171). The Littman Library of Jewish Civilization.

Tal, N. (2024). The teaching of traumatic narratives: Out-of-the-classroom engagement with non-canonical "chosen traumas." *History Education Research Journal, 21*(1), 11. https://doi.org/10.14324/HERJ.21.1.11

Tal, N., and Hofman, A. (2021). Beyond the curriculum: Teaching history in Israeli classrooms, 1970s–1980s. *History of Education, 50*(6), 837–854. https://doi.org/10.1080/0046760X.2021.1906456

Thomas, M. S., Crosby, S., and Vanderhaar, J. (2019). Trauma-informed practices in schools across two decades: An interdisciplinary review of research. *Review of Research in Education, 43*(1), 422–452. https://doi.org/10.3102/0091732X18821123

Winthrop, R., and Kirk, J. (2008). Learning for a bright future: Schooling, armed conflict, and children's well-being. *Comparative Education Review, 52*(4), 639–661. https://doi.org/10.1086/591301

World Zionist Organization (2015). *Annual Report for 2013: The Office of the Comptroller.* https://www.wzo.org.il/Upload/media/Files/2013-%20Eng.pdf

"Can we talk about it?": Implementing Israel Education during Wartime at Jewish Summer Camps

Tal Vaizman[*]

It hit me straight in the face as I stepped out of the car at the center of the camp compound: "The camp stands with Israel." The Israeli flag decorated the banner on the main building, accompanied with that firm declaration. Was that about to reflect all that is to come?

In the summer of 2024, I set out to visit two overnight Jewish summer camps. This was not the average year, marked by the ongoing war between Israel and Gaza, following the October 7 massacre. Hostages were held captive for months, many perished, over 100,000 residents were evacuated from northern Israel, and soldiers engaged in seemingly unending conflict. Some displaced Israeli youth attended camp, while soldiers served as Israeli counselors. This was not the average summer.

Will these events impact Israel education at camps? The effects could be varied. Camp culture typically adheres to traditional methods of Israel education with consistent delivery and content shaped and affected by current events (Lorge and Zola, 2006; Sales and Sax, 2004). However, the atmosphere

---

[*] This study was made possible through the generous support of the Collaborative for Applied Studies in Jewish Education (CASJE) at The George Washington University (GWU). I am deeply grateful to the Foundation for Jewish Camp (FJC) for their valuable collaboration throughout this project. Special thanks go to the camp leaders and all the participants who generously shared their time and thoughts.

and socialization within camps may be influenced by ongoing news, altering Israel's role in discussions and its significance in campers' Jewish identities.

This chapter discusses the social and educational dynamics affecting implementation of Israel education by Israeli staff following October 7, as observed at two secular Jewish camps. Absorbing Israelis as counselors during the most sensitive time in Israel history, camps' ability to implement Israel education affected not only campers' exposure to delicate topics, but the people involved in the educational process. Those adjustments are also affected by the campers' wishes, experiences, and characters, and this too requires coordination and consultancy between senior and Israeli staff. Israelis' role as mediators, facilitators, and experts is discussed in this chapter, exploring their relationship with administration, the freedom to lead, and flexibility vs. planned educational curriculum. The collected data reveals that the informal and spontaneous interactions between Israeli counsellors and American campers can oftentimes provide greater opportunities for meaningful encounters than formal and structured programming.

Background

Overnight Jewish summer camps are crucial in shaping campers' attitudes and understandings about contemporary Jewish issues, including the Israeli-Palestinian conflict. Despite the informal nature of these settings, the educational impact is significant, influencing how young Jews engage with complex global issues.

While Jewish education and Israel education may run parallel, they often intersect within camp settings, contingent upon the extent to which Israel is integrated into the Jewish identity of both the camp environment and its participants. Fostering Jewish culture at camp has become one of the first priorities for most camps in the 2000s (Sales et al., 2011). Informal Jewish education at camp may be broad and open-ended, emphasizing personal growth and meaning-making over structured curriculum (Chazan, 2002). Chazan claims that the emphasis shifts from merely transmitting Jewish culture to fostering personal Jewish development, allowing individuals to actively engage in their own journeys of growth. However, much like traditional formal education, Jewish education may systematically focus on transmitting knowledge in certain times, and on mere socialization (as non-educational interaction) at other times (Cremin, 1977). Camps, however, are dynamic environments where every moment can be educational, and camp settings offer a unique space for personal and communal Jewish development (Reimer, 2018).

In contrast to Jewish education, which is grounded in spirituality, tradition, morality, narratives, and often domestic practices (Reimer, 2003; Sales and Sax, 2004), Israel education necessitates a strong foundation in historical knowledge alongside a dynamic awareness of contemporary events. Davis and Alexander (2024) claim that while informal settings like camps are essential for addressing Israel education, there is a need for educators to develop a deep pedagogical content knowledge (PCK) about how to teach the Israeli-Palestinian conflict. They argue that though understanding the political and cultural dimensions of Israel is integral, it is also vital for the educators to be skilled in engaging with campers in ways that foster critical thinking and encourage meaningful dialogue. It becomes increasingly important given that high school students in Jewish day schools report not being taught to critically engage with the complexities of the conflict, with their educators simplifying or omitting the nuances in order to foster a sense of loyalty to Israel (Zakai, 2022). This reality underscores the necessity for camps to integrate comprehensive and nuanced discussions about Israel into their programs, rather than relying solely on superficial cultural content (Pomson and Deitcher, 2010). This includes engaging campers in meaningful discussions about the Israeli-Palestinian conflict and its implications for Jewish identity and values (Isaacs, 2011).

Traditionally, Jewish camps focused on fostering a positive cultural connection to Israel, often emphasizing cultural aspects over political realities (Rothenberg, 2016). They often recruit Israeli emissaries, serving as experts on "Israel education," to be cultural ambassadors, bringing authentic Israel to camp—usually in a concise or symbolic way (Benor et al., 2020). The "Israel-lite" approach, as Rothenberg describes, presents a romanticized, depoliticized image of Israel that can lack depth and critical engagement, with some camps now feeling challenged to address Israel's political complexities while maintaining a positive environment (Beinart, 2010).

Jewish camps are renowned for their vibrant Jewish culture, which includes shared rituals, songs, and communal activities (Kent, 2012). Sale and Saxe (2004) describe the basic goals achieved by Jewish camps: creating a supervised setting for Jewish adolescents to socialize in, to expose them to Jewish culture and rituals, and to create a Jewish community beyond home. The sense of belonging that campers experience within a Jewish community at camp is often unmatched in their home communities, making it one of the greatest values of Jewish camps (Reimer, 2018). Fostering a strong sense of community and overcoming the challenge of a "light" cultural framework as an educational setting, it can be leveraged to enhance Israel education.

Despite the historical challenge of how to introduce a nuanced Israeli culture, contemporary challenges like political apathy complicate Israel education at camps. Friedman and Zisenwine (1998) highlight the political apathy observed among campers, while Pomson et al. (2014) suggest that this avoidance may stem from a lack of knowledge and a tendency towards superficial treatment of the topic by camp leadership. This superficiality is often manifested in what Benor et al (2020) referred to as "Hebrew infusion"—the use of the language in a symbolic way, absent a deep understanding or cultural transference. Despite most camps' tendency to believe that the Hebrew language and Jewish culture should unite Jewish people to some degree regardless of their religious practices (Sarna, 2006), in practicality Hebrew words are often used in isolation rather than within complete, meaningful sentences (Benor et al., 2020). In times of emojis, acronyms, and concise messaging in any language, harnessing Hebrew into cultural exchange—Israeli songs, dance, banners—might result in further superficiality.

Moreover, changes in current events in Israel, particularly involving the conflict with the Palestinians, may change Israeli-Jewish American relations as manifested in camps. Religious camps often maintain a connection to Israel based on religious texts and a belief in the Jewish people's spiritual and national return to the land of Israel—seeing Israel as not just a political entity, but rather the fulfillment of biblical prophecy (Sales and Sax, 2004). While such approach may sustain political turbulences, secular ideological camps' connection to Israel might be more affected by timely events. Secular Zionism is experiencing a decline, often viewing Israel through the lens of an occupying force—which may lead to a growing focus on Orthodox Jews as the primary future supporters of Israel, as well as the main audience for Israeli education (Beinart, 2010). The prevalence of misinformation and the role of social media further complicate the educational landscape, as adolescents encounter both authentic and fabricated information online (Tandoc et al., 2017).

Methodology

This study employed an ethnographic approach to examine two Jewish summer camps: A liberal Zionist Maryland-based camp (MBC), affiliated with a socialist youth movement, and an unaffiliated Pennsylvania-based camp (PBC). The camps were chosen because of their secular backgrounds, with the goal being to explore Israel connections outside of religious affiliations. In particular, I was interested in how the camps orchestrated cultural exchanges, socialization amongst youth, and the role management played in guiding these interactions. This was also an opportunity to explore two camps that differ in political stances and in their ratios of Israeli counselors to North American counselors. Data collection took place on two occasions at each camp: during staff training and a two-to-three-day visit to each site. The research population included campers aged thirteen and older, counselors, and senior staff, with all names altered per Institutional Review Board (IRB) protocols. The ethnographic methodology utilized a multi-faceted data collection strategy, combining observations, interviews, focus groups, videography, photography, and analysis of educational and practical materials used at the camps. This approach captures and analyzes cultural practices and social interactions (Pink, 2013) and allows for a rich, nuanced understanding of camp culture, social dynamics, and educational practices.

Participant observation formed a core component of the research. I immersed myself in the camp environment, observing daily activities and routines. This method provided invaluable insights into the lived experiences of campers and staff, allowing me to observe behaviors, interactions, and cultural practices in their natural setting.

Interviews were conducted using a flexible, conversational style. Potential participants were approached in the field to discuss their experiences. Guided by my observations, unstructured interviews followed a predetermined framework, facilitating focused discussions on relevant issues while using familiar terminology (Bauer and Gaskell, 2000). This informal approach encourages open sharing of thoughts and feelings. I also participated in group activities like lessons, cooking, dancing, and singalongs, observing interactions and asking follow-up questions for deeper exploration. Focus groups were organized to facilitate discussions on specific topics (Gubrium and Holstein, 2001), enabling the exploration of shared experiences and collective meaning-making among campers and staff. The dynamic nature of these groups often yielded rich conversations and unexpected insights.

Visual methods, including videography and photography, were employed because they capture the physical environment, activities, and non-verbal aspects of camp life (Becker, 2002). These provided additional context and depth to the observations and interviews (Heath et al., 2010). I also collected and analyzed educational and practical materials used in the camps, such as activity plans and informational documents. These artifacts offered insights into the formal and informal curriculum of the camps. During data collection, I logged fieldnotes, documented firsthand impressions, and made records of casual conversations (Emerson et al., 2011).

Data analysis followed an iterative, inductive approach typical of ethnographic research. I paid close attention to conduct and appearance, noting how participants behaved and presented themselves in various contexts. Tone and manner of speech were carefully considered, as they often conveyed underlying attitudes and emotions not explicitly stated (Lieblich et al., 2010). A crucial aspect of the analysis involved "reading between the lines"—interpreting subtle cues, unspoken assumptions, and cultural nuances that might not be immediately apparent. This required me to draw on their immersive experience in the field or their understanding of the broader cultural context of Jewish summer camps.

The data was organized into emerging units of meaning (Bazeley, 2013). This thematic analysis involved identifying recurring patterns, concepts, and ideas across the various data sources. Themes were refined and consolidated through an iterative process of reviewing and comparing data.

This comprehensive ethnographic approach allowed for a holistic examination of the Jewish summer camp experience, capturing both the explicit and implicit aspects of camp culture, social dynamics, and educational practices.

Findings

Staff and campers revealed that Israel education is crucial to camp culture, existing during both structured and informal programming. Both camps included Israel in staff training, though the integration varied. Counselors engaged in preparing lessons and activities related to Israel, emphasizing the importance of social interactions on the topic. Notably, significant differences arose between the camps, shaped by their specific agendas and the presence of Israeli staff.

Camp Culture and Agenda: A Setting for Israel Education

The two camps have distinct backgrounds and responses to current events, influencing their educational focus. MBC camp, aligned with a socialist youth movement, emphasizes a progressive educational philosophy rooted in social justice and cultural engagement, fostering community through experiential learning and a focus on Jewish identity. In contrast, PBC, without a specific affiliation, prioritizes community building, personal growth, and Jewish values, while promoting social responsibility.

In recent years, MBC has increasingly aligned with the progressive left in the United States, advocating for freedom of expression and diversity, distancing itself from Zionism and unconditional support for Israel. The camp environment displayed varied clothing styles and a subdued presence of Israeli culture. Although MBC maintains historical Zionist connections, support for both Israelis and Palestinians often overshadowed support for the State of Israel, which remains a contentious issue.

This leftward shift was described by the MBC staff. Aaron, an educational leader, noted: "This movement has been doing a lot of soul searching... The idea of identifying as a Zionist conflicts with a liberal progressive left thinking." Edgar, his co-leader, added, "Since 2019 a lot of people tried to remove or reassess Zionism as a pillar of the movement." Aaron pointed out, "People that have no connection to Israel might describe themselves as antizionists and the campaign in Gaza as a genocide."

Steve, a veteran counselor, reflected on the camp's shifting ideological landscape: "This place goes in and out of different cultural areas... There were conflicts. [Members] kind of left in protest, but, by leaving, that energy kind of died. It [holds] leftist ideologically, but more balanced. People can see multiple perspectives." The MBC staff's reflections on their camp's ideological stance suggest a transitioning faze, from being fully supporting of Israel, to a conflicting leftist approach, and perhaps back to a more balanced view. Steve's insights illustrate the camp's cautious educational approach to the contentious topic of Israel. The camp has faced conflicts, rifts, and departures, leading leaders to cultivate an environment that encourages dialogue and prevents any single viewpoint from dominating.

For MBC campers, the camp experience this year offered a diverse Jewish space that alleviated feelings of alienation some experienced as Jews in non-Jewish spaces during the school year. Here, among friends, they sought common ground, even as they upheld individualism and diversity. The year's theme, "Jewish Joy," seemed detached from reality but Aaron explained the choice was purposeful and fitting: "We're trying to focus on what we can do together, how we can create a healing space as the war continues."

Despite these efforts, being Jewish was not universally joyful for the staff, affecting their concern for the campers. "Being Jewish felt hard this year," wrote one counselor during an anonymous reflection exercise, while Aaron acknowledged, "We're hoping that things will go well, and kids won't feel very emotionally charged... it puts a lot of pressure on the staff." This mindset shaped the counselors' approach to camp amid the ongoing conflict in Israel, which could not be ignored but was also a sensitive and polarizing issue. Leading up to camp, interest in Israel-related activities surged, with twenty-seven volunteers for pre-summer planning, compared to six or seven in previous years. However, concerns about safe spaces for discussion arose as counselors feared differing opinions might create friction, leading to the establishment of inclusive discussion guidelines.

In contrast, taking a stand at PBC appeared strikingly different. The Israeli flag prominently decorated the main building, and staff wore yellow shirts in support of hostages every day, symbolizing their clear stance: "We stand with Israel." PBC's lack of movement affiliation allowed for greater freedom in addressing the conflict and shaping their educational agenda. While MBC grappled with community inclusion, PBC strove to balance education about sensitive topics like Israeli current events with fun experiences and opportunities for socialization, something that was often perceived as requiring minimal effort by the Israelis. In a group discussion, an Israeli counselor remarked, "This is not an educational place," while another replied, "It was never educational. We've been here before," suggesting that enjoyment took precedence over education.

The banner on PBC main building

This year, counselors, especially Israelis, faced heightened expectations. Ehud noted, "The expectation was that after the war, we'd talk more about the situation." Elisha, an American counselor, explained why at PBC this might be a challenge, since many campers relied on camp as their only Jewish outlet, limiting educational depth: "Especially since October 7, these kids didn't have the chance to express or receive any sort of comfort in their Judaism at all. Having a place here ... they feel safe in their Judaism, and that means a lot to them, even if we can't educate them for more." While both Ehud and Elisha would have welcomed a deep educational discussion, Elisha's familiarity with PBC's population allowed him the understanding of the senior staff's reluctance to wade into discussions about October 7.

All staff who were interviewed acknowledged the good intentions and concern from American leadership, though perspectives varied based on individual experiences. Some appreciated the camp's flexibility and provision of materials, viewing symbolic gestures like the Israeli flag as emotional support. Others critiqued these gestures as superficial, desiring more substantive leadership. Discussions surrounding Israel often clashed with the camp's emphasis on fun and a positive atmosphere, especially during wartime. Additionally, the educational culture regarding Israel was heavily influenced by the presence of Israeli staff, who were numerous at PBC but few at MBC.

Whose Responsibility Is It?

It is logical for experts on a team to lead programs relevant to their field. However, MBC had only four Israeli counselors (see Table 9.1), whose experience might make them "natural experts," resulting in hesitant discussions during staff training about Americans' preparedness to talk about Israel. Ehud and Aaron, the educational leaders, voiced concerns about addressing Israel as a topic, and Aaron said, "We'd like to allow people to identify, discuss their common values in relation to the conflict." Their focus was more on the "how" than the "what," while trying to frame the complex conflict around common values.

Table 9.1 *Camps' Staff in the Summer of 2024*

	Staff Hired 2023	Emissaries	Proportion %
MBC	87	4	4.6
PBC	290	31	10.7

Hesitation regarding Israel education arose not just from fears of friction but also from uncertainty about the campers' knowledge and backgrounds. Typically, Israel education encompasses history and culture (Ladon, 2024; Golden and Kadden, 2024), but, after October 7, counselors were cautious about over-planning due to the ongoing conflict. A discussion about how to approach the issue with the Bogrim (senior) class was conducted among their counselors in an intimate room. One counselor remarked, "We don't know all their backgrounds, what schools they come from, what experiences they had . . . so maybe once the campers are here, we'll know how to conduct the dialogue." Controversial topics like *aliyah*[1] were also avoided; one counselor said, "I don't know if I'd feel comfortable doing that," and another explained, "There was controversy around it so that's why it was canceled" in reference to a previous year. While there was clear interest in dialogue, fear of controversy remained prevalent.

Acknowledging these concerns, Bria, another counselor, said: "I don't really know what [campers'] feelings about [Israel] are, but I'm definitely prepared to talk to them about it." Despite her willingness to have dialogue about Israel, her uncertainty about campers' feelings about Israel reflected a wider psychological barrier felt by other leaders. Not confident in the campers' feelings about the conflict, they felt uneasy planning ahead. The vibe in the room had a sense of "If we are not sure—why risk it?" Nessa added, "We should leave an open space for discussion. It's important that we don't force opinions on them but show them our values." Zane expressed concern over potential emotional reactions: "It's important to acknowledge that there are going to be disagreements about the conflict. It's very personal for many people and tends to get heated . . . so it should be something that we talk about, but I don't want it to be 'the thing of the summer.'" Bria further noted, "I really want to be able to talk about it without it feeling hard. It's important that we share our experiences, thoughts, and feelings, even if there are disagreements, from a place of understanding."

Avoiding discomfort was a recurring theme. Concerns about feelings and reactions influenced decision making more than the intrinsic relevance of topics. It seemed as though for the counselors, discussions about Israel might not have been essential for Jewish life or American-Israeli relations in the camp setting, while they were seen as significant for campers' well-being by the educational staff. Ironically, counselors emphasized fostering the campers' characters by instilling values, while recognizing that discussions promoting independent thought could lead to friction. When educational values clashed, the counselors prioritized acceptance and friendships.

At the educators' meeting, the issue of Israel was presented as an emotional need for campers but programs were only scheduled occasionally. Amit, the only Israeli present, sensed that the issue might be overlooked: "I think we need to be in control over the situation. I know there are things I want to talk about. Our [camps'] values are important, but we, the Madrichim[2], should bring what is important to us." Her remarks highlighted the counselors'

---

1   Refers to the immigration of Jews to Israel, an act considered significant and deeply rooted in Jewish history and tradition.
2   A Hebrew word commonly used in Jewish summer camps addressing the staff in charge of leading campers.

intent to address campers' needs while not fully accommodating the Israeli counselors. Amit pointed out that they also had needs and educational perspectives. The Israeli-American ratio influenced the discussion, placing less responsibility on the sole Israeli and limiting her contributions.

"What is so wrong with a bit of struggle and disagreement?" was the question raised among the Israeli counselors at PBC. There, their numbers were significant, making their perspectives harder to ignore. Responsibility for Israel education often fell on them, creating a gap between expectations and reality. While Israeli staff were more than willing to take on the responsibility, they expected support and dedicated time slots, two factors that that they did not always receive. Unlike at MBC, American staff at PBC allowed the Israeli counselors to lead and plan programs, but camp guidelines restricted certain discussions by age group. Moreover, lessons were not always scheduled in advance, leaving it up to the Israeli counselors to request slots or utilize ShabOption.[3] And so, while the Israelis expected to be educational leaders, the realities on the ground at times made it difficult for them to perform those roles.

Challenges were both practical and psychological. Though unofficially responsible for the Israel program, some Israeli counselors felt mistrusted, unconsulted, and underappreciated. Omri commented, "They don't care about previous experience like mine, in [our] youth movement... in the IDF. For them, 'you're a child so don't cross the street by yourself.'" He highlighted a communication gap with management, noting that supervisors often didn't inquire about his background, limiting the utilization of his skills. "They don't know where I come from. Therefore, they cannot use my skills. I know I have a lot to offer." He cynically reflected on his early hopes to make a difference, stating, "the first time I was here I thought I could make a difference... I decided I can't change a thing, so I came to have some fun."

The idea of fun was prominent in discussions, viewed as essential to the camp experience yet limiting educational potential. Omri noted, "It's very hard to change things here. Everyone is very strict, no flexibility. They want their escapism, and I get that." Some frustration stemmed from the time slots allocated to Israeli counselors. Dudi, a former camper now counselor, remarked, "They asked me to share my experience in the IDF, but it was clearly a low priority... It was at the end of a night... eventually didn't come through. There was no attempt to reschedule. They want to preserve the 'fun' experience, rather than letting it [the conflict] into the bubble they created."

---

3   Short for "Shabbat Option," a slot dedicated to various activities from which campers chose one or several options to attend on Shabbat.

Israel Education in Practice

Games. At both camps, games were used to engage campers in educational experiences. Activities such as theatrical plays or competitions enable campers to connect with historical periods and cultural practices. Fox (2023) notes that camp educators employed role playing games like *Hityashvut* and *Aliyah Bet* to simulate Jewish migration and address concerns about assimilation among American Jews. These activities foster physical and emotional connections to Jewish heritage, history and identity, demonstrating the deeper cultural significance behind these seemingly simple camp experiences.

Israeli counselors at PBC expressed frustration over their limited influence on camp programming and being able to address current events. "Why don't you make a game of it?" I suggested to Omri, who worked at the camp's farm. "As they work with the soil, you can tell them about the kinds of crops the Israeli pioneers used to grow, the soil, the hardship—let them pretend." A smile appeared on his face. "I'm going to use that," he said. Such games require minimal resources and can significantly enrich campers' daily experiences. Music also serves as an effective educational tool. Adina, an Israeli counselor, recounted how a co-counselor created a playlist of Israeli and American songs that campers enjoyed, exposing them to Israeli culture.

Ehud described a simple game where campers shared songs meaningful to them, fostering personal connections and cultural insights:

> Everyone wrote the name of a song meaningful to them. We threw it in a hat, picked one out, played about thirty seconds of it, and everyone had to guess whose song it was. Then the person explained how this song was meaningful to them. I used a Hebrew song by Machina, "Lama li politika achshav" (What good is politics now). I later saw one of the campers playing it through his speaker while walking around.

Ehud's song was a symbolic choice, giving the campers insight to a cultural expression from the 1980s that is still relevant today. By sharing it, he created a new interpretive community (Vaizman, 2023) based on Israeli pop culture. Despite limitations imposed by camp priorities, the impact of this game extended beyond the immediate experience, leveraging campers' social connectivity through their phones.

Addressing traumatic events like October 7 in a game is difficult due to several factors: (1) the sensitivity of the subject matter, (2) management restrictions on discussing issues with younger campers, (3) American counselors' discomfort in broaching the topic, and (4) the challenge of oversight in such discussions. Even in a cabin setting, American counselors may feel unequipped to facilitate the program, while Israeli counselors' personal experience might suggest that a more serious, conventional educational format would be better.

Thus, Israel education at camp is presented in different pedagogical approaches, with cultural elements like food, dance, and geography being done with games and creativity, and politics and current affairs topics more often being done in a more traditional or formal education context. Even when games are integrated into more serious lessons, like a trivia game about the West Bank at PBC, staff work to not undermine the topic's seriousness.

Programmed Lessons and Pedagogical Approaches. The challenges of Israel education in both camps stem from their pedagogical methodologies and the personal experiences of the staff. A key distinction in their approaches is the preference for "educating about" versus "educating for."

"Educating about" involves conveying knowledge on specific subjects like Israel's geography, history, or culture, and lessons are delivered by individuals with expertise. In contrast, "educating for" emphasizes cultivating skills, attitudes, and competencies to achieve broader objectives, focusing on character development in informal settings like camps. This approach uses subject matter as a medium and those directing the discussion act primarily as a facilitator rather than a source of knowledge.

While both camps aim to foster character development and meaningful experiences, at PBC, character is built into camp experiences and is not prioritized over educational content. In contrast, MBC emphasizes character and ideals above all else. Each lesson followed a specific methodology aligned with the camp's prevailing philosophy: Camp MBC applied "educating for," addressing controversial and divisive topics to foster values, while Camp PBC focused on filling knowledge gaps among campers and staff through "educating about." Pedagogical approaches were chosen not for their inherent value, but rather for the camp's philosophy and the leaders', who mostly grew up embracing it, ability to deliver the lesson accordingly.

The differences in educational practices regarding the "West Bank" lessons at PBC and MBC reveal their differing approaches to Israel education. At PBC, the lesson took place indoors with over seventy participants sitting in two circles around an Israeli counselor. It began energetically, with the leader outlining expectations for engaging with the provided materials. Conversely, MBC's session occurred outdoors led by an Israeli counselor and an American counselor. It took about five minutes for MBC to initiate discussion, and the atmosphere was quieter.

Both camps started by sharing information about the West Bank but did so in different ways. At MBC, the lesson commenced with a reading from a personal account about a checkpoint during a riot, inviting subjective interpretations. In contrast, PBC employed a matching game where participants connected events to specific years, emphasizing historical facts over personal perspectives.

Following the reading at MBC, a brief discussion ensued about the author's intent, but engagement was limited. Despite attempts to encourage participation through questions about power dynamics, the discussion remained subdued. The session included a video about Palestinian workers crossing checkpoints, yet campers' interaction continued to be minimal. The Israeli counselor even remarked on the limited participation, hoping for a more dynamic dialogue, but it was to no avail. A different lesson about the West Bank at MBC addressed evacuations from both Israeli and Palestinian perspectives using podcast interviews, fostering more engagement from the campers. In contrast, PBC's lesson focused on identifying terms like "PLO," leading to a more structured approach where the leader dominated the conversation, reinforcing a clear distinction between knowledgeable participants and those there to learn. The discussion also covered the historical context of the term "West Bank," which was absent from MBC's lesson.

PBC's educator clarified terms and provided relevant information like the IDF's role in the West Bank. The latter part of the lesson addressed the geography of the West Bank, reinforcing factual knowledge while limiting personal perspectives. Questions from participants highlighted the knowledge disparity within the group, with a focus on clarifying information rather than engaging in a broader dialogue.

Initiatives. Israeli presence and camp agenda influenced the special initiatives taken by Israeli counselors, which were more accepted at PBC, despite implementation difficulties. Israeli staff were encouraged to initiate programs, but changes to schedules or acquiring supplies posed challenges.

Two distinctive and well-received initiatives at PBC were a memorial board created by several Israeli counselors and placed in the lounge, and a live Zoom meeting they arranged with a hostage's granddaughter. Avital was particularly impressed by the camp's willingness to incorporate the latter: "This is not 'fun, fun' American camp, but listening to a difficult conversation." The

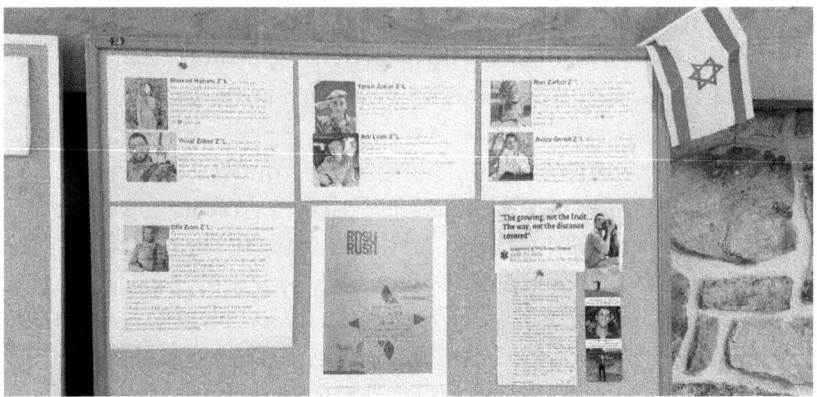

PBC memorial board

meeting, intended for campers aged fifteen and up, was attended by administrators as well. Regarding the memorial board, Avital noted: "These are our initiatives, and the camp embraces them. You don't need to hold a certain position to initiate."

Despite a number of successful initiatives, implementation challenges persisted. Recognizing that their American campers were unfamiliar with Israeli childhood games, Adva and her co-counselor decided to create an activity for this purpose. They required balloons, candles, and flour, and completed the necessary forms on time. Their manager expressed enthusiasm, stating, "Wonderful, so great!" However, when they arrived to collect their supplies, half of the items were missing. The manager casually mentioned that some materials were unavailable, unconcerned with the implications for their program. Though they drove to Walmart to purchase the supplies, Adva was left feeling frustrated: "They want to give you the space and often do, but they don't fully commit." The activity was a success, and Adva and her co-counselor were pleased with the results. However, they were left with a bitter taste: "We were so happy to see the Israeli kids so excited, because it's Israel, and all the campers explored some Israeliness. But! Eventually, the feedback from the supervisor and higher management was absent. They saw the flour on the floor and that's what they were worried about."

The Israeli counselors at PBC recognized a disconnect between the camp's desire to engage with Israeli culture and its ability to facilitate its implementation. It fell to them to initiate, be creative, and advocate for their needs, often experiencing disappointment in the support they received. Despite understanding their role in introducing Israeli culture, they frequently encountered a lack of actionable support and insufficient preparation. Avital commented, "If there wasn't an Israeli delegation here, I don't think anything would have happened. It would have been completely American," suggesting that Israel would be left out of the program.

Despite some stating that they had no expectations from the administration, disappointment was palpable and often clearly expressed. In response to the inquiry on whether the state of things and their personal motivations might hinder their emissary role, particularly in this challenging year, Shaked said: "The Agency[4] expects us to bring our personal stories, allow even one person a sense of 'home at the other side of the world.' And it sometimes

---

4   The Jewish Agency sends emissaries to summer camps in North America to strengthen the bond between Israel and Canada and the United States. See "Shlichim," https://www.jewishagency.org/il/shlichim/.

works." The Israelis in the focus group claimed, that though qualified to lead lessons, that was not what the agency expected, nor trained them for, as Meidad bluntly claimed: "They [agency] don't discuss Israeli issues, how to market it, present it best." Their grievances further stressed that the responsibility for explanatory and educational tasks is on their shoulders and by means of social interactions, rather than on scheduled lessons and planned activities.

Socialization and the Clash of Cultures

Given the challenges of implementing formal programs about Israel—due to their controversial nature, the absence of designated time slots, inconsistent support from senior staff—engaging in socio-cultural exchange was often a more effective means to introduce Israeli themes at camp. This was especially evident at PBC because interactions between Israelis and Americans were more frequent given the large number of Israeli staff and because campers shared tents with Israeli staff. Nevertheless, cultural differences, fear of offending, and concerns about disrupting the atmosphere often hindered meaningful dialogue.

The complexities of addressing the ongoing Israeli war further complicated the situation, as recent events heightened the need for personal sharing by the Israeli counselors. The importance of receiving support from American colleagues through genuine interest was acknowledged by many Israeli staff. Despite the interest, most agreed that cultural differences impeded deeper conversations. Adina, a staff member at PBC observed, "They are scared to address the issue," to which Shaked replied, "It depends; some have visited Israel multiple times, while others are younger counselors. Generally, conversations with Americans are shallower." Ehud expressed surprise at the American culture within the camp, stating, "It's very hard to deliberate with the Americans here. There's a position and no interest in understanding the other's view."

Establishing personal connections proved crucial for sharing opinions and cultural insights. Once relationships were formed, individuals were more receptive to listening and learning. Adina mentioned that her friendships with Americans facilitated their understanding of the Israeli perspective. Lea added, "This is part of why we're here—not only to address the issue directly but to establish personal connections and share our stories." Adina echoed this sentiment: "They see things as black or white. Good Israeli or Bad Israeli. The more we can show them good Israeli, the better."

The fact that arguing over political differences was out of the question as part of camp culture frustrated some Israelis, who viewed arguments as a natural part of socialization. Adina remarked, "I got into a huge argument with a fellow Israeli counselor, and I know everything is good, and he told me so. If an American did that, it would be like 'we're not friends anymore!'" Ehud added, "You're walking on eggshells. They are brought up to know that every person is pure and should not be harmed. They're not willing to allow campers to experience the world outside of the bubble they created." Lea shared an experience of confronting an Israeli co-counselor about a poor job they did, noting that an American would never feel comfortable being so direct: "No *dugri* ['directly' in Israeli slang]. They are offended when we talk to them like that." Such interpretations meant that the Israeli counselors could not be their full selves, often sidelining discussions about Israel in casual conversations.

For some, it often felt personal. "As an Israeli, when someone tells me where they're from, I'll immediately ask a follow-up question about their family. Yesterday was the first time an American asked me 'Is your family ok?' and I've been here a month," Avital said. "It seems reasonable to address someone from a country in a state of war, but it's probably the fear of being insensitive." Adva recounted a day when she cried after watching the news: "Noticing my red eyes, my co asked if I was ok. I told her, but she just hugged me and moved on. Even when given the chance to ask more, they won't take it. They fear it."

Conclusion

In the summer of 2024, overnight Jewish camps faced significant challenges in implementing Israel education due to the polarized opinions resulting from the war following October 7. This polarization affected Jewish identity and raised concerns about campers' knowledge. Traditional practices like the use of Hebrew terms continued in a "Hebrew infusion" approach, as described by Benor et al. (2020). However, symbolic support for Israel was minimal at the progressive MBC camp, which retained ties to its socialist past. In contrast, PBC displayed more visible support through actions like singing "Hatikva" and wearing yellow for hostages, although deeper support often faced administrative hurdles.

Israel education varied between camps. MBC integrated planned lessons focused on values like humanity and respect, largely due to a lack of "Israeli experts" and the camp agenda's constraints. Conversely, PBC had abundant expert resources, but lessons were sporadic and often excluded many campers. Initiatives like games involving Israel occurred informally in smaller settings at PBC, while MBC, with its cautious spirit and fewer Israeli counselors, was less adaptable.

Camps play a pivotal role in Jewish education, especially in relation to Israel. While traditional approaches have focused on cultural connections, there is a growing need to address political realities and contemporary issues. By adopting a more comprehensive and nuanced approach and by delegating and relying more on Israeli counselors, camps can better prepare young Jews to engage with the complexities of the Israeli-Palestinian conflict and its impact on their identities.

The concept of "meaningful Israel education" may vary among camps, campers, Israeli staff, and Jewish educators. After October 7, more than before, what some see as meaningful may be interpreted by others as harmful, polarizing or risky especially considering camps' desire to offer a safe and joyful experience to campers. However, and although not generalizable to all overnight summer camps, clear conclusions emerge about Israel education from studying these two very different secular camps:

1. the camp's philosophy towards modern Israel and its willingness to engage in open discussions about sensitive topics directly contributes to Israeli staff members' ability to enact effective programs;
2. camp administrators need to allow for flexibility in scheduling to accommodate meaningful conversations about Israel;
3. the presence of knowledgeable and committed Israeli staff members needs to be better leveraged to allow them to effectively serve as cultural ambassadors and subject matter experts;
4. the cultural gap between Israelis and Americans should be addressed, leveraging the opportunity for meaningful cultural exchange through socialization.

When these conditions are optimally present, particularly in secular and modern camp settings, Israel education can foster genuine connections based on knowledge, dialogue, and cultural exchange. This approach moves beyond traditional, often idealized presentations of Israel to create more nuanced and authentic understanding among representatives of two cultures, meeting over a summer experience.

References

Bauer, M. W., and Gaskell, G. (2000). *Qualitative researching with text, image and sound: A practical handbook for social research*. Sage. https://doi.org/10.4135/9781849209731

Bazeley, P. A. T. (2013). *Qualitative data analysis: Practical strategies*. Sage.

Becker, H. S. (2002). Visual evidence: A seventh man, the specified generalization, and the work of the reader. *Visual Studies*, 17(1), 3–11. https://doi.org/10.1080/14725860220137327

Beinart, P. (2010). The failure of the American Jewish establishment. *New York Review of Books*, 57(10), 10–21.

Benor, S. B., Krasner, J., and Avni, S. (2020). *Hebrew infusion: Language and community at American Jewish summer camps.* Rutgers University Press.

Chazan, B. (2002). *The philosophy of informal Jewish education.* Jewish Agency for Israel.

Cremin, L. A. (1977). *Traditions of American education.* Basic Books.

Davis, B., and Alexander, H. (2024). "You never told me": The pedagogical content knowledge (PCK) of Israel education. *Contemporary Jewry*, 44(2), 369–395. https://doi.org/10.1007/s12397-024-09562-w

Emerson, R. M., Fretz, R. I., and Shaw, L. L. (2011). *Writing ethnographic fieldnotes* (2nd ed.). University of Chicago Press.

Fox, S. (2023). *The Jews of summer: Summer camp and Jewish culture in postwar America.* Stanford University Press.

Friedman, D., Zisenwine, D. W., and Chazan, B. I. (1998). *Israel in Jewish summer camps.* CRB Foundation, Department for Jewish Zionist Education of the Jewish Agency for Israel, Charles R. Bronfman Centre for the Israel Experience, Mifgashim.

Golden J. and Kadden Y. (2024). Knowledge, connection, and stance toward a more enduring israel engagement. In S. Zakai and M. Reingold (Eds.), *Teaching Israel: Studies of pedagogy from the field* (pp. 151–176). Brandeis University Press.

Gubrium, J. F., and Holstein, J. A. (2001). *Handbook of interview research: Context and method.* Sage.

Heath, C., Hindmarsh, J., and Luff, P. (2010). *Video in qualitative research.* Sage.

Isaacs, A. (2011). Israel education: Purposes and practices. In H. Miller, L. D. Grant, and A. Pomson (Eds.), *International handbook of Jewish education* (pp. 479–496). Springer.

Kent, E., and Cantor, T. I. (2012). Communal song at Jewish summer camp and the creation of community. In D. Coffman (Ed.), *CMA XIII: Transitioning from historical foundations to 21st century*, 106–111. Sage.

Ladon, J. (2024). Voices on the page and in the room: A pedagogy of Jewish text study in Israel education. In S. Zakai and M. Reingold (Eds.), *Teaching Israel: Studies of pedagogy from the field*. Brandeis University Press.

Lieblich, A., Tuval-Mashiach, R., and Zilber, T. (2010). Between the whole and its parts and between content and form. In L. Kacen and M. Krumer-Nevo (Eds.), *Data analysis in qualitative research* (pp. 21–42). Ben-Gurion University of the Negev Press.

Lorge, M. M., and Zola, G. P. (Eds.) (2006). *A place of our own: The rise of Reform Jewish camping*. University of Alabama Press.

Pink, S. (2013). *Doing visual ethnography* (3rd ed.). Sage.

Pomson, A., and Deitcher, H. (2010). Day school Israel education in the age of Birthright. *Journal of Jewish Education*, 76(1), 52–73. https://doi.org/10.1080/15244110903572965

Pomson, A., Wertheimer, J., and Wolf, H. H. (2014). *Hearts and minds: Israel in North American Jewish day schools*. Avi Chai.

Reimer, J. (2018). Shabbat-at-camp at three Jewish camps: Jewish learning through ritual participation. *Journal of Jewish Education*, 84(4), 359–388. https://doi.org/10.1080/15244113.2018.1522578

Rothenberg, C. E. (2016). *Serious fun at a Jewish community summer camp: Family, Judaism, and Israel*. Lexington Books.

Sales, A. L., and Saxe, L. (2004). *"How goodly are thy tents": Summer camps as Jewish socializing experiences*. UPNE.

Sales, A. L., Samuel, N., and Boxer, M. (2011). *Limud by the lake revisited: Growth and change at Jewish summer camp*. Avi Chai. https://avichai.org/knowledge_base/limud-by-the-lake-revisited-growth-and-change-at-jewish-summer-camp-2011

Sarna, J. D. (2006). The crucial decade in Jewish camping. In M. M. Lorge and G. P. Zola (Eds.), *A place of our own: The rise of Reform Jewish camping in America* (pp. 27–51). University of Alabama Press.

Tandoc Jr., E. C., Lim, Z. W., and Ling, R. (2018). Defining "fake news": A typology of scholarly definitions. *Digital journalism*, 6(2), 137–153. https://doi.org/10.1080/21670811.2017.1360143

Zakai, S. 2022. *My second favorite country*. New York University Press.

Testifying to October 7: Israeli Voices and Experiences at North American Jewish Overnight Camps

Matt Reingold

One of the time-honored traditions of North American Jewish overnight camps is the presence of a *mishlachat*, a group of post-army Israelis who spend their summer working alongside North Americans as counselors. The position is not new, with camps employing Israeli staff since the 1930s. Though the songs and dances may change from year to year, these young Israelis come to camps in order to help facilitate campers' connections with Israel, to form relationships with campers, to represent Israel as a presence in the diaspora, and to increase the level of Hebrew spoken at camp throughout the summer (Bunin Benor, Krasner, and Avni, 2020).

In the aftermath of Hamas's terror attack on October 7 and the ensuing war in Gaza and in the north of Israel, camps, like other Jewish organizations around the Jewish world, needed to adapt their programmatic offerings in order to provide their constituents with appropriate and meaningful content that responded to the acute trauma. This chapter looks at the role and place of Israelis at overnight camps in the first summer after October 7 and the enhanced responsibilities they assumed in conveying the magnitude of what befell their homeland. Unlike earlier literature that showed that Israeli experiences with trauma and military service were often not afforded space at summer camp (Bunin Benor, Krasner, and Avni, 2020), interviews with senior staff at nine North American overnight camps reveal the ways that the

Israeli experience was not only welcomed but became central to camps' identities and programming in the summer of 2024. At some camps, this came as a result of giving Israeli staff new roles and responsibilities. At other camps, it happened by way of carefully orchestrated programs where the Israeli staff testified in front of their fellow staff and some campers about what happened to them on October 7. A third way that the Israeli experience took priority in summer 2024 happened when camps decided to host large groups of displaced and/or traumatized Israeli campers—often at their own expense—as a way to give back to Israel at a time when the country was suffering.

Literature Review

Jewish Communities after October 7

The months following Hamas's terror attack on October 7, 2023, yielded a number of reports that have tried to document the ways that diaspora Jewish communities have been impacted by what happened in Israel. One such study focused on American university students and determined that they are experiencing antisemitism at a rate that surpasses findings from 2016, confirming an assumption that antisemitism in the diaspora worsens when tensions in Israel are heightened. The study authors also identified a correlation between perceptions of hostility and perceptions of safety and belonging on campus. The greater the degree of perceived antisemitism, the less likely students feel a part of their university (Wright et al., 2023). A 2024 study of Canadian Jews' experiences with antisemitism after October 7 yielded similar results, with respondents reporting feeling less safe today than five years earlier. Furthermore, the data revealed a correlation between the level of emotional attachment to Israel and feeling less safe in Canada: the higher the attachment to Israel, the less safe one felt (Brym, 2024). A study of Australian Jews' in the weeks after October 7 revealed that social media use played a significant role in exacerbating respondents' levels of anxiety vis a vis the outbreak of violence in Israel and antisemitism in Australia (Bankier-Karp and Graham, 2024). Lastly, Matt Reingold and Shira Reznik (2024) determined that, for a group of students attending a Jewish high school, the nature or value of school changed as the students came to see the school as not only a space that provided academic or social opportunities but also a space that provided emotional value in a time of Jewish national crisis.

Jewish Overnight Camps

Jewish overnight camps began in America over 130 years ago (Fox, 2023) and, as of 2024, the Foundation for Jewish Camp counts over 150 residential Jewish summer camps in operation across North America (*Find a camp*, 2024). The immersive experience away from the distractions of city life afforded camps the opportunity to create "intensive experiential programming in the context of the social ideologies they wished to promote" (Koffman, 2018, p. 417). Though camps' affiliations and ideologies have changed over time based on the prevailing cultural norms (i.e., less examples of communist camps exist today than in the 1950s), camps allow for "simplified Jewish communities" where campers can experience a brand of Jewish religious, cultural and political life (Koffman, 2018, p. 417). Data collected since the 1970s has demonstrated that Jewish summer camps are transformative spaces for Jewish youth and lead to greater investment in Jewish communities, commitment to Israel, and higher rates of endogamy, factors that have contributed to Jewish summer camps' continued appeal well into the twenty-first century (Fox, 2023).

In their earliest incarnations, Jewish summer camps provided American Jewish youth an opportunity to escape urbanity and return to nature in an American fashion (Sarna, 2006). In the 1920s, Zionist camps began to be established in America, gaining prominence in the 1940s alongside American support for the establishment and success of the State of Israel (Fox, 2023) Formal Jewish programming and religious services—which are considered normative practices at most Jewish overnight camps in the present—did not begin until Camp Cejwin instituted Shabbat programming in 1920 (Krasner, 2011). The observance of Shabbat at Cejwin gave way to the creation of Jewish denominational camps in the 1940s and 1950s when both the Reform and Conservative movements began opening Jewish summer camps in America where campers would be immersed in the values and ideologies of their Jewish denomination (Fox, 2023). Much like today's Jewish camps, the nature, emphasis, and quantity of a camp's Jewish programming differed vastly based on a camp's Jewish and political ideologies. Despite these differences in *practice*, Sandra Fox (2023) has shown that there is consistency across camps in using their sites as a space for promoting "nationalism, language, and various forms of Jewish practice" (p. 6) in order to create meaningful Jewish experiences.

One of the key features of Jewish life at Jewish summer camps is the opportunity to participate in Jewish learning (though the practice of these programs differs widely at different camps). Absent the incentive of grades to entice student engagement, summer camps rely on creative and experiential programming alongside staff enthusiasm to create a culture that is committed to Jewish learning (Reimer, 2018). Hebrew also features prominently in daily life at some camps, with the language being used in songs, prayers, games, building names, direction signs, and even as phrases thrown into English sentences.

As a component of Jewish programming, Israel also receives attention at many Jewish summer camps. This happens at flagpole activities where the Israeli flag is raised and its national anthem "Hatikvah" is sung and also in formal programming time dedicated to the study of Modern Israel. Though day school attendance or time spent in Israel are the greatest predictors of Israel engagement, attendance at Jewish summer camp has also resulted in increased Israel engagement (Aharon and Pomson, 2018).

Shlichut

A hallmark of many Jewish summer camps is a *mishlachat*, a group of Israelis who are members of the staff team. This Israeli presence is borne out of a desire to "bring Israel to camp ... as Israel-experience surrogates [who] materialize aspects of Israel in the camp setting ... [by] bottling up the homeland experience and, taking it on the road, and meting it out in experiential ways that are both enjoyable and educational" (Bunin Benor, Krasner, and Avni, 2020, p. 198). Etymologically, the word *mishlachat* is connected to the words *shaliach/shlichim* (emissary/emissaries) and *shlichut* (mission), which refer to Israeli emissaries who leave their homeland in order to work in the Jewish diaspora. This role predated the founding of the State of Israel in 1948 (Cohen, 2011) and evolved into a cadre of professional educators who left Israel for two to four years under the aegis of the Jewish Agency to teach Judaic studies courses in schools and for bringing Israeli culture and society to students as a "bridge" between the local school and Israel (Pomson and Gillis, 2010). At times, however, the role can cause conflict such as when the *shaliach* is seen as a representative of Israel writ large and is expected to promote Israeli policies with which they personally disagree; this can result in the *shaliach* experiencing a disconnect between their lived and professional identities (Aharonov, 2015). More recently, the *shinshinim* program has been created to bring pre-army Israeli youth on one-year contracts to work in schools, synagogues, and camps, and evidence shows that the program creates meaningful opportunities for students to develop their engagement with Israel (Hameiri, 2018). As Pomson and Gillis (2010) explain, "the *shaliach* resembles the trader who brings to the local economy products it does not produce itself" (p. 46), and Israeli emissaries therefore play an important and necessary role in diaspora Jewish communities.

Most Israeli staff at summer camps are very different from those employed in schools. First, they are not professional educators; they are often post-army university students. Second, they are not coming for years at a time; they are working for the summer before returning home to Israel. But, like their fellow in-school *shlichim*, Israeli staff have been working at North American Jewish overnight summer camps since the 1930s (Bunin Benor, Krasner, and Avni, 2020) and have many of the same roles and responsibilities of bringing a slice of Israeli life to diaspora Jews. This includes ensuring Hebrew is spoken and heard at camp and of "fostering campers' sense of connection to Israel and its Jewish population" (Bunin Benor, Krasner, and Avni, 2020, p. 201) through immersive and engaging Israel programming. By the end of the twenty-first century's second decade, there were more than 1400 Israelis working at overnight camps in North America, and the number continues to grow (Bunin Benor, Krasner, and Avni, 2020).

Methodology

Data was collected from thirteen senior staff members from nine North American Jewish overnight camps about the Israel programming that was offered in summer 2024, the first summer after Hamas's terror attack on October 7, 2023. By design, a religiously and politically diverse group of camps were included in the study in order to gain a more complete understanding of the range of programs that were offered. The breakdown of participating camps was as follows: three camps were aligned with liberal/progressive streams of Judaism, one was a Conservative Jewish camp, two identified as Modern Orthodox, one self-identified as non-Zionist,[1] and two advertised as pluralistic Jewish camps.

---

1   Note: This camp is *not* antizionist; they sing Israel's national anthem daily, hire Israeli counselors, and raise the Israeli flag. Their self-designation as non-Zionist is because of their decision to not offer Israel-related programming or to spend any camp time dedicated to discussing Israel, Israeli politics, culture, etc.

Interviews were conducted at three points during the summer. The first interview occurred in the week before the first summer session began; by this point, all hiring, planning, and visioning for summer 2024 was complete. The second interview took place at the approximate midpoint of each camp's summer; this was an opportunity to discuss staffing and the implementation of the program vision thus far and to assess what, if any, additional plans were being considered for the remainder of the summer. The third interview took place within two weeks of the end of camp; during this conversation, the senior staff were asked about staffing, the programming that occurred during the second half of the summer, and their reflections on the summer as a whole.

A different semi-structured interview protocol was written for each of the three interview windows since the nature of each conversation was different. All senior staff were asked the same initial questions during the same interview window. As it was a semi-structured interview, I asked clarifying and follow-up questions based on the answers provided. Prior to each interview, I reviewed previous transcripts and asked tailored follow-up questions based on statements made by camp staff about future programs. The data presented in this article comes from responses given throughout the three interview windows where stories about Israeli staff and campers were discussed. During the first interview, interviewees were asked: "Based on previous summers, in what ways does the camp include Israelis in camp life?," "Why do you bring Israelis to camp?," and "In what ways will Israelis be present at camp for this summer?" In the third interview, the interviewees were asked: "Did the Israelis make any specific and meaningful contributions this summer?" and "What particular benefits were there to having Israelis this summer?" The data for this chapter comes from the answers to these specific questions and also from responses offered to other questions where Israelis were mentioned.

At the conclusion of all of the interviews, the transcripts were coded and analyzed using grounded theory methodology with the goal of arriving at new understandings of the role and value of having Israelis at camp in the summer after October 7. As a research method, grounded theory is an "approach to qualitative data collection and analysis, ultimately generating a theoretical explanation for the phenomenon being studied" (Olshansky, 2014, p. 1). The interviews were transcribed and coded using open coding to identify "distinct units of meaning" (Goulding, 2002, p. 74). I then used focused coding to generate descriptive categories and higher-order categories (Liska Belgrave and Seide, 2019) that explain the different ways and whys Israeli staff and campers contributed to a camp's Israel experience in the summer of 2024 at North American Jewish summer camps.

Results

Bringing Israeli Staff to Camp

Ahead of the 2024 summer camp session, the rationales offered by senior staff for why they want Israelis as counselors at their camps were similar to the ones reported by Bunin Benor, Krasner, and Avni (2020). The primary reason given by the interviewees was that Israelis gave their campers an opportunity to deepen their relationship or connection with the country by meeting its people. Carly,[2] the director of education at Camp Kodesh, explained that Israel is not something *new* for her campers. It is something that is talked about at home and at school. At camp, though, having Israelis "helps the camper feel connected. Now he knows someone. He can say, 'Oh, my staff is from Israel. I feel connected. I care about him.' These connections are the thing that makes them feel connected and close to Israel." At Camp Ruach, Emily, its director of camper care, said that it is the Israeli staff who "give camp its meaning." This is because of the central place Israel has in the camp's identity. "Having that interaction with people," she explained, "is really important to building a connection to the place." Much like Carly, Emily also believed that the relationships with individual Israelis are what lead to relationships being formed with Israel the country. She explained:

> Having that interaction with people I think is really important to build a connection to the place. When you know someone who actually lives in a certain area, you build a connection through speaking with them, hearing about their experiences, and getting to know them. Then when you think about Israel, you're thinking about all of your people there, all of the friends you've met.

In addition to enhancing campers' relationships with Israel, a secondary reason for having Israeli staff was offered by three of the interviewees. The

---

2   All camp and staff names are pseudonyms.

presence of Israelis alongside North American staff creates a diverse and multicultural experience for campers. Zack, the director of Camp Dvash, explained that "their presence is to show the diversity of Israeli society." Phil, the co-director of Camp Etz Chayim, relayed that his Israeli staff do not do specific programming about Israel in their capacity as Israel emissaries. Rather, they are regular counselors who fill whatever role they are best suited to. The benefit to having Israelis is that they are part of the camp's "cultural exchange." They offer "kids and staff access to real Israelis" who can be interacted with and appreciated as regular people.

It was only at the end of the summer, when the senior staff were asked to reflect on the roles Israeli staff assumed during the summer of 2024 where new insights into the value of having a *mishlachat* emerged. Seven of the nine camps identified specific and tangible added benefits to having Israeli staff on site in the summer after October 7.[3] In the paragraphs that follow, I will outline the identified benefits before homing in on what I call the testimony session, a program that was ubiquitous at many of the camps and that became, according to many of the senior staff, a central element to the positive Israeli-North American exchange that occurred during the summer of 2024.

The senior staff identified three new benefits to having Israelis on their staff team in the summer after October 7. First was an opportunity to engage with Israeli voices and perspectives about October 7 itself. Though certainly similar to the idea that Israelis offer a cultural connection, at camps that wanted to find ways to address October 7 as part of their programming[4] the opportunity to hear from Israelis themselves was very important and resulted in experiences that could not have been had otherwise. For

---

3   Of the two who did not, one was the previously mentioned Camp Etz Chayim which did not ask its Israeli staff to assume any type of responsibility or ownership of Israel programs. The second was Camp Dvash, a Modern Orthodox camp. Its director explained that Israelis already had an outsized and very significant presence at camp prior to October 7, and the October 7 events did not alter that in any way.

4   Three camps included in this study did not facilitate programming that touched on October 7. Camp Etz Chayim made no mention of October 7 in any capacity because it felt committed to offering campers an experience that did not mention the tragedy. This was done to offer a respite from the types of conversations and programs campers experienced during the school year. Camp Ruach felt that its campers were too young (ages six to thirteen) to fully understand what happened. Camp Matok believed that the post-October 7 politics that arose in North America were divisive, and they instead chose to lean into unity as their summer 2024 value and avoided discussions about October 7. To varying degrees, all of these camps did offer Israel programming, just not October 7 programming.

example, at Camp Eretz Zahav's Tisha B'Av ceremony commemorating the destruction of the Jewish Temple in Jerusalem, Israeli staff played an outsized role, telling stories about October 7 and the subsequent war in Gaza. Bram, the camp's assistant director, said that hearing "first-hand experiences was beneficial" and that he realized the camp was using its Israeli staff to tell personal stories in a way where, "in previous years, we may have not gone to them." The traumatic Israeli experience was able to give new meaning to a day in which other, more historical and remote, tragedies were already being commemorated.

The second new benefit to having Israeli staff at camp after October 7 was that their presence helped to counter the negative messaging about Israel that campers at progressive and liberal camps had been exposed to in the months after October 7. The Israel that dominated Western news cycles was, according to Michelle, the head of Camp Tikvah's *mishlachat*, a warzone. Having a *mishlachat* allowed "campers this summer to see not just Israel in the news headlines but to think about the counselors they played sports or did art or went in the lake with. When I think of a warzone, I picture something different from my life. So, for the kids to see someone from a warzone, but they are their counselors, it is grounded and not just people in a random country in a warzone. It's us." At Camp Gan Eden, Jill, its assistant director, said that "it felt important to experience real life Israelis when Israel is dominating the news and when it's often negative. It's important for our kids that when we talk about Israel, we are talking about real people." In a similar vein, Lucy, the head of Camp Kodesh's *mishlachat*, reflected on what *she* sees on social media about Israel and how very different it is from what her North American colleagues and campers see:

> Me as an Israeli, when I go to social media, I see pro-Israel and pro-IDF posts, but I know my camp people are exposed to pro-Palestinian content and they can get influenced by the content they see there. Seeing and meeting and connecting to Israeli staff gives you the opportunity to see firsthand from an Israeli and their experience. It is really, really important.

Michelle, Lucy, and Jill are not highlighting specific programming or messaging that the *mishlachat* provided their campers. Instead, the mere *presence* of Israelis was, in their opinion, sufficient to give campers alternative and positive messaging that differed from what they had seen and heard online and in the news since October 7.

The senior staff also believed that having Israelis at camp allowed for a deeper and more nuanced understanding of how October 7 affected Jews inside and outside of Israel. At Camp Gan Eden, Jill said:

> Ahead of camp, we heard from the Israelis that the war doesn't have anything to do with [North Americans]. Then it became they didn't realize how much kids are facing in schools and communities because of the war. It was important that our Israeli staff understood what our campers are experiencing day to day.

At times, these realizations were hard for Israelis, especially when they introduced stances on Israel that differed from how the Israelis thought about their own society. At Camp Matok, Richard, its director, recalled an Israeli staff member who was upset about how his North American colleagues were thinking about Israel and questioned whether they even understood what was happening in Israel. By the end of the summer, though, the staff member went out of his way to thank him for facilitating those conversations and helping him better understand how North Americans think about Israel. The opportunity to hear from North Americans about Israel resulted in the Israelis being able to work with their campers because they understood them better but it also allowed them to understand the complex ways that North American Jews relate to Israel and have been affected by October 7. Despite the differences in opinions that existed at some camps, there was a belief that the Israelis returned home with more nuanced understandings of what it means to be a Zionist in the diaspora.

Mishlachat in Action: The Testimony Program

In this next section, I want to zoom in on one specific type of program that the *mishlachat* facilitated at North American overnight camps. At five of the camps, Israeli staff led an oral testimony program where they shared with North American staff and/or campers about their experiences on October 7.[5] This is a program that only Israelis could offer but for which they received

---

5   Each of the four camps that did not hold a testimony program did so for different reasons. At Camp Etz Chayim, Phil, the co-director, cited the camp's purposeful decision to not do any October 7 programming because campers and North American and Israeli staff

no outside training or guidance. It is also a program that the camp directors identified as being core to enabling North Americans to better understand the Israelis at camp. And yet, historically, this type of program has been eschewed in camp settings. In their study of North American camps, Bunin Benor, Krasner, and Avni (2020) noticed that Israelis tend to speak "in generalities" about traumatic incidents in their country in order to "downplay the seriousness of war and its effects" (p. 211). Even in the summer of 2014, when three Israeli teenagers were kidnapped and murdered by Hamas terrorists leading to a seven-week war, camps tended to minimize or avoid discussing what was happening in Israel, lest it "depress the effervescent atmosphere that campers expected" (p. 212). The impact of this relative silence, however, conveyed to Israeli staff that what was happening in Israel ultimately mattered less than having a fun time at camp. The occurrence of October 7 testimony programs at more than half of the camps surveyed in this study is indicative of how camp leadership saw the summer of 2024 as something very different from previous summers and they therefore needed to pivot with regards to the types of *mishlachat*-led programs they would offer.

The programs I will describe below are reminiscent of the ones that many Jewish communities around the world organize as part of Holocaust Education Weeks, Holocaust commemoration events, and March of the Living programs. These types of programs place Holocaust survivors center-stage where they bear witness to the traumatic experiences that they suffered under Nazi rule. Testimony has many uses: "story telling, witnessing, and evidence" (Nutkiewicz, 2003, p. 18). Despite these positive uses, survivors are confronted by competing desires: to forget what happened to them (though it is likely impossible to do so) and to memorialize the past and in so doing offer contemporary listeners a keener understanding of the past in order to inform

---

wanted a break from October 7. At Camp Matok, the director chose to minimize October 7 conversations because they could be divisive and he prioritized unity as the driving value for the summer of 2024. As a result, he said his Israelis did not ask to share their stories. Camp Gan Eden actively encouraged its staff members (North American and Israeli) to openly talk about their different perspectives on Israel, October 7, and the ways the war was managed by Israel. Jill, the camp's assistant director, acknowledged that this at times left the Israelis feeling that Israel was not understood by their colleagues. The Israelis chose to not speak about what happened to them on October 7, a decision Jill said she could not explain. Lastly, though Camp Nefesh did a lot of October 7 programming, its director felt that, since no Israelis directly asked him for permission to address a large group, he did not want to initiate a program like that in order to maintain the positive energy that existed at camp.

the present. Michael Nutkiewicz (2003) sees in the opportunity to testify in front of a living audience (rather than recorded for some sort of posterity) the opportunity to mediate between the two desires, to offer the survivor a space where they can share their memories which cannot be forgotten and to offer listeners access to "continuity, personal and communal resiliency, and access to autobiographical and communal memory" (p. 22). The dual tensions and the perceived benefits from listeners were all also present at the camps that decided to coordinate testimony programs.

The opportunity to talk about their experiences was something that Israeli staff saw as both difficult and important. Walter, Camp Tikvah's director, said that his Israeli staff "felt the need to tell their stories of what happened to them," and he felt it was important to give them the space to do so. At Camp Ruach, Israeli staff told their stories in pairs across an afternoon during staff training. The experience was, according to Emily, the director of camper care, difficult for the Israelis, "but they wanted to share." Lucy, the head of Camp Kodesh's *mishlachat*, explained that testifying allows the Israelis to "give space and respect for the people they want to talk about and to have a chance to talk about how they felt and how it affected them."

With the Israelis themselves wanting to tell their stories, the directors of five of the camps helped facilitate opportunities for stories to be told. At Camp Ruach, the directors felt that a testimony program was only appropriate for staff to hear because their campers' ages are between six and thirteen, and so it needed to happen during staff training week. Conversely, at Camp Eretz Zahav, testimony stories were primarily limited to being told on Tisha B'Av because of the day's somber nature, and were shared with both staff and campers who were already in high school. Camp Kodesh dedicated a Shabbat afternoon program for staff and older campers to listen to a few of their Israeli staff talk about what happened to them on October 7. Though they occurred at different points during the summer, the testimony events organized by Camps Ruach, Kodesh, and Eretz Zahav established clear boundaries for when the Israelis were allowed to talk about October 7.

A very different approach was taken by Camp Tikvah, borne out of a desire to not limit or restrict the Israeli staff's right to tell their stories. As a result, some members of the *mishlachat* told their stories during staff training, but others told their stories during evening programs. Though it respected the Israelis' feelings, this model did present senior staff with challenges of when and how to implement a testimony program once campers arrived and regular programming began. Furthermore, when Walter told the *mishlachat* that their stories would not be part of mandatory staff programming during the summer because staff should have the right to decide whether they want to hear traumatic stories, it led some of the Israelis to feel that their experiences were not being sufficiently validated. Walter cited, as an example, one late-night program that the *mishlachat* conducted exclusively in Hebrew:

> We also had a staff speak in Hebrew about his close friend being killed in a battle where the staff member was also shot and spent months in rehab. When he finished talking and there was a montage with music, the speaker and at least two other soldiers in the room sobbed uncontrollably for ten minutes as everyone else tried to figure out what to do.

In hindsight, Walter still felt that his decision to make the program optional was correct because not everyone was comfortable having to be a part of that type of program. A second challenge presented by Camp Tikvah's model involved members of the *mishlachat* being unsure of when or how to talk about what happened to them with their own campers. Michelle, the head of the camp's *mishlachat*, relayed how members of the *mishlachat* were struggling with balancing the "part of us that always wants to bring [October 7] up and talk about it and the part of us that wants to have fun in summer camp." Michelle also recognized that revealing one's experiences on October 7 exposes oneself, and the camp's porous boundaries of when and how to talk about October 7 made her concerned about not "putting counselors in a position of being so vulnerable in front of campers." Despite her reservations, Michelle worked with her Israeli staff to find age-appropriate ways and time-sensitive moments for her staff to talk about October 7 throughout the summer.

With regards to content, the stories told by *mishlachat* members tended to be either about personal experiences from in and around the Gaza envelope and about time spent as a soldier fighting in Gaza. At Camp Ruach, "a couple girls from kibbutzim around Gaza shared their experiences and [talked] about their friends or teachers held hostage or killed." At Camp Eretz Zahav, one of the members of the *mishlachat* served in the Israeli army's *chevrah kadisha*, the group responsible for gathering the remains of fallen soldiers' bodies. On Shabbat afternoon of counselor training week, this staff member spoke with all of the camp staff about the fighting he saw in Gaza and the specific tasks he performed when recovering Israeli soldiers' bodies. Though only five of the nine camps that participated in the study allocated formal program time for Israeli staff to speak about their October 7 and war experiences, the fact that this occurred at all is surprising. Previous research has seen camps being reticent towards opening their spaces up to the types of traumatic stories that Israelis face as citizens of a country that has been a frequent target of terror and war (Bunin Benor, Krasner, and Avni, 2020). However, in the aftermath of October 7, survivor testimonies have become common in Jewish spaces. As Bram, Camp Eretz Zahav's assistant director, explained, campers who also attend Jewish day schools have been hearing October 7 stories for almost a year. Therefore, what occurred at Camps Eretz Zahav, Ruach, Kodesh, Dvash, and Tikvah was both a continuation of the type of programming from during the school year, which focused on personal experiences to build connection to Israel and Israelis, and also a departure from how camps have traditionally operated in the past.

There was consensus across all five of the camps that the decision to include testimony programs was valuable because it helped form relationships between the *mishlachat* and those who listened. In turn, these connections helped North Americans arrive at a deeper understanding of who the Israelis with them at camp were and of Israel as a country. Despite being difficult for the Israelis to verbalize and for the North Americans to hear, at Camp Kodesh it "was special for them to hear Israelis' views. Even if they don't know any of the people they are hearing about, they can say it's their staff who were affected by the war and it connects them to Israel and makes the connection stronger. It leads to more empathy." At Camp Eretz Zahav, which has a high percentage of students who attend Jewish day school and who had been learning about October 7 all year, the opportunity to hear from someone the North American staff and campers *personally* knew was transformative. Bram explained: "It has more meaning when you hear face to face from someone you know and will spend two months with." Camp Ruach's director Andrea believed that, when her *mishlachat* made themselves vulnerable in front of their colleagues during staff training, "it built connections from day one. It made people feel closer to them and connect with them on a deeper level which led to relationships and collaborations and a positive impact on their integration."

Both Holocaust survivor testimony programs and *mishlachat* testimony programs afforded victims of trauma the opportunity to share their story in front of a living audience, so there is certainly commonality. Furthermore, in both programs, there is evidence to suggest that it is both a difficult yet important experience for the survivor and a difficult yet important experience for the listener. In these regards, what happened in the summer of 2024 at these five camps contains parallels with Nutkiewicz's (2003) observations about Holocaust survivor testimony. That differences between Holocaust and October 7 testimony exist should be expected—no two traumas are the same—but I want to call attention to two features that are particularly of relevance when considering what happened at Jewish overnight camps in 2024. Were campers and staff to hear from Holocaust survivors at camp, they would do so as individuals who are significantly younger than the person holding the microphone and telling them a story. Such was not the case in the programs described in this section. The Israelis who told their stories were of the same generation as those who listened and, in the case of fellow staff, of nearly identical ages. They were, therefore, *peers* with most of the people who heard their stories. As Michelle noted in relation to sharing with people younger than the *mishlachat* (but this is equally applicable to people close in age to them), this creates *vulnerability* because they do not know how people will then consider them or treat them. Furthermore, what also does not occur following a Holocaust survivor program is the establishment of enduring relationships. When the session is complete, people may offer thanks and gratitude but the nature of the program is such that there is no ongoing interaction between the testifier and those who listen. In the case of the summer camps—irrespective of whether the program happened before camp started or during sessions—the expectation is that the relationship between the Israeli staff and North Americans will continue.

These two distinctions—age and ongoing relationships—could have proved to be disastrous in harming camp dynamics. However, as the Israeli and North American head staff all acknowledged, this did not happen. Instead, the opportunity to share transformed camp, offering the Israelis a safe and supportive cocoon where they could unburden themselves, and giving the North Americans an opportunity to better understand the Israelis' experiences and what has shaped them over the past year, while also being cognizant of the fact that this is the same Israeli who staffs boats or who knits. What resulted were staff teams that were stronger, more cohesive, and more attuned to what it has meant to be Israeli since October 7.

Bringing Israelis as Campers to Camp in 2024

The existing literature about Israeli presence at overnight camps has focused on staff, but one of the unique features of overnight camps in summer 2024 was the desire by most of the studied camps to create space—often at their own expense—for Israeli campers to participate in summer programming amongst Jewish peers. Aside from Camps Eretz Zahav and Dvash, which were already operating at capacity, the remaining seven camps all allocated space and resources for Israeli campers. For some of the camps, like Kodesh and Nefesh, this involved making space for additional Israelis, while for other camps, like Tikvah and Gan Eden, this involved carving out space for Israeli campers for the first time.

Overwhelmingly, the Israeli youth who came to North American camps arrived as having been directly affected by October 7 and the subsequent war, or having been displaced from their homes following Hezbollah rocket fire in the north. At Camp Nefesh, space was made for eighty Israeli youth from the region surrounding Gaza. This included children who were themselves physically harmed on October 7, with one participant having been shot in the eye and another having been shot in the neck. One of the Israelis who attended Camp Gan Eden was the sibling of someone who was taken hostage on October 7 before being murdered by Hamas in Gaza. Two of the camps included in this study arranged for Israeli support staff to also be present on site in the event that any of the Israelis required specific interventions or were struggling to adapt to camp and would want an adult who understood their experiences.

Camps adopted different approaches to integrating Israeli campers into camp life. According to Sam, the director of Camp Nefesh, the camp knew what to expect because it had previously hosted approximately forty Israeli campers every summer. He explained that the challenges that Israelis face are different than the ones that North Americans experience:

> There's definitely a [North American] way of adapting to an overnight camp experience that the Israelis don't have. The adapting for Israelis is to the environment—cold nights and mosquitos. For [North Americans] there's more homesickness and social issues. The Israelis want to make friends.

To mitigate against these differences and begin to build relationships, the camp placed Israeli campers in bunks with North American peers from the get-go. At Camp Ruach, which hosted sixteen Israelis who were displaced from their homes in the north, the decision was made to house the Israelis in their own cabins (separated by gender) so that they could have a fully

Israeli space of their own to return to at the end of the day and be surrounded by people with shared experiences. By the end of the session, to the camp director's delight, the campers became so integrated that North Americans and Israelis freely moved between their respective cabins, with them "sitting on [each other's] beds and chatting."

The decision to host Israeli youth at camp was a costly one, but the directors agreed with it because they felt that this was an opportunity for their camp to make a meaningful contribution to Israeli society during a period of intense trauma and tragedy. The costs varied at each camp as some did receive outside funding from Jewish and Israeli organizations, but the directors needed to account for lodging, food, program supplies, and additional staffing. Despite these costs, senior staff at camps overwhelmingly bought into the idea. Michelle, the head of Israeli staff at Camp Tikvah, explained that her camp's ability to host displaced Israeli youth provided them with "an amazing experience to get away from Israel and the ten months they have been evacuated." In a similar vein, Richard, who directs Camp Matok, saw hosting Israeli campers as "a way of supporting Israelis in the midst of this really hard time." Hosting Israeli youth thus became an act of solidarity and alignment with Israel, of giving back to the country that they and their camp care deeply about.

Whereas camps' primary reason for bringing Israeli staff to camp was to provide benefit to their North American campers, the overwhelming rationale for bringing Israeli campers to camp was to provide benefit to these Israeli youth.[6] The benefit, according to Camp Etz Chayim's co-director Molly, is to "have a break, get to have fun with kids their own age, and not the cloud of everything that's happened." To that end, her Israeli campers specifically requested not to be asked about their wartime experiences, and Molly committed to them that no staff would put them in a position where they would be asked to relay what happened to them on October 7. At Camp Ruach, the benefit was to participate in fun and even silly programming that allowed the Israelis to just be kids. Andrea, the camp's director, explained: "We had a dance program and the Israelis were ballet dancing in tutus. They left trauma and war and such terrible horrible circumstances and they left their homes and are ballet dancing amongst new friends who were strangers. At camp,

---

6   When staff mentioned the benefits to North American campers, it was always done secondarily. The benefits were similar to the ones identified about what the *mishlachat* offers: seeing Israelis as real people and bringing Israeli culture to North America.

everything is secondary." Sam, the director of Camp Nefesh, saw the Israelis' attendance at camp as an opportunity for catharsis and cleansing, a shedding of all that they had been holding on to for the past year. He relayed a story about an impromptu rainy-day program where a staff member decided to host a dance party with Israeli music and the outpouring of emotion that resulted from the spontaneous dancing: "All the Israelis and [North Americans] were singing and crying. I have a *shaliach* who said he was in tears. He said that I have no idea what has been inside these kids for the last nine months and it was now exploding. And I saw it come out on the staff and the kids and everybody." Stories such as these reveal that camp directors understood the value of their program as offering Israeli youth a chance to escape, temporarily, the trauma they endured over the past year. Being able to offer Israeli children a space in camp was an opportunity for their camps to show that their commitments to Zionism and to Israel extended in multiple directions. Hosting Israeli campers—and not just Israeli staff—allowed the camp staff and campers to give something of value to Israel at a moment when the state was in need of help from global Jewry.

Conclusion

As in previous years, Israeli staff at Jewish overnight camps in the summer of 2024 were the ones primarily responsible for cultivating positive Israel-connections for campers. This was done through interactive programming designed to bring Israel to life in the hearts and minds of campers. But the October 7 terror attack also resulted in new roles for Israeli staff at camp while also ushering in new ways of interaction amongst North American campers and Israeli peers. The Israeli staff, in addition to the roles they had previously assumed, also took on the role of bearing witness to what happened on October 7 by sharing their stories (a program that those who testified also benefited from), leading the camp in October 7-related programming and prayers, and being examples of who and what Israelis are, which helped to counter the negative messaging that is seen in the North American media and on social networks. With Israeli campers, the camps were able to put their positive messaging and affinity towards Israel into action by offering Israelis a dose of what they do best: an opportunity to become immersed in daily life at camp. Doing so allowed the camps to make a tangible and meaningful impact on Israeli youth and to model what it means to love and care for Israel and

Israelis. Despite the horrors of October 7 and the ensuing war, what occurred at the North American Jewish overnight camps that participated in this study is evidence of the enduring relationship between Israel and the Jewish diaspora. The creative ways that senior camp staff developed their programming in order to provide meaningful opportunities for Israelis and North Americans to interact with each other in response to October 7 is demonstrative of the importance of the diaspora-Israel relationship and the power of the overnight Jewish summer camp experience.

References

Aharon, N., and Pomson, A. (2018). What's happening at the flag pole? Studying camps as institutions for Israel education. *Journal of Jewish Education*, 84(4), 337–358. https://doi.org/10.1080/15244113.2019.1522564

Aharonov, Y. (2015). The educational mission of the shaliach: A case study in Australia. *Journal of Jewish Education*, 81(2), 189–211. https://doi.org/10.1080/15244113.2015.1027869

Bankier-Karp, A. L., and Graham, D. (2024). Surrounded by darkness, enfolded in light: Factors influencing the mental health of Australian Jews in the October 7 aftermath. *Contemporary Jewry*. https://doi.org/10.1007/s12397-024-09584-4

Brym, R. (2024). Jews and Israel 2024: A survey of Canadian attitudes and Jewish perceptions. *Canadian Jewish Studies / Études Juives Canadiennes*, 37. https://doi.org/10.25071/1916-0925.40368

Bunin Benor, S., Krasner, J., and Avni, S. (2020). *Hebrew infusion: Language and community at American Jewish summer camps*. Rutgers University Press.

Cohen, E. H. (2011). *The educational Shaliach 1939–2009: A socio-history of a unique project in formal and informal education*. Tel Aviv University.

Find a camp (2024). Foundation for Jewish Camp. https://jewishcamp.org/families/find-a-camp/

Fox, S. (2023). *The Jews of summer: Summer camp and Jewish culture in postwar America*. Stanford University Press.

Goulding, C. (2002). *Grounded theory: A practical guide for management, business and market researchers*. Sage.

Hameiri, L. (2018). Israel engagement in practice: An Empirical look at the impact of the year of service emissaries. *Journal of Jewish Education, 84*(1), 56–78. https://doi.org/10.1080/15244113.2018.1418102

Koffman, D. S. (2018). Playing Indian at Jewish summer camp: Lessons on tribalism, assimilation, and spirituality. *Journal of Jewish Education, 84*(4), 413–440. https://doi.org/10.1080/15244113.2018.1522580

Krasner, J. (2011). *The Benderly boys and American Jewish education*. Brandeis University Press.

Liska Belgrave, L., and Seide, K. (2019). Coding for grounded theory. In A. Bryant and K. Charmaz (Eds.), *The Sage handbook of current developments in grounded theory* (pp. 167–185). Sage.

Nutkiewicz, M. (2003). Shame, guilt, and anguish in Holocaust survivor testimony. *The Oral History Review, 30*(1), 1–22. https://doi.org/10.1525/ohr.2003.30.1.1

Olshansky, E. F. (2014). Overview of grounded theory. In M. D. Chesnay (Ed.), *Nursing research using grounded theory: Qualitative designs and methods in nursing* (pp. 1–8). Springer.

Pomson, A., and Gillis, M. (2010). The teacher-as-stranger as model and metaphor. *Teacher Development, 14*(1), 45–56. https://doi.org/10.1080/13664531003696576

Reimer, J. (2018). Shabbat-at-camp at three Jewish camps: Jewish learning through ritual participation. *Journal of Jewish Education, 84*(4), 359–388. https://doi.org/10.1080/15244113.2018.1522578

Reingold, M., and Reznik, S. (2024). Navigating crisis together: Canadian Jews, Israel, and October 7. *Contemporary Jewry*, 1–18. https://doi.org/10.1007/s12397-024-09572-8

Sarna, J. D. (2006). The crucial decade in Jewish camping. In M. M. Lorge and G. P. Zola (Eds.), *A place of our own: The rise of Reform Jewish camping* (pp. 27–51). University of Alabama Press.

Wright, G., Volodarsky, S., Hecht, S., and Saxe, L. (2023). *In the shadow of war: Hotspots of Antisemitism on US college campuses*. Brandeis University's Cohen Center for Modern Jewish Studies. https://doi.org/10.48617/rpt.1072

Section Four

AFTER OCTOBER 7: THE FUTURE OF JEWISH EDUCATION

Meeting the Challenges of the Moment: How to Think about the Purposes of American Jewish Education after October 7

Jon A. Levisohn[1]

A. Introduction

For American Jews, including the author of this chapter, the story of October 7 is both a story about what happened over there and also, inevitably, about what happened here. It begins with the shock and horror of the morning of Shemini Atzeret, as the news filtered into our gatherings in synagogues of an unprecedented Hamas assault on Gaza Envelope border communities, of a catastrophic failure of Israeli military intelligence and defense, of casualties that climbed every hour, of horrific atrocities, and of an unthinkable number of civilian kidnappings. The story continues with the efforts to come together in solidarity and mutual support over here, echoing on a smaller scale the massive outpouring of citizen-driven efforts across the political spectrum over there. Then, even as the military response by

---

1   This chapter has benefitted greatly from the critical feedback of Erica Brown, Lila Corwin Berman, Aaron Dorfman, Ziva Hassenfeld, Ethan Hersh, Jill Jacobs, Josh Levisohn, Tamara Mann Tweel, Joe Reimer, Matt Reingold, Jon Spira-Savett, and Dan Smokler, who of course are not responsible for the final version. The chapter will use the colloquial term "American" to refer to "of the United States of America," which will be the focus of the chapter. Naturally, the analyses of the present and historical condition of liberal democratic culture in the United States and of the Jewish situation within that liberal democracy may not exactly track with other countries in North America or elsewhere.

Israel was still taking shape, American Jews experienced abandonment and a startling absence of empathy from erstwhile friends and allies. As the Israeli military response built in its ferocity and its devastation, the story over here developed as well, as the American Jewish community encountered countless instances of explicit antisemitism, both verbal and physical, on college campuses but also in k-12 education, in workplaces, on social media, and in the public square, as well as what often felt to many like a collapse of the norms of civil discourse. In a very significant way, for many American Jews, the sense of being at home in America felt threatened or even undermined entirely.

What does this look like? There are countless examples of vandalism, of exclusionary rhetoric, and of physical and even deadly violence. But consider the case of an American Jewish college student who discovers that her roommate has moved out because the roommate cannot tolerate living with a "Zionist." This anecdote is particularly meaningful because, over the course of the twentieth century, American Jews have come to feel completely comfortable on college campuses. Yes, college campuses have leaned left, but then again, most Jews do too. Yes, the rules in college dorms and quads can be hard to navigate if you're a first-gen student, but, by this point in American Jewish history, most Jews have parents or even grandparents who hold college degrees. Yes, Israel has been a polarizing topic for many years, among a sub-set of the most politically active students. But the idea that your Jewish identity would be reduced to your sympathy with and connection to the historical project of Jewish self-determination, and that that sympathy with the Zionist project would itself then be reduced to its most aggressive military expression, and that that identity would be then be a source of stigma that legitimates the most basic forms of social exclusion precisely in a cultural location where inclusion is so valued, or, alternatively, that inclusion would suddenly be conditional upon the performance of a demonstrative repudiation of your commitments and familial connections—this feels new.[2] Campuses have

---

2 This is not the place for comprehensive documentation of the explosion of antisemitism in 2023, nor for consideration of the pre-2023 rise in antisemitism that preceded it, nor for a debate about exactly what constitutes antisemitic speech or action. Some, of course, are skeptical that antisemitism on the left is real. It is true that, historically, left-wing antisemitism was not as deadly as antisemitism from white nationalists on the right, but recent events demand a reconsideration of this judgment. We can stipulate that some (even many) instances of speech that are called antisemitic, by individual Jews and by Jewish organizations, reflect hyper-sensitivity about criticism of Israel and a knee-jerk suspicion of expressions of sympathy for Palestinian suffering. Jewish organizations do themselves no favors by muddling these categories and engaging in zero-sum thinking (or

often been locations of political activism, including extreme rhetoric, about Israel and many other topics. But, as others have noted (Prell, 2025), rarely if ever have they been locations where the targets of that political activism and that rhetoric have been fellow students.

American Jewish educators and American Jewish educational institutions have responded as well as they can, mobilizing on behalf of Israeli victims, creating new learning opportunities for both Jewish and non-Jewish students, serving as safe spaces where students' and families' experiences could be validated and understood. Many of the chapters in this volume provide extensive documentation of those efforts. But this chapter asks a more prescriptive question about how American Jewish educators and American Jewish educational institutions *should* respond to the challenges. How should we think about the purposes of Jewish education in this post-October 7 moment?

In order to think through this question, we first need to think about the validity of the question. We will do that, briefly, in Part B. We then need to understand what we mean by "the moment," which will be considered in Part C. But education is never only about reacting and adapting to the world as it is; education is also, always, a process of building the world as we want it to be. So, in Part D, we will propose and develop two central purposes for Jewish education today—purposes that encompass both adapting to what is and building for the future.

B. Why the Question is Valid

Charles Taylor (2007) famously characterizes our time and our culture as "a secular age," by which he means a time when reasonable people adopt profoundly different worldviews, and within which we are *aware* of that diversity.

---

zero-sum activism) about the conflict. Nevertheless, the explosion of hostile, exclusionary, and violent words and actions towards Jews represents a phenomenon that cannot be ignored. The important question is not whether this or that specific incident is "really" antisemitic, much less whether this or that person is "really" antisemitic. But patterns of hostility to Jews, exclusion of Jews, use of violent rhetoric against Jews, and actual physical violence towards Jews and Jewish institutions—all this demands our attention. On the social exclusion by non-Jews of Jews, see Hersh & Lyss (2024). Other relevant recent scholarly documentation includes Samuel et al. (2024); Wright et al. (2024); the ADL (2024) report; the Sheskin (2024) report; the AJC (2024) report; Krasner et al. (2025); Silverstein and Block (2025); and Katz et al. (2025), among many other studies. On some of the conceptual and historiographical questions surrounding antisemitism, see Judaken (2021); Persico (2024); and Ury and Miron (2024).

Religious affiliation and practice have not disappeared in this secular age, but they have been privatized and have become matters of choice.[3] Under these conditions, religious communities try to promote their own traditions rather than other options, to advocate for the eternal truths of their religion against the fads of the moment. This seems like a natural way to think about the purposes of religious education. Accordingly, the question of how religious education can "meet the moment," any moment, is misplaced. What religious education ought to do, in this moment, is what it ought to do in every moment, at least since the Enlightenment. Religious education ought to teach the particular religious tradition so that students will remain committed to it.

However, this way of thinking about religious education in general, and Jewish education in particular, is inadequate for a number of reasons.[4] First, it ignores the historical evolution of the tradition itself. Second, in the particular context of contemporary American Jews and Judaism, it misunderstands the condition of the vast majority of contemporary Jews (other than the most traditionalist), who are surely deeply immersed in "secular" culture but do not interpret that culture as being locked in a zero-sum contest with Jewish religious culture.[5] Third, this way of thinking about religious education does not accommodate the breadth of Jewish culture, and instead unreflectively focuses on those elements that sociologists of religion call "official religion."

But, in addition to these concerns, there is an additional reason why this way of thinking about religious education is inadequate, which was certainly

---

3   On the decline of the "secularization thesis" in sociology of religion, see, for example, Cox & Swyngedouw (2000) and Stark (1999). To be sure, other argue that the reports of the death of secularization are greatly exaggerated. See, for example, Kasselstrand, Zuckerman, & Cragun (2023).

4   I have pursued these arguments in a number of places, including Levisohn (2013) and Levisohn (forthcoming a).

5   There are undoubtedly moments when individual Jews face decisions where values collide. Maybe it is a choice between going to Hebrew school or playing in the soccer playoffs. Or maybe it is a choice about a particular Jewish ritual observance, such as a question about whether to set aside the practice of Shabbat or Kashrut in order to participate in some other cultural or professional activity. But those specific "choice points" are fairly rare in the overall lives of contemporary American Jews. It is a mistake to imagine that the moral life leads up to and is signified by these choices. It is a mistake, in other words, to imagine that the choices made are reliable assessments of some deep truth about the chooser. If a student chooses to tuck away her Star of David rather than display it proudly, that is perhaps a marker of her lack of self-confidence in the face of potential hostile responses. But it also might just be prudence in this moment. We can feel compassion for the chooser, and lament the need to make the choice, without claiming that the choice reveals something important about the chooser's "identity."

visible prior to October 7 but has become more acute afterwards. The conception of Jewish education as a response to the secularity of the modern age, with the goal of "keeping Jews Jewish" or "strengthening Jewish identity" or encouraging "Jewish choices," is not sufficiently attuned to what it means to be an American Jew in the present moment, and what challenges those Jews face—spiritual challenges, intellectual challenges, emotional challenges, even threats to physical safety and security. What we actually need is a better and deeper diagnosis of those particular challenges, in order to design educational opportunities that enable them to face those challenges, to live with them, and to flourish despite them.

David Bryfman, in a number of articles and presentations drawing on the academic movement known as "positive psychology" (see, e.g., Bryfman, 2016, 2017), has argued for attention to what he called "thriving," which is to say, the idea that Jewish education ought to focus on creating the conditions for individual Jews to live flourishing lives. This educational approach is attuned to specific challenges in the contemporary environment that threaten to undermine thriving or flourishing—the growth of social media, for example, or the relentless pressures of materialism and an excessive focus on achievement in middle-class culture. It is not surprising that Bryfman's own response to the question of Jewish education after October 7 extends his earlier commitment. "Educators," he writes, "must confront the task of asking ourselves for what world we are educating our children" (Bryfman, 2024, p. 54). Bryfman is not demanding that we predict the future. However, the world for which we are educating our children, after October 7, represents a distinctive set of challenges that we need to think through and understand as deeply as possible.

So what does it mean to orient Jewish education not as a reaction to modern secularity, not as an effort to help American Jews to "make Jewish choices" simply by teaching "Judaism," but rather as a series of educational opportunities intentionally and specifically designed to enable Jews to cope with and thrive within this moment—a moment marked by a particular set of challenging social-cultural circumstances, by hostility in the spaces that once felt most comfortable, by fear for physical safety, and, as a result, the regular questioning of how visibly to display one's Jewishness, by the erosion of norms that we have come to take for granted, and, most fundamentally, by a sense that America is not the comfortable home that it once seemed to be? This chapter will pursue this conceptual-philosophical question not by relying on empirical evidence about how Jewish educators and Jewish educational institutions have in fact responded to the present moment, but rather by developing an argument about how they should.

C. What is This Moment?

In April 2024, seven months after October 7 and its aftermath both in Gaza and throughout much of the West, Franklin Foer (2024) staked out a strong position about the historical significance of the current moment in American Jewish life, which he called "the End of the Golden Age" of American Jews. What did he mean?

Foer opens his article with graphic depictions of antisemitic hostility faced by American Jews in public educational spaces, from progressives, because of Israel. Notably, his examples are not cases of public pro-Palestinian activism that cross some contested line between legitimate and illegitimate critique. Instead, the salient characteristic of these cases is that Jews are assigned collective responsibility for the actions of Israel, which then triggers a collapse of interpersonal norms of respect, civility, and inclusion. This seems, to Foer, new—not that the phenomenon has never existed but that what used to be a marginal phenomenon has become normalized. And this is why left-wing antisemitism is much more relevant, for Foer, than the right-wing antisemitism associated with white nationalism. While the latter is certainly part of problem of the erosion of liberal democratic norms (and, furthermore, has a longer history of deadly violence), the former undermines the sense among American Jews of being comfortable and secure in the places that they live and work.

Thus, what has sometimes occurred in the most fervently ideological leftist spaces, i.e., not just a critique of Israel but a demonization of Israelis or Zionists, has become conventional among non-ideological and only vaguely progressive spaces like liberal-leaning suburban K-12 schools, professional organizations, and town halls. What Foer implies but does not state explicitly is that the debates over where antizionism crosses over into antisemitism actually miss the important development, which is not about the severity of the critique of Israeli actions but about the unexamined ideological framing that situates people into competing camps—oppressor and oppressed, colonizer and decolonizer, Zionist and antizionist, Jew and whoever is the subject of the Jew's power. The world is made up of good guys and bad guys.

According to that illiberal framing, demonization of your opponent is not a vice but a virtue.[6]

Foer describes antisemitism as "a tendency to fixate on Jews, to place them at the center of the narratives, overstating their role in society and describing them as the root cause of any unwanted phenomena" (p. 24). He also names the centrality of conspiracy theorizing within antisemitic discourse on the left, just as it is on the right, which entails not just a tendency to believe in conspiratorial explanations for social and political phenomena but also a tendency *not* to believe in or trust traditional institutions or the "mainstream media." But most importantly, the target of extremist antisemitism (on both the left and the right) is not just Jews and Judaism but also the liberal ideal, "an ideal that American Jews championed and, in an important sense, co-authored ... that combined robust civil liberties, the protection of minority rights, and an ethos of cultural pluralism" (p. 25). This liberal ideal is sometimes the explicit target of extremists, who argue that its moderation and its tendency to seek consensus is an excuse to maintain the status quo and to protect the powerful. For moderates, the ability to work with diverse (and powerful) interests to get stuff done is worthy of praise. For extremists, it is a sign of weakness.

Importantly, while the liberalism that seems to be slipping through our fingers is certainly political (and generally leans towards identification with the Democratic Party, as American Jews overwhelmingly have done), Foer is focused on an "ideal," an "ethos," a broader, cultural understanding, or what he also calls "the democratic temperament," more than specific actions or policies. In this way, he is following the lead of scholars of American democracy such as Joshua Cherniss, who likewise describe liberalism not in

---

6   This, in part, explains the use of Nazism as a rhetorical weapon against Israel and against Jews, and why Holocaust education is ineffective (or worse) as a cure for antisemitism. The underlying issue is whether critics are locked into a demonization paradigm. Van Jones (2024), in a CNN interview, offers a pithy distinction: "You protest a policy. You don't protest a people." That distinction lacks conceptual nuance, but it is a useful contrast to the contrary unnuanced position that perceives only structures and not human beings. Or consider the constructive response to the slogan "Zionists are not welcome here" by the Harvard Chaplains Executive Committee on November 21, 2024, in their "Statement on Campus Inclusivity and Religious Expression": "We have noticed a trend of expression in which entire groups of students are told they 'are not welcome here' ... We find this trend disturbing and anathema to the dialogue and connection across lines of difference that must be a central value and practice of a pluralistic institution of higher learning." Such statements by morally serious people disrupt the demonization paradigm; while they may not be effective in swaying the most ideologically committed, they are welcome efforts to restore principles of liberal democratic discourse among moderates.

terms of specific policies but rather in terms of a "liberal ethos" characterized by moderation, responsibility, tolerance, integrity, respect, and intellectual humility. This liberal ideal or temperament is non-partisan, or it was, encompassing moderates in both the Democratic Party and the Republican Party, ideological opponents who regularly sparred on questions of policy but shared fundamental commitments to liberal democracy. In this way, Foer is also building implicitly on the work of scholars such as political scientist Robert Putnam, who has spent his career documenting the rise and fall of social capital and social trust, and the impact of those patterns on democracy, especially through his famous titular concept of "bowling alone" (Putnam, 2000; and also see Putnam and Garrett, 2020).[7]

Now, however, Foer writes that "the Golden Age of American Jewry has given way to conspiracy, reckless hyperbole, and political violence" (Foer, 2024, p. 25). Again, there are incidents and data to which he points, as he makes his case—but the argument is really about a shift in the culture. What matters more to Foer's argument is not the explosive growth of violent attacks on Jews (whether from the right or from the left) but the even more explosive growth of violent rhetoric about Jews, reflecting "a society that has lost its capacity to express disagreements without resorting to animus" (p. 34). Yossi Klein Halevi (2024) makes a parallel argument: More than actual antisemitic actions, "the deeper trauma for diaspora Jews is psychological: the sense that their acceptance in society—from universities to the political system to the streets—is eroding."

Foer's articulation of a post-war Golden Age of American Jewry builds on earlier, familiar ideas about a fundamental alignment between American Jewish aspirations and commitments and the social, economic and political conditions of post-war America.[8] For example, in a classic argument, Jonathan Woocher (1986) wrote about the "civil religion" of American Jews, which,

---

7   Putnam's analysis suggests that the underpinnings of liberal democracy have been eroding for longer than we might have thought, since the late 1960s. Putnam and other academic theorists can help us understand, more deeply than Foer's article, the ways in which a liberal democratic ethos is not merely an ideology but is supported by other social and cultural structures. Notably, his more recent work (Putnam and Garrett, 2020) is an effort to learn from trends in the past in order to develop effective interventions now.
8   In reviewing a set of historiographical sources in chronological order, this paragraph will use the past tense, to give a sense of how these ideas were articulated over a period of time. The following paragraph will return to the convention of referring to sources in the present tense.

while distinct in certain respects from American civil religion in general, also comfortably incorporates "Americanness as a virtue." Regarding antisemitism in particular, Jerome Chanes (1999) declared that "America is different" (p. 127). Marc Dollinger (2000) wrote that "Jews . . . helped direct the nation toward a vision of democracy rooted in tolerance, pluralism and the rule of law" (p. 3). Sylvia Barack Fishman (2000) developed the concept of "coalescence" to describe the way that American Jews increasingly merge American and Jewish commitments, with the result that "American Jews today inhabit a universe that is substantively different from the contexts of Jewish lives in earlier periods of Jewish history" (p. 31). According to Deborah Dash Moore's (2001) summary, "After World War II, when Judaism entered the American pantheon of the religions of democracy and Jews joined the middle class and moved out to the suburbs, Jews lost much of the stigma attached to them" (p. 48). Hasia Diner (2004) emphasized that the conceptual alignment between Jewish and American identity assumes a kind of fluidity or progressivism: "[Jews] did not believe that they had to accept America as it was, nor did they see Judaism as a fixed entity that they could not mold to fit their needs. They could put their impress on both . . . to bring the two into harmony" (pp. 1–2). And Steven Windmueller (2013) called this a "Jewish contract with America," by which he means a distinctively harmonious arrangement for Jews along several dimensions. "During this [post-war] period," he wrote, "Jews were able to see themselves no longer as social outsider or an immigrant class but rather as an integral part of the American experience" (p. 14).

At the same time, for some historians, Foer's way of thinking about the relationship of American Jews to America—the very idea of a post-war Golden Age—may sound suspiciously close to a position that it sometimes called "American Jewish exceptionalism." The term suggests an unnuanced and uncritical reading of American Jewish history, one which tends to ignore the ways in which the American Jewish experience has not always been so harmonious. Strong expressions of American Jewish exceptionalism tend to retroject Jewish acceptance and achievement from the post-war period to earlier periods, and in fact tend to overlook the persistence of exclusionary practices and policies well into the post-war period. Such a reading of American Jewish history fails to appreciate the ways in which it has not been so harmonious for all kinds of Jews—especially Jews who were not middle-class, who were not politically and religiously moderate, and who were not white-presenting men. The idea of the Golden Age also understates important changes in the American Jewish community over the course of this period, such as those that emerged from the profound critique of the sexism and materialism of the American Jewish establishment in the 1960s, those that followed the rise of neo-conservativism in the 1980s, and those generated by the wave of anxiety around assimilation and continuity in the 1990s. It ignores the way in which American Jewish life has always suffered from a tension between integration and group distinctiveness, often compromising the latter on the altar of the former. In celebrating the achievements of American Jews, it tends to under-appreciate the structures and social policies that enabled those achievements in the post-war period; it also under-appreciates the ways that those structures and policies were not available to other minority groups in equal fashion, or, indeed, the ways that American Jews sometimes chose to endorse policies that advanced Jewish communal achievement at the expense of others. As a result, for some advocates of American Jewish exceptionalism, what is "exceptional" and praiseworthy is not America and what it has provided but actually the Jews themselves. American Jewish exceptionalism also tends to be associated with its cousin, American exceptionalism, which is sometimes taken to be a quasi-theological legitimation for jingoistic patriotism—so exceptionalism is not just historiographically naïve, it may also be dangerous.[9]

Thus, we have good reasons to be cautious about overly romantic claims about the American Jewish experience. Jews have not always been welcome. Jewish status as citizens was not always assured and not always equally distributed. Even what it means to be a citizen—what rights are granted by that status—is subject to ongoing negotiation. And yet, when Hasia Diner (2004) concludes the introduction to her one-volume history of American Jews, she writes: "Whatever their political opinion about Israel, or indeed about any subject, [American Jews at the turn of the twenty-first century] saw graphically how America and its Jews had created a very special relationship" (p. 9). Perhaps not exceptional, but certainly "very special." More recently, Shuli Rubin Schwartz (2021) is comfortable opining that "this country has offered Jews a sense of at-homeness unprecedented in Jewish history." And

---

9   This paragraph is informed by scholarship on American Jewish exceptionalism including Michels (2010) and Sorkin (2010); by other critics such as Liebman (1973) on American Jewish ambivalence; Dollinger (2000) on the development of American Jewish liberalism; Liefer (2024) on the myth of Jewish achievement; Soloveitchik (2024) on the naïveté of American Jewish illusions; and Beinart (2024) on the tension between Zionism and liberalism; and by personal correspondence with Lila Corwin Berman.

Joshua Leifer describes a "faith in the unique benevolence of America as demonstrated by the singularity of the American Jewish experience [that] has been shared across the American Jewish political and religious spectrum" (2024, pp. 9–10). Leifer's book is a critique or, perhaps better, a lament—but it affirms the prominence of this way of thinking for American Jews during the post-war period.

Rachel Gordan's (2021) analysis of what we might call the anti-exceptionalist trend in contemporary American Jewish historiography is particularly helpful here. For Gordan, historians' efforts to document the ways that the American Jewish experience is not quite so exceptional are historiographically astute, but they miss the important point that American Jews have *felt* that America is exceptional, that Jews found and built a home in post-war America—and felt at home—in a way that is different than other times and locations of the Jewish diaspora. That is the enormously influential story that American Jews have told themselves in this place, about themselves in this place.

And that is the story that is, now, being revisited—not just because of a proliferation of incidents of antisemitism but more fundamentally because of an erosion of a set of liberal democratic norms, "the liberal ethos." The post-war period was not just a time of astonishing economic mobility for Jews and astonishing social acceptance. It was not just the period where American Jews made important contributions to American science and law, entertainment and culture. It was not just a period that witnessed a convergence between the interests of Jews and the interests of moderate middle-class America. The dramatic rise of higher education, the emergence of middle-class professions, the move to the suburbs, the decline of social antisemitism—all this contributed to the Golden Age, to be sure; but, for Foer and other observers, the essential element is a liberal democratic ethos encompassing individual autonomy, religious pluralism, political moderation, inter-group coalitions, trust in institutions, and personal integrity. When American Jews said that they felt at home in America, it was due to the prominence of this ethos. Foer ends his argument as follows: "If America persists on its current course, it would be the end of the Golden Age not just for the Jews, but for the country that nurtured them" (2024, p. 35). For Leifer, "the pillars [of Americanism, Zionism and liberalism] that once defined American Jewish life have ceased to be viable" (2024, p. 14). For his part, Yehuda Kurtzer (2024) does not disagree, but adopts a more optimistic—because more activist—stance. "We American Jews have believed for a long time," he says, "that America is a site of a covenantal relationship, that the best way to be American was to believe in the possibility of America and then work really hard to actualize that belief." He concludes with a call to action: "What is it going to take of us to sustain this magnificent era of Jewish history in the face of what others would call a decline?"

The preceding paragraphs were written in late 2024, leading up to the re-election of Donald Trump. For some Jewish observers, that political development was welcome not least because it promised to bring about a wave of triumphant retaliation against antisemitic extremists on the left. Indeed, under the banner of combatting antisemitism, the administration has pursued punitive measures against individuals, groups, and institutions. But if you diagnosed the underlying problem as Foer did, namely as the erosion of liberal democratic norms, then the election signaled a dramatic acceleration of the same worrisome dynamic. By the spring of 2025, one year after the publication of Foer's essay about the end of the Golden Age that has served as the focus of the preceding discussion, the condition of American democracy is grim. Democratic norms have not merely eroded but imploded: pervasive attacks on due process, explicit defiance and demonization of the judiciary, rejection of the separation of powers, transparent targeting of political opponents and the press, invocation of fraudulent concerns about national security to justify denial of rights, political interference in independent institutions, and celebration of authoritarianism abroad. For some, Foer's judgment about the end of the Golden Age may have seemed hyperbolic; a year later, his essay seems to have underestimated the speed and severity of the collapse.

D. Two Central Purposes for Jewish Education Today

There are surely those who would argue with the preceding representation of the current moment. Perhaps we are romanticizing the prior acceptance of liberal democratic norms in post-war America, or overstating their decline. Perhaps American democracy is more resilient than we fear. Perhaps this moment of extremism will pass, and the voices of moderation will re-emerge. But for those who believe that something fundamental has indeed changed for American Jews—not that it changed overnight, because we can point to many precursors, but that the dynamics on display since October 7, both on the left and the right, are indicators of how dramatically the culture has changed—how should we think about the purposes of Jewish education?

The answer to a set of emotional and psychological challenges cannot be as simplistic as a course in positive psychology or a dose of counseling. Nor should we set aside the project of educating students within the Jewish religious and cultural tradition, as if the urgent demands of the moment should be allowed to crowd out the deeply significant ongoing project of situating students with a tradition, helping them to navigate within, feel ownership over, and develop their own contributions to that culture.[10] However, in what follows, we will propose two central purposes for Jewish education in the present moment—not as replacements for that broader project but as complements to it and specific manifestations of it. The first central purpose: *Jewish education must prepare our young people for the reality of contemporary America*, a reality that is different and far more hostile than the one in which many of us grew up. The second central purpose: *Jewish education must equip our young people with the tools to change that reality*. We need a conceptual framework that helps us to articulate the project of change and what qualities we seek to cultivate to encourage that change to happen. Contemporary Hebrew has two helpful rhyming words to label these two purposes: *ha-matzui*, that which is, and *ha-ratzui*, that which is desired, or, in other words, the world as it ought to be. Jewish education in this moment must be an education both for the *matzui* and for the *ratzui*. Neither one is sufficient without the other.

In order to better understand the first purpose, it may be helpful to call attention to two comparisons. The first comparison is to contemporary American Islamic education, an education that occurs within a context of cultural hostility to Islam.[11] Randa Elbih (2012), for example, writes about Islamic education after 9/11, which was a profoundly important turning point for the Muslim American community (although of course Islamophobia was present beforehand):

> The distorted Islamic identity presented by the media and the educational curriculum has more than just an external effect; it also affects the construction of Muslim Americans' self-identification . . . This, coupled with peer pressure and

---

10 For articulations of the purposes of that "ongoing project," see Levisohn (2021) and Levisohn (forthcoming b).
11 The following paragraphs are adapted from Levisohn (2025).

> wanting to fit in, result in negative self-identification, rejection to [sic] their Muslim identity, assimilation to mainstream society, or developing an identity split. (pp. 160–161)

For Elbih, Islamic education has to anticipate and preempt the hostile image of Islam that students will encounter, an image of themselves that is discordant with their own self-perception, or, worse, that generates self-loathing. Habiba Farh (2018) writes, "Islamic school teachers ... have to teach students how to cope with the hostile Islamophobic environment students are living in." Mona Abo-Zena and Abdelrahman Hassan (2024) propose that Muslim youth should be "socialized to recognize being excluded and/or discriminated against" (p. 57). Islamic education in America cannot be satisfied with just teaching Islamic values, texts and practices, and hoping that students will navigate their way as Muslim Americans successfully on their own.

The second comparison is from an earlier moment in American Jewish education, the inter-war and immediate post-war period in which, as Krasner (2019) documents, the negative impact of antisemitism on "Jewish identity" was a prominent concern. Krasner points in particular to the work of the psychologist Kurt Lewin, who argued for "the centrality of Jewish education in promoting Jewish psychological wellbeing" (p. 41). Jewish education in that period was oriented around the psychological concern for being "well-adjusted" in the face of hostile or assimilatory pressures.

These two comparisons—to Islamic education in the post-9/11 period and to American Jewish education of two or three generations ago—are intended to highlight the way that contemporary Jewish education may need to change. For a long time, Jews have been at home in America. Jewish educators were surely aware of white supremacists and radical left antisemites, but the focus of those Jewish educators has tended to be on the downsides of Jewish comfort and acceptance, i.e., how to maintain Jewish distinctiveness. Given the legal sanctions against discrimination or hostility against Jews, and the political power of Jews on the left within the Democratic Party and on the right among evangelical defenders of Israel, Jewish educators did not think that preparing students for a hostile environment in America might need to be a priority. We have not been exercising these muscles. We need them now.[12]

---

12 As noted, the focus here is on how to educate Jews regarding antisemitism, not how to educate non-Jews in order to eliminate or reduce antisemitism—not because the latter is unimportant but simply because this chapter and this volume is about Jewish education,

What would this look like? This chapter is not the place to outline a scope and sequence, but we can consider some principles. It is not enough for young Jews to have "pride" or "strong identities," nor is it enough for them to know a lot about Jewish texts and traditions, as valuable as those are. American Jewish students need to learn about and understand the historical and contemporary patterns of antisemitism—not in order to turn them into warriors on the front lines, and not to build up high protective walls behind which they can retreat. Instead, they need to learn about contemporary antisemitism in order to prepare them for the gaslighting, conditionalization, erasure, demonization, and denial of the right to self-definition that is part of contemporary political discourse in the cultural spaces that most Jews occupy.

Gaslighting occurs when someone denies that an act or expression that is experienced as hostile and directed towards Jews *as Jews* is antisemitic.[13] Conditionalization and cooption occurs when Jews are required to identify as "good Jews" by repudiating or disidentifying with other Jews as a condition of acceptance into organizations or social circles.[14] Erasure occurs when Jews, as a group, are denied a status and a history that other groups rightfully are granted.[15] Demonization occurs when criticism of Jews or

---

i.e., the education of Jews. To be sure, the Jewish community has recently been investing astonishing amounts of money in "fighting antisemitism." These efforts, alas, seem to be ill defined and under-theorized. There are public relations campaigns and social media initiatives, training programs for non-Jewish educators, and a dominating emphasis on the Holocaust. However, if contemporary antisemitism is downstream from political radicalism and broader cultural dynamics such as erosion of social trust—and if, for political radicals, demonization of one's opponents is not a vice but a virtue, as suggested above—then it would seem our efforts ought to be focused on understanding the underlying dynamics and on re-establishing the vibrancy of political moderation in the face of extremism, rather than just hoping that naming-and-shaming will work to change hearts and minds. It will not.

13 Compare Jason Rubinstein's (2023) insightful essay, in the form of a communal letter to the Yale Hillel community, in which he offers a definition of antisemitism as resistance to an assertion of power by Jews as Jews. Also see Rosenberg (2022) for a concise argument about the way that left-wing ideology regarding power serves to insulate attacks on Jews from being recognized as antisemitic; and Kelner (2024) for a critical-systemic analysis of the power dynamics that produce antisemitism.

14 Jill Jacobs has been a particularly articulate voice on this point; see, for example, Jacobs (2024, p. 10).

15 The arguments by defenders of Israel against the so-called "double standard" to which Israel is held by progressive activists or international jurists can lead to evasion of serious critiques that deserve to be addressed directly. However, the underlying Kantian principle is fundamental to sound moral reasoning: One should not employ arguments against selective targets that cannot be generalized. Thus, when critics of Israel complain about a "Palestine exception" (e.g., a "Palestine exception" to principles of free speech), that

of Israel suggests that there is something about the object of critique that represents, not unwise or unjust policies, but evidence of the demonic in the world (even if the demonic is sometimes secularized in the familiar terms of contemporary radical political theory).[16] Denial of the right to self-definition occurs when Jews are not permitted to explain for themselves what they mean by, for example, the term "Zionist," and instead have definitions assigned to them.

These are five prevalent patterns. An education in anti-antisemitism, for Jews, ought to engage with these patterns (and others) so that contemporary Jews have the agency to navigate progressive spaces as they wish, to engage with others to the extent that they want to do so, with an understanding of the underlying moral and political dynamics. Knowledge, to borrow a phrase, is power; understanding how antisemitic tropes and themes are playing out in one's immediate context can help turn a vague sense of unease into an empowered stance. Again, the point here is not to equip Jewish students to do battle against antisemites, nor to motivate a retreat or a retrenchment. In fact, it is important to note that focusing on patterns and tropes de-personalizes the conversation; it is almost always more helpful to explore the ways in which a statement or argument draws on antisemitic tropes rather than purporting to assess whether a person is, in their heart (as it were), antisemitic. Instead, the point is to prepare young Jews for an environment in which these patterns have become common.

There is a further element to this first central purpose of preparing Jewish students for the reality of contemporary America, which is to consider the tension between victimization and resilience. In our contemporary moral discourse, and this occurs both on the left and on the right, nothing is more powerful than to be a victim—and so nothing is more appealing. Jews surely have the right, now and in the past, to call attention to their own victimization. But the long-term health of Jews as individuals and as a community (just like the long-term health of other minoritized communities) will be better served by a focus on resilience, in both historical terms and psychological

---

complaint is legitimate and worthy of attention. And at the same time, nothing should justify a "Jewish exception," treating Jews as a collective in ways that progressives would not tolerate regarding any other group, either intellectually (Kelner, 2024) or inter-personally (Hersh & Lyss, 2024).

16 See Tomer Persico's (2024) analysis of the relationship between radical hostility to Israel and a quasi-theological hostility to "the West," or what he calls "a rejection of the West ... as inherently violent, oppressive, imperialist, patriarchal, or just plain evil."

terms, rather than entering the Oppression Olympics,[17] demanding attention to our own victimization, competing for the prize of Most Victimized. This is not a posture of passivity, but rather, of emotional and psychological strength.

To this point, we have focused on the first central purpose of Jewish education in this moment: *Jewish education must prepare our young people for the reality of contemporary America.* To educate for that reality entails a deep understanding of the surprising hostility of the contemporary environment; a sober investigation of how other communities, or the Jewish community at other times, has created educational structures to help students to cope with such environments; the development of a sophisticated curriculum to help students understand the patterns and dynamics of contemporary antisemitic discourse—including gaslighting, conditionalization, erasure, demonization, and denial of the right to self-definition; and, finally, attention to resilience rather than victimization. For Jewish educators, this will require a significant shift, especially because, for most, this is not the reality that they themselves experienced as they grew up. But this is not enough. The second central purpose is: *Jewish education must equip our young people with the tools to change that reality.* The reality, we have been arguing, is characterized by the decline of a liberal democratic ethos. More than specific incidents of antisemitism, it is that decline that has undermined our confidence in America and challenged our feeling of being at home. If this is accurate, then changing the reality must involve the restoration—or if we want to avoid romanticizing the halcyon past, then simply "strengthening"—of liberal democratic norms. Our shorthand for this focus is "American Jewish civic education."[18]

---

17 The term "Oppression Olympics" seems to be credited to Elizabeth Martínez (Martínez & Davis, 1994). She and others have critiqued the Oppression Olympics as part of a broader argument in favor of coalition-building across communal boundaries without regard for who is most oppressed.

18 The following paragraphs benefitted greatly from ideas generated by and within the American Jewish Civics Seminar, co-sponsored by A More Perfect Union: Jewish Partnership for Democracy and the Shalom Hartman Institute of North America, in 2024–2025. Naturally, none of the participants in that seminar are responsible for this particular formulation. It is also important to call attention to an underlying premise here about the nature of Diaspora Judaism, which stands in conflict with the classical Zionist approach of *shelilat ha-golah,* the so-called "negation of the diaspora"—the idea that the success of the Zionist project in the Land of Israel necessarily entails the repudiation not just of the historical reality of diasporic Jewish flourishing but also its potential flourishing into the future. For many Zionists, although of course not all, the aspirational investment of emotional, intellectual, and spiritual energy (and resources) into the flourishing of diasporic Jewish community for the future was and is anathema. An American Jewish civic education represents exactly that kind of aspirational investment. How exactly we ought

As we will see in a moment, American Jewish civic education is not, first and foremost, an education in American (or American Jewish) history, although certainly understanding that history can serve its purposes.[19] It will not focus primarily on technical details about the American political system—the three branches of government, how a bill becomes a law, and so on. It will overlap with the kind of education that is necessary for all Americans, in its themes and the dispositions that it promotes, in order to rebuild our liberal democratic norms without ignoring its flaws and failures, but it is focused on the role that Jews can and should play in particular. Thus, it particularistically considers not just what it means for a Jew to be an American but also what it means for a Jew to be an American Jew. It therefore focuses on how and why and under what conditions Jews engage with others and with the broader polity—implicitly rejecting a policy of retrenchment in the face of a challenging environment. One way of thinking about American Jewish civic education is that it incorporates a set of essential conversations that the American Jewish community can and should be having, and into which younger American Jews can and should be inducted.[20]

What should be the focus of this American Jewish civic education to meet the present moment? Again, we are not proposing a particular curriculum, much less a scope and sequence. But we can envision five central themes, which are surely interconnected, each of which represents not merely an idea (although they will be articulated as ideas) but more like a stance or a disposition to act in certain ways. Each theme is represented by a phrase from within the Jewish textual tradition, which marks the theme as distinctively

---

to think about the relationship between the Jewish community in America and the Jewish community in Israel is an important topic of conversation. It may well be that there are some possibilities for Jewish flourishing that are possible only in one rather than in both, which affect the choices that individuals may make. But American Jewish civic education assumes that the American Jewish community is not going anywhere, nor should it.

19 The paragraphs above on the question of American Jewish exceptionalism, for example, and the substantive historical evidence that support those historiographical discussions, are directly relevant to how young American Jews think about the project of America and Jews' role in that project.

20 This way of thinking about American Jewish civic education—the essential Jewish communal conversations into which young members of the community ought to be inducted—is indebted to Sivan Zakai, both in personal conversation and in her scholarly work (e.g., Zakai, 2022). The idea of a culture as comprising an intergenerational "great conversation" was popularized by thinkers such as Robert Maynard Hutchins and Mortimer Adler (see, e.g., Hutchins, 1952) but that tradition tends to be rather more universalistic, as if there is one such conversation rather than diverse conversations.

"Jewish" and thus implicitly undermines any purported dichotomy between Jewish and other ("Western" or "liberal" or "universalist") values, but, more importantly, points towards the extended conversation about the issues within that tradition. These five themes as follows:

1. *Dina de-malkhuta dina* ("the law of the land is the law [for Jews as well]");
2. *Ger ve-toshav* ("both a stranger and a resident");
3. *Mipnei darkhei shalom* ("[we adopt this socially engaged policy] because of the ways of peace");
4. *Mahloket le-shem shamayim* ("argument for the sake of Heaven");
5. *Kohi ve-otzem yadi* ("my power and the strength of my hand [are the source of this abundance]").

In what follows, we will discuss each theme in turn.

First, the theme of *Dina de-malkhuta dina* is much more than just a technical question of whether Jews must obey the laws of secular rulers.[21] That is just the minimum requirement. It also encompasses the deeper political-theoretic conviction that the rule of law is central to a functioning and healthy shared society, and that the stability and security of law is foundational to human and communal flourishing. Our ideal, to borrow the famous phrase from John Adams, is "a government of laws, not of men." Citizens must have confidence that laws are written for the purposes of justice, that they will be administered fairly to all—and when they fall short of these ideals, as they always have and inevitably will, that there are mechanisms for amendment and improvement.[22]

---

21 For an extensive technical discussion of *Dina de-malkhuta dina*, including the relevant rabbinic sources, see Schachter (1984). Josh Levisohn (personal correspondence) points out that, in the classical sources, the source of the law in question is an external power, whereas, in a liberal democratic framework, Jews participate in the creation and administration of the law. This is just one way that the use of *Dina de-malkhuta dina* here builds on and expands the discussion within classical Jewish sources, rather than being limited to them.

22 The question of how to balance incremental reform with respect for and conservation of institutions—especially law but also other social institutions—is, naturally, one on which people will differ. The Jewish tradition does not tell us how to navigate that question. But the suggestion here is that both are important values, and that deliberating about their relative weight in particular situations is how liberal democracy ought to operate. American Jewish civic education ought to explore this debate rather than resolving it.

In this way, *Dina de-malkhuta dina* subverts a merely transactional conception of the relationship with secular power. That kind of transactionalism has certainly been commonplace at other times in Jewish history.[23] And it would be naïve to ignore the ways that the American Jewish community has benefitted and continues to benefit from transactional relationships with the American political and legal system. But as an ideal *Dina de-malkhuta dina* reminds us that this is not our goal. Instead, we should aspire to and acknowledge our responsibility for a legal regime on which all citizens can rely and in which they can trust, a legal regime under which Jews thrive because everyone thrives.

The second theme of American Jewish civic education, *Ger ve-toshav*, draws upon Joseph Soloveitchik's interpretation of the description of Abraham in Gen. 23:4 (see Besdin, 1979, ch. 16). Soloveitchik turns the phrase from a mere linguistic curiosity—why does Abraham describe himself with both terms?—to a principle about how to live both within society and apart from it: "We are very much residents in general human society while, at the same time, strangers and outsiders in our persistent endeavor to preserve historic religious identity" (Besdin, 1993, p. 177).[24] This status may be "paradoxical," as Soloveitchik also calls it, but it is fundamental to contemporary multicultural societies—societies that not only respect religious (and other) communities, but even more, that recognize those communities as foundational building blocks of healthy societies. In 1915, at a moment in American history that saw widespread anxiety about the fragmentation of national identity, Theodore Roosevelt famously declared that "there is no room in this country for hyphenated Americanism."[25] Americans, he believed, ought to be un-hyphenated. But over time, Roosevelt's position lost the political-theoretic battle to the contrary position articulated by Horace Kallen (1915) in favor of "cultural pluralism" in that very same year. Being a Jew in America, like being Irish-American or Italian-American or African-American, is not a strange or secondary way of being American. The hyphen (whether or not there is an

---

23 The institution of *shtadlanim*, intercessionary leaders of the Jewish community, is a relevant paradigm here (Thulin, 2017).
24 I am indebted to Mark Gottlieb for this citation. See also the discussion by Soloveitchik's great-nephew, Meir Soloveitchik (2025).
25 The quote comes from a speech by Roosevelt at the Columbus Day celebration in New York on October 12, 1915, at the Knights of Columbus, as reported by (presumably among other outlets) the *New York Times*, "Roosevelt Bars the Hyphenated," October 13, 1915.

actual hyphen, which is just a matter of linguistic convention) is an asset, not a liability. Yet this is always, at the same time, a challenge—a challenge to build a Jewish community that contributes to the larger society, that is able to advance its own interests (because this is also entirely normal) while also maintaining interest in, commitment to, and responsibility for the broader polity.

The third theme, *Mipnei darkhei shalom*, is a principle that is cited in rabbinic literature as the basis for a variety of rulings and policies that promote social cohesion, not only within the Jewish community but also within the broader community; it "creates an environment of peaceful and mutual respect between all persons irrelevant of their race and religion" (Fishbane, 2018, p. 73). As in the time of the Mishnah, so too today: Those of us who live within and enjoy the benefits of strong communities must also participate actively in institutions and initiatives that bring us outside of the Jewish community and enable us to engage substantively with others from whom we differ in terms of background and even in terms of ideology.

Those from whom we differ are, in the end, our fellow citizens. It is certainly strategic to develop the norms and the habits of coalition building, where interests align, but it is also a moral requirement. This "end of the Golden Age" moment is a hard time to work on this, given the feeling of many Jews that our erstwhile coalition partners—the people we thought would be our allies—have disappointed us. That feeling is legitimate. And we have been disappointed in our partners before, just as, if we are honest with ourselves, they surely have been disappointed in us as well. But to allow potential or actual disappointment to deter the building of coalitions is a mistake. We should recognize that this is just another moral-purity argument against coalition building, i.e., the flawed argument that we should only collaborate with those with whom we already agree about everything important. If we are going to rebuild our liberal democratic ethos, we have to believe—we have no choice but to believe—that our fellow citizens are not our enemies. They are, figuratively and literally, our neighbors; and, as political theorist Nancy Rosenblum (2016) cogently argues, "neighborliness" is a kind of everyday democratic virtue that enables and promotes encounter across difference.

Here we might also learn from the work of another political theorist, Danielle Allen (2023), who, channeling Martin Luther King, Jr., argues for a political stance that responds to violations of political norms with a spirit of generosity rather than resentment. "To put the general idea simply," she writes, "the work is to call in, not call out" (p. 214). She recognizes that adopting this stance puts the onus on those who have been marginalized or who feel victimized to be magnanimous towards their opponents. This is a lot to ask. But she insists that this is the only way forward. For the Jewish community, likewise, calling out antisemites cannot be the endgame; we have to seek to build relationships, even—especially—with those who seem ideologically distant.[26]

The fourth theme in American Jewish civic education is *Mahloket le-shem shamayim*. If we believe that religious (and other) communities are the building blocks of a healthy democratic society, then we also have to hold ourselves accountable for the democratic health of those communities themselves. This means, among other things, considering how well we enable dialogue across difference within that community; how minority opinions are not just tolerated but respected and recognized; how we encourage robust discussion while avoiding factionalism and fragmentation.

The principle of *Mahloket le-shem shamayim* does not solve all problems; after all, the tradition teaches that "disputes for the sake of Heaven are destined to endure" (m. Avot 5:17). Political theorist Joshua Cherniss (2023) suggests that "acceptance of plurality and conflict" is one of the core principles of liberalism; we should be committed, he says, to "mediating and stabilizing, but not suppressing, conflict." This means that we should try not to fear disagreement, and instead learn to approach disagreement with curiosity alongside conviction, with resilience rather than fragility.[27] This is harder to do under our contemporary conditions of political polarization, both with regard to American politics and, within the Jewish community, with regard to Israel. No one should diminish how serious the disagreements really are, and how hard it is to stay in conversation with people who seem not to share your most foundational beliefs—and of course, inevitably, this goes in both (or all) directions, whether the foundational belief is respect for all human life, or the physical protection of my own family, or, indeed, the principles articulated here such as respect for the rule of law. To stay in conversation with those who seem to be traitors to a just cause that we hold dear is a lot to ask. Still, the ideal of *Mahloket le-shem shamayim* functions as a self-fulfilling prophecy: If we can work our way through to the belief that our opponents

---

26 Robert Putnam's argument on behalf of the importance of social trust is also relevant here; see Putnam (2000) and Putnam & Garrett (2020).

27 As an example of productive initiative in this area, see the work of Robbie Gringras and Abi Dauber (in their 2022 volume and the programmatic activities through their organization, For the Sake of Argument).

are arguing for their version of the ideal community (or nation), and engage them accordingly, that goes a long way towards making it so.

Finally, the fifth theme of American Jewish civic education is *Kohi ve-otzem yadi*. In its original context in Deut. 8:17, the phrase is a critique of the delusion that one's material attainments are due to one's own efforts; as Shai Held (2017) comments on this passage, "Real piety requires us to surrender the illusion of self-sufficiency" (p. 229). With a little bit of rhetorical license, we can think about it as a call for humility from the powerful. Whatever Jews have acquired, in terms of material and financial success, intellectual achievements, political accomplishments, or even military might—we ought to consider those accomplishments with a bit of critical distance, recognizing that they are not the testaments to our moral virtue that we may think they are or want them to be. This entails gratitude for the opportunities that have been provided, to be sure, but not just gratitude. It also demands honesty about contemporary realities and a stance of ethical responsibility.

This is particularly important for American Jewish civic education at a time when the Jewish community, in both the United States and in Israel, has acquired levels of power that are historically unprecedented. A mature education in Jewish civics does not repudiate that power as if power is inherently unethical, and does not participate in the sophomoric celebration of powerlessness. It recognizes that one can have power in certain respects while also being subject to injustice or the power of others, rejecting the groundless bifurcation of the world into the powerful and the powerless. But if that is true, it also demands—and our students will demand, and will be right to demand—far more rigorous attention to the ethics of power than we typically give.

What does it mean, for us and for our children, that American Jews have acquired so much financial and material success? That power operates both within the community and beyond its borders. When Jews or their interests are threatened, we wield that power—whether through the organized Jewish community or through the actions of powerful individuals, sometimes in aspirational efforts to build a better future for all, and sometimes in more transactional ways. Likewise, in Israel, the Jewish community employs the levers of power, including the apparatus of a sovereign state and its military might, sometimes in aspirational efforts to build a better future for all, and sometimes to advance its interests more narrowly and more shortsightedly.

This is a conversation that we must undertake, with as much honesty and ethical rigor as we can muster. Commentators on the original source of *Kochi ve-otzem yadi* in Deuteronomy emphasize that it follows verses that describe a reality (of Divine beneficence) that is being ignored or forgotten.[28] In other words, the phenomenon that initially presents as a lack of humility is actually generated by a lack of awareness of or attention to realities on the ground. The corrective, then, is more awareness of and more attention to those realities, which all too often are hidden from us unless and until we ask the questions and actively seek to understand what is being done in our name. The American Jewish civic education envisioned here would invite students into an informed, mature, and ethically rigorous conversation about our power and how we use it.

Notice that this fifth theme is intentionally framed as a question about the Jewish community, not a question about universalist obligations to others. Jews should certainly feel obligated to others beyond the borders of the community, as discussed above in the context of *Mipnei darkhei shalom*. But the pursuit of this fifth theme is about what kind of Jewish community we envision and want to create, both here in America and in Israel, within the complicated contexts in which we find ourselves. In America, we are participating in a democratic polity made up of diverse groups with diverse interests; our narrative is inevitably bound up with the narratives of others. In Israel, we are navigating a conflict with another national group with whom we are fated to share the Land, and over whom we have and continue to exercise power; there too our narrative is one in which others are already present.[29] This is the landscape within which we live. These are the realities. What is our vision for the ethical exercise of power, in the Jewish community, in relation to those outside of the community?

These five themes or principles, as noted above, are not a scope and sequence. They certainly do not dictate particular policies. If we are focused on what kinds of people we are hoping to develop through our Jewish educational interventions, we might rephrase them as elements of Jewish civic virtue.[30] And, by sourcing and proposing them, we are not making a claim

---

28 See, e.g., Naftali Tzvi Yehuda Berlin, in his *Ha'amek Davar* on Deut. 8:17.
29 Bryfman (2024) put the point as follows: "Irrespective of politics and ideologies, we must continue, as educators, to grapple with the inconvertible fact that there is another people with claims to much of the same land as the Jewish people" (p. 54).
30 As noted above and again below, the argument of this chapter is not intended as a replacement for the "ongoing project" of Jewish education. The suggestion here, that Jewish civic education is about the development of a set of civic virtues, may be a helpful way of squaring the circle: Regardless of the specific content of our lessons, whether they are lessons about American history or about Jewish texts, we ought to maintain a focus on

about comprehensiveness; there are surely other useful and relevant themes as well. But these five might help us to recapture some of what seems to have been lost, to rebuild some of the liberal democratic ethos, to create or recreate a healthy American Judaism that can thrive within—and that can contribute to—a thriving American democracy. In this way, they represent a Jewish educational response that meets the challenges of the moment.

E. Conclusion

In a short essay about Jewish education after October 7, Erica Brown (2024) proposes that "we are in the midst of a world-shaping moment in Jewish history... an inflection point that we have yet to comprehend" (p. 51). A bit later on, she opines that "it is still too early to apprehend how we have changed as a nation and as individuals; this will be the work of many years to come." Her note of humility in the face of what seem like profound changes is welcome and admirable. If the present essay has overstepped its bounds in offering prescriptions on the basis of diagnoses that themselves are premature, Brown offers a welcome reminder that all of this needs to be couched in tentative terms. But she continues by proposing an analogy to a science teacher in a classroom who struggles to teach as a storm breaks outside, distracting the students with its fierce winds and lashing rain against the windows.[31] The teacher, losing control of her lesson plan, leans into the distraction, bringing the students to the windows, and conducts an impromptu science lesson about weather. "We are in that storm," writes Brown. "We need to take our students to that window and talk about the storm" (p. 52).

The analogy seems apt. We are in the storm, and we need to talk about it. We need to talk with our students about what living in stormy conditions feels like, and we need to talk about how to prepare for the passing of the storm. All this is certainly not a replacement for Torah, for the richness and vibrancy of the Jewish tradition, for the meaningful anchoring that ritual and community can and do provide; as noted above, we should never lose sight of

---

the kinds of qualities that we are seeking to cultivate—respect for the rule of law, a bifocal commitment to one's own community and the broader polity, an inclination towards cooperation with others, curiosity and resilience in the face of disagreement, a critical stance towards one's own power. The overarching framework reminds us that these are Jewish qualities, derived from Jewish sources, and part of an ongoing Jewish conversation.

31 Brown believes that the analogy should be credited to Joseph P. McDonald.

the "ongoing project," the pedagogical imperative to help our students to feel at home and empowered within Jewish languages, cultures and spaces. But neither can we assume that a Jewish education that served for other moments will serve this one. For this moment, we need a Jewish education that prepares our young people for an environment that is far more hostile than the one in which most of us were raised, and we need a Jewish education that elevates the goal of rebuilding a democratic ethos, and an American Jewish democratic ethos, to among its highest priorities.

References

Abo-Zena, M., & Hassan, A. (2024). Reflecting personal, family and community ethnographies to understand how fasting Ramadan fuels the religious development of Muslim youth. *Journal of Islamic Faith and Practice*, 5:1, 53–83.

ADL (2024). Antisemitic attitudes in America 2024. ADL Center for Antisemitism Research. https://www.adl.org/resources/report/antisemitic-attitudes-america-2024

AJC (2024). 2024 survey of American Jewish opinion. https://www.ajc.org/news/survey2024

Allen, D. (2023). *Justice by means of democracy*. University of Chicago Press.

Beinart, P. (2024). The great rupture in American Jewish life. *New York Times*, March 22, 2024.

Besdin, A. R. (1979). *Reflections of the Rav*, vol. 1: *Lessons in Jewish thought adapted from the lectures of Rabbi Joseph B. Soloveitchik*. KTAV Publishing House.

Brown, E. (2024). We are not the same. In H. Deitcher et al. (Eds.), *Until the day breaks and the shadows flee away: Directions in Jewish education after October 7* (pp. 53–55). Ministry for Diaspora Affairs and Combating Antisemitism of the Government of Israel.

Bryfman, D. (2016). When you're happy and you know it: The true purpose of Jewish education. *eJewishPhilanhtropy*. https://ejewishphilanthropy.com/when-youre-happy-and-you-know-it-the-true-purpose-of-jewish-education/

Bryfman, D. (2017). From continuity, to renewal and renaissance, to . . . Jewish thriving. *Ayeka*. https://www.jewishedproject.org/news/continuity-renewal-and-renaissance-jewish-thriving

Bryfman, D. (2024). Israel education just can't be the same after October 7. In H. Deitcher et al. (Eds.), *Until the day breaks and the shadows flee away: Directions in Jewish education after October 7* (pp. 53–55). Ministry for Diaspora Affairs and Combating Antisemitism of the Government of Israel.

Chanes, J. (1999). Antisemitism and Jewish security in contemporary America: Why can't Jews take yes for an answer. In R. Rosenberg Farber & C. I. Waxman (Eds.), *Jews in America: A contemporary reader*. Brandeis University Press.

Cherniss, J. L. (2021). *Liberalism in dark times: The liberal ethos in the twentieth century*. Princeton University Press.

Cherniss, J. L. (2023). Joshua Cherniss on liberalism beyond institutions. Address at the Hebrew University of Jerusalem. YouTube, June 7. https://www.youtube.com/watch?v=Gb0LRMXIar4.

Cox, H. G., & Swyngedouw, J. (2000). The myth of the twentieth century: The rise and fall of secularization. *Japanese Journal of Religious Studies, 27*(1/2), 1–13.

Dash Moore, D. (2001). Intermarriage and the politics of identity. *The Reconstructionist,* Fall, 44–51.

Diner, H. (2004) *The Jews of the United States, 1654 to 2000*. University of California Press.

Dollinger, M. (2000). *Quest for inclusion: Jews and liberalism in modern America*. Princeton University Press.

Elbih, R. (2012). Debates in the literature on Islamic schools. *Educational Studies, 48*(2), 156–173.

Fahr, H. (2018). Research memo (unpublished).

Fishbane, S. (2018). Mipnei Darkhei Shalom: The promotion of harmonious relationships in the Mishnah's social order. In L. J. Greenspoon (Ed.), *Is Judaism democratic? Reflections from theory and practice throughout the ages.* Purdue University Press.

Fishman, S. B. (2000). *Jewish life and American culture*. SUNY Press.

Foer, F. (2024). The golden age of American Jews Is ending. *The Atlantic,* April.

Gringras, R., and Dauber Sterne, A. (2022). *Stories for the sake of argument*. FSA Publications.

Gordan, R. (2021). The sin of American Jewish exceptionalism. *AJS Review* 45(2), 282–301.

Hersh, E., & Lyss, D. (2024). *A year of campus conflict and growth: An over-time study of the impact of the Israel-Hamas War on U.S. college students.* Jim Joseph Foundation. https://jimjosephfoundation.org/wp-content/uploads/2024/08/Hersh_Final_Report_Campus_Conflict_and_Growth.pdf

Held, S. (2017). *The heart of Torah*, vol. 2: *Essays on the weekly Torah portion: Leviticus, Numbers and Deuteronomy.* Jewish Publication Society.

Hutchins, R. M. (1952). *The great conversation: The substance of a liberal education*, vol. 1. Encyclopaedia Britannica.

Jacobs, J. (2024). *Criticism of Israel and antisemitism: How to tell where one ends and the other begins.* https://truah.org/resources/criticism-of-israel-and-antisemitism-how-to-tell-where-one-ends-and-the-other-begins/

Jones, V. (2024). Interview. *CNN*. https://www.youtube.com/watch?v=QQa71Pe6sy0

Judaken, J. (2021). Anti-semitism (historiography). In S. Goldberg, S. Ury, & K. I. Weiser (Eds.), *Key concepts in the study of antisemitism.* Palgrave Macmillan.

Kallen, H. (1915). Democracy versus the melting pot. *Nation*, February 25.

Katz, V. S., Forman, E. R., & McGuire, N. H. (2025). Unsettled ground: How Jewish undergraduates are negotiating identity shifts and (un)civil campus discourse after October 7. *Journal of Jewish Education*, March 25. https://doi.org/10.1080/15244113.2025.2481249

Kelner, S. (2024). Turning critical theory on its head: Academia's Palestine exception. *Sapir*, 15, pp. 1–9.

Klein Halevi, Y. (2024). The end of the post-Holocaust era. *Times of Israel*, October 7. https://blogs.timesofisrael.com/the-end-of-the-post-holocaust-era/

Krasner, J. B. (2019). On the origins and persistence of the Jewish identity industry in Jewish education. In J. A. Levisohn & A. Y. Kelman (Eds.), *Beyond Jewish identity: Rethinking concepts and imagining alternatives.* Academic Studies Press.

Krasner, J., Weiner, C., Greenwald, M., & Rothchild, L. (2025). Between home and homeland: Jewish college students confront the Israel-Gaza conflict and campus divides. *Journal of Jewish Education*, May 14. https://doi.org/10.1080/15244113.2025.2488844

Kurtzer, Y. (2024). Our golden age. *Identity/Crisis.* https://www.hartman.org.il/our-golden-age-identity-crisis/

Leifer, J. (2024). *Tablets shattered: The end of an American Jewish century and the future of Jewish life.* Dutton.

Levisohn, J. A. (2013). Rethinking the education of cultural minorities to and from assimilation: A perspective from Jewish education. *Diaspora, Indigenous, and Minority Education: Studies of Migration, Integration, Equity, and Cultural Survival, 7*(1), 54–68.

Levisohn, J. A. (2021) Producers, not possessors: A direction for Jewish education in turbulent times. Applied Research Collective for American Jewry, New York University. https://static1.squarespace.com/static/60bf7eeb36252e1b53064736/t/615240af64c392449dfbcc55/1632780465237/Levisohn_Mech+%281%29.pdf

Levisohn, J. A. (2025). What we've learned about teaching and learning in Jewish day schools, and what we still need to learn. In J. Krasner et al. (Eds.), *Teaching and learning in Jewish day schools* (pp. 329–351). Brandeis University Press.

Levisohn, J. A. (forthcoming a). Teaching and learning the norms of Judaism beyond the Beit Midrash. In C.-S. Popa (Ed.), *Teaching and learning the norms of life and faith: Pedagogues, educators and their heritage in Abrahamic religions.* Mohr Siebeck.

Levisohn, J. A. (2025) Becoming a speaker of Jewish language, *Journal of Jewish Education.*

Martínez, E., & Davis, A. Y. (1994). Coalition building among people of color. *Inscriptions, 7,* 42–53.

Michels, T. (2010). Is America 'different?' A critique of American Jewish exceptionalism. *Journal of American Jewish History, 96*(3), 201–224.

Persico, T. (2024). Western self-hatred and the offering of Israel. *Café Americain,* May 10.

Prell, R.-E. (2025). A new era of cultural vitality for American Jews? Annual Grob Lecture at the University of Virginia. YouTube, February 27, 2025. https://www.youtube.com/live/8N9ZsNSTy2U

Putnam, R. D. (2000). *Bowling alone: The collapse and revival of American community.* Simon & Schuster.

Putnam, R. D., & Garrett, S. R. (2020). *The upswing: How America came together a century ago and how we can do it again.* Simon & Schuster.

Rosenberg, Y. (2022). Why so many people still don't understand anti-semitism. *Atlantic*, February 19.

Rosenblum, N. (2016). *Good neighbors: The democracy of everyday life in America*. Princeton University Press.

Rubin Schwartz, S. (2021). At home in America's home? *eJewishPhilanthropy*, December 7. https://ejewishphilanthropy.com/at-home-in-americas-home/.

Rubinstein, J. (2023). *Reckoning with antisemitism at Yale*. Joseph Slifka Center for Jewish Life at Yale, Yale University. https://slifkacenter.org/wp-content/uploads/2023/10/Reckoning-with-Antisemitism-at-Yale.pdf

Samuel, N., et al. (2024). Campus voices: Jewish students' experiences of antisemitism at US colleges. Cohen Center for Modern Jewish Studies, Brandeis University. https://www.brandeis.edu/cmjs/research/antisemitism/pdfs/campus-voices-120924.pdf

Schachter, H. (1984). "Dina de'malchusa dina": Secular law as a religious obligation. In A. S. Cohen (Ed.), *Halacha and contemporary society*. KTAV Publishing House.

Sheskin, I. (2024). *Antisemitism in the United States: The impact of October 7*. Combat Antisemitism Movement. https://combatantisemitism.org/wp-content/uploads/2024/10/CAM-Antisemitism-in-US-Survey-Since-October7.pdf

Silverstein, Y., & Block, C. (2025). Making the invisible visible: A taxonomy of contemporary antisemitic experiences on college campuses. *Journal of Jewish Education*, April 10. https://doi.org/10.1080/15244113.2025.2482060

Soloveitchik, M. Y. (2024). The golden age of American Jewry hasn't ended. It may have just begun. *Mosaic*, December 30. https://mosaicmagazine.com/observation/history-ideas/2024/12/the-golden-age-of-american-jewry-hasnt-ended-it-may-have-just-begun

Soloveitchik, M. Y. (2025). Jewish identity vs. identity politics. *Sapir, 16*, pp. 1–14.

Sorkin, D. (2010). Is American Jewry exceptional? Comparing Jewish emancipation in Europe and America. *Journal of American Jewish History, 96*(3), 175–200.

Stark, R. (1999). Secularization, R.I.P. *Sociology of Religion, 60*(3), 249–273.

Taylor, C. (2007). *A secular age*. Harvard University Press.

Thulin, M. (2017). Shtadlanut. In *Encyclopedia of Jewish history and cultures online.* Brill. https://referenceworks.brill.com/view/entries/EJHC/COM-0806.xml

Ury, S., & Miron, G. (2024). *Antisemitism and the politics of history.* Brandeis University Press.

Windmueller, S. (2013). The Jewish contract with America. In D. Schnur (Ed.), *American politics and the Jewish community* (pp. 3–38). Purdue University Press.

Woocher, J. (1986). *Sacred survival: The civil religion of American Jews.* Indiana University Press.

Wright, G., et al. (2024). Antisemitism and polarization: the political dynamics of American Jewish concerns about traditional and Israel-related antisemitism. *Politics, Groups, and Identities, 12*(2), 457–475.

Zakai, S. (2022). *My second favorite country: How American Jewish children think about Israel.* New York University Press.

Solidarity, Criticism, and Complexity: Jewish Educators Responding to Difficult Times

Ezra Kopelowitz

Jewish Education and the Weave of Jewish Collective Belonging

Jewish educators' pedagogical responses to the fallout from the Hamas invasion of Israel on October 7, 2023, are an opportunity for understanding the role of educators in nurturing their learners' sense of belonging to the historic and global Jewish people. This chapter draws on survey research, interviews, and focus groups conducted in summer and fall 2024 that were designed to understand how educators approached teaching about Israel and other topics related to the fallout after October 7. Jewish educators exhibited three dominant approaches:

1. **solidarity**: emphasizing the need to foster love for and support of Israel and the Jewish people;
2. **criticism**: a focus on moral standards for Jewish life, which in the post-October 7 context translates into criticism of the Israeli government's conduct of the war and the response of the organized Jewish community;
3. **complexity**: balancing the desire for Jewish solidarity with encouraging learners to grapple with the complexity of the unfolding events, and the diverse reactions among Jews and beyond.

Each approach offers an important insight into one thread in the weave of Jewish collective belonging and the way Jewish educators understand their role in the post-October 7 context. This chapter argues that the solidarity, criticism, and complexity approaches, each on their own, are insufficient as educational responses. In times of socio-political crisis or when responding to a challenge to which there is no single agreed-upon Jewish path forward, an integrated educational approach is needed. Building on educators' responses to October 7, I suggest an integrative approach to Jewish education that draws on theories of peoplehood.

The Research

This chapter draws on research commissioned by the Jim Joseph Foundation and implemented in partnership with the Jewish Education Project and M²: The Institute for Experiential Jewish Education.[1] The study aimed to understand where Jewish educators stood nine months into the crisis (June/July 2024) and to suggest ways the organized Jewish community could support their work. The mixed-methods research was designed to generate a formative understanding of Jewish educators' responses to October 7.

Survey

The survey sought an understanding of educators' perceptions of October 7 as a historically significant event, their felt need to respond, understanding of major issues, confidence and capacity to act, and the support they require (Kopelowitz et al., 2024).[2] It was conducted from June 6 to July 31, 2024, with 1,281 responses obtained from lists distributed via sixteen Jewish educational organizations[3] and to individuals who responded to an earlier survey. Respondents were predominantly from the United States (eighty-six percent), with representation from fifteen other countries. They encompassed a

---

[1] I thank Rabbi Dena Klein, chief Jewish education officer of the Jewish Education Project, who served as a thought partner, providing invaluable feedback and support.
[2] The report is available for download on the websites of the Jim Joseph Foundation, the Jewish Education Project, M²: The Institute for Experiential Jewish Education, and the Center for Jewish Peoplehood Education. The survey dataset is available upon request.
[3] Supporting organizations include: ADCA, BBYO, For the Sake of Argument, Hillel International, the Jewish Education Project, Moishe House, M², NCSY, Pardes, Society for Humanistic Judaism, the Lookstein Center, UnitedEd, URJ (includes NFTY), USCJ, USY, and the Wexner Foundation.

broad range of years working in the field, age, educational sectors, learner age groups, and denominational affiliations (see Appendix 1).

Interviews

Ten in-depth interviews with senior Jewish education professionals were held in August 2024 to gain an in-depth understanding of how the selected group of master educators were grappling with the educational challenges described by the survey respondents. Five of the interviewees were nominated by the Jim Joseph Foundation and the Jewish Education Project due to their thought leadership in the field, and another five were selected due to the depth of their response to the survey and diverse approaches to Israel in Jewish education. A list of those interviewed is found in Appendix 2.

Focus Groups

Three online focus groups with sixty-four senior Jewish educators were held in September 2024 to receive formative feedback on the research team's analysis of the survey results and interview findings.

Educators Reaction to the Fallout from October 7

Widespread Agreement as to the Significance of the Fallout from October 7

As a group, the educators responding to the survey were in widespread agreement as to the historical significance of October 7 for Jewish education, with 99% of the respondents agreeing that we are in a critical historical moment for the Jewish people (see Exhibit 12.1). Eight to nine months in, 94% agreed that "I have an important role to play in helping my learners grapple with this historical moment" (see Exhibit 12.2).

Diverse Emotional and Educational Response

The fallout from October 7 evoked diverse emotions and educational goals among the Jewish educators who responded to the following four survey questions.

1. In your role as a Jewish professional in these difficult times, which of the following feelings do you frequently experience? Check all that apply.
2. In the post-October 7 context, what, in your opinion, are the dominant emotions your learners/constituents are expressing at this point in time that as a Jewish professional you need to consider? Select up to three choices.
3. In the post-October 7 context, which of the following questions do your learners/constituents ask most frequently? Select up to five choices.
4. In the post-October 7 context, which of the following are your principal educational objectives? Select up to three choices.

The educators' emotional reactions to the fallout from October 7 are overwhelmingly negative, with 65% reporting anxiety and 55% despair. Positive emotions, such as confidence (12%) and clarity (14%), were reported far less frequently. These negative emotions extended to the educators describing their learners experiencing confusion (60%), anger (46%), despair (39%), and concern for physical safety (37%). Positive learner emotions, such as hope (16%) and a sense of connection (15%), were uncommon, highlighting the difficult environment in which educators feel they are working.

The educators' reports on their students' questions provided context to intensely negative emotional environments and fears for personal safety. They reported that the most frequent questions learners asked centered on antisemitism: "How do I deal with antisemitism?" (58%), "Why do people hate us?" (40%), and "Where am I safe?" (20%). Three additional question categories appeared, all grappling with the disruptive nature of the post-October 7 context:

1. Jewish Solidarity: "How can I best support Israel at this time?" (36%) and "How can Jews best support one another at this time?" (18%);
2. Political Divides: Questions having to do with relationships across political divides, such as how best to maintain connections with Jews (33%) and non-Jews (30%) "who think differently than me about Israel";
3. Ethical Dilemmas: Questions focused on dilemmas stemming from Israel's conduct in the war, including the morality of Israel's actions in Gaza (26%) and balancing solidarity with empathy for Palestinians (19%). Questions reflecting the desire for active protest such as "How can I protest Israel's actions?" (6%) were less common.

The diversity of reactions extended to the educators' professional goals. 37% selected "providing knowledge," followed by a focus on solidarity and connection to Israel, with 34% aiming to strengthen Jewish solidarity and 25% nurturing a sense of connection to Israel. Around a third of respondents sought to facilitate respectful conversations (31%) or encourage complex thinking (29%). Emotional resilience was another focus, with educators seeking to convey hope or counteract despair (23%). Goals tied to promoting moral and ethical engagement, such as addressing moral dilemmas (14%), grappling with challenges through a values lens (12%), or conveying empathy for Palestinian suffering (7%), were less common. Goals focused on supporting ethically or morally driven activism were the least cited whether focused on support for Israel advocacy (11%) or supporting protests against Israeli policies (2%).

Dominant Educational Approaches—Solidarity, Complexity and Criticism

The diverse answers to the survey questions discussed in the previous section show that no single educational goal emerged from the Jewish educators' responses to the fallout from October 7. Rather, when the educators' goals and their assessment of their learners' emotions and questions are analyzed for statistical correlations (Exhibit 12.3), three distinct educational approaches can be identified.

Based on the respondents' educational goals, the questions that educators are asking, and their recollections of learners' questions, these approaches can be labeled as "solidarity," "complexity," and "critical" educational strategies. These labels were created and refined drawing on a parallel analysis of the written survey responses (shown below), and formative discussions of the data with the research stakeholders and educator focus groups. The final formulation of the labels resonated with the stakeholders and educators, reflecting their personal understanding of prevailing Jewish educational worldviews and practices after the October 7 crisis in general, and Israel in Jewish education in particular.

The Solidarity Approach—59% of Respondents

Emphasis: Focuses on fostering Jewish mutual support and emphasizes unity and collective pride in Israel.

- **Attributed Learners' Emotions:** "Identification with Israel" (71%).
- **Attributed Learners' Questions:** "How can I best support Israel?" (60%), "Why do people hate us?" (59%), "How can I explain to others Israel's moral high ground in executing this war?" (29%).
- **Unique Educational Goals:** Strengthening connections to Israel (42%), and "To support advocacy for Israel" (20%).

The Complexity Approach—25% of Respondents

Emphasis. Aims to balance support for Israel with helping learners navigate the confusion and divisiveness of the post-October 7 period by engaging in critical thinking and dialogue.

- **Attributed Learners' Emotions:** "Confusion" (80%).
- **Attributed Learners' Questions:** Key questions include "How can I maintain relationships with Jews who think differently about Israel?" (57%) and "Are Israel's actions in Gaza morally defensible?" (46%).
- **Unique Educational Goals:** Respectful conversations (56%) and encouraging complex thinking (50%).

The Criticism Approach—16% of Respondents

Emphasis. Like the complexity educators, these educators are also concerned with respectful conversation. They allow for the expression of opposing viewpoints and encourage complex thinking. These integrate with the following unique attributes that center on moral accountability, challenging communal norms with a focus on empathy for Palestinians and policy critiques.

- **Attributed Learners' Emotions:** "Antipathy towards Israel" (62%).
- **Attributed Learners' Questions:** "How can we hold Israeli and Palestinian lives as equally valuable?" (66%) and "How can I identify with the Jewish people when Israel is inflicting pain on Palestinians?" (53%).
- **Unique Educational Goals:** Empathy for Palestinians' suffering (35%) and supporting protests of Israeli policy (15%).

Collective Belonging and Desired Educational Outcomes after October 7

The solidarity, complexity, and critical approaches each provide a unique angle in answering the following two questions:

- How do individuals understand themselves as belonging to the Jewish people?; and
- What is the role of Jewish educators in nurturing that connection?

To understand the significance of the different approaches, the following analysis shows how they align with three foundational approaches to collective belonging in sociological theory. Each educational approach, while providing critical insight into the nature of Jewish collective belonging, has drawbacks from an educational perspective. I offer a fourth approach, labeled here as peoplehood education, which incorporates elements of each of the three other approaches and offers a more robust framework for educators whose goal is to nurture the connection of their learners to one another, their community, and the Jewish people in the post-October 7 context and beyond.

Four Approaches to Collective Belonging and Jewish Education in the Post-October 7 Context

Solidarity Approach

Theoretical Foundation. The solidarity approach to education aligns with the Durkheimian school in sociological theory, which posits that shared and agreed upon values, rituals, symbols, and collective memories are central to building and maintaining group cohesion. Durkheim (1995) argued that this shared basis of group life generates a collective consciousness, binding individuals into a moral or sacred community that transcends their individual interests and sense of self. The assumption is that all members of the group *should* hold this "sacred" basis of group life in common for their social group to survive and thrive.

Expression after October 7. As is seen in exhibit 12.3, in their reaction to the fallout from October 7, most Jewish educators are solidarity educators.

Solidarity educators emphasize fostering pride, unity, and mutual support by highlighting what they perceive as the shared and agreed-upon building blocks of Jewish collective identification. In this educational worldview, Israel is a symbol of Jewish resilience and hope in the Jewish fight against common enemies, challenges such as antisemitism at home, and forces of evil such as Hamas.

For solidarity educators, Israel integrates into Jewish education as a means for inculcating and reinforcing a "love of Israel"[4] and, in so doing, strengthening Jewish peoplehood. The open text responses from participants identified as solidarity educators show a focus on acquiring knowledge with focus on the ability of Israel and the Jewish people to overcome adversity. These areas of knowledge are taught in classroom environments and/or reinforced by ceremonies focusing on the celebration of Israel's independence, Israeli music and culture, or commemoration and contribution having to do with Israel in times of war or tragedy.

Discussions of the war are often intentionally brief and contextualized to maintain the focus on Israel as a source of inspiration, or focus on advocacy in support of Israel. The primary educational focus is on strengthening Jewish solidarity through activities that cultivate a shared sense of purpose and belonging. Educators both create intimate educational settings and involve themselves in broader political action, as the following examples from two educators[5] show:

> We continue to teach children about Israel in a positive light without dwelling on the war. We initially did age-appropriate discussions about what was going on. Then we proceeded to teach love of Israel as part of our curriculum. Truthfully, the kids don't talk much about the war. We are very focused on solidarity with Israel, bringing *shinshinim*[6] to do program-

---

[4] On the focus on "love of Israel" in Jewish education see Novak Winer (2024, pp. 283–285); Zakai (2016); Kopelowitz and Pitkowsky (2024, pp. 313–315); Grant and Kopelowitz (2012, pp. 7–8); Pomson et al. (2009).

[5] All quotes detailing the educational strategies are taken from written responses to a survey question that asked respondents in three parts 1) to detail their greatest post-October 7 related challenge, 2) to describe their educational response, and 3) to provide an example.

[6] *Shinshinim* (שינשינים) are Israeli high school graduates who defer their military service for a year to volunteer as informal educators in Jewish communities abroad, fostering connections between Israel and the Jews living outside of Israel.

ming, and singing "Hatikvah" and "Am Yisrael Chai" every school session.

I am working to help Jews who have been swept up by the antizionist media propaganda and the hateful pro-Palestinian mobs on campus to step away from the trend, learn more, and love their Jewish family here and in Israel. I address it through classes, sermons, video messages, special speakers, supporting Jewish students and faculty who are being harassed, meeting and organizing with local and state elected officials (including school boards and college chancellors).

Drawback. The emphasis of these two educators is on solidarity in the face of adversity. There is no intention to develop a systematic approach for supporting learners in navigating the diversity of Jewish and other responses to difficult questions and challenging situations. The outcome is that learners are not given the opportunity to form their own understanding of what "the ideal Jewish response" should be.

Complexity Approach

Theoretical Foundation. Ethnomethodology (Garfinkel, 1984; Sudnow, 1972) is a school of thought developed in opposition to Durkheimian sociology and conflict theory. Like the Durkheimian school, the focus is on the way shared meaning and understanding anchor an individual's relationship to a social group. "Shared meaning" is generated in a fluid and dynamic process resulting from interaction between members of a social group. However, unlike conflict theorists, ethnomethodologists do not assume that social change must be rooted in conflict. Rather, the generative nature of social interaction is simply the outcome of the very nature of humans interacting with one another.

The way we understand what is occurring around us is not dependent on an overarching ethical or moral principle that determines right from wrong. How "I understand who I am" as a member of a social group is generated from communication with others in particular contexts. In the communicative act, words, concepts, shared memories, values, sacred objects, and associations are used to enable each person to recognize the other as a member of a common social group, and to understand one's place in the group. But the meaning and implications of those shared associations depend on context and the dynamic of the interaction. The result is an understanding of collective belonging that assumes a moral core in terms of shared knowledge, memory and sacred objects. However, the interpretation of what that core means to individuals has never ending variations that generate social change.

Expression after October 7. Using ethnomethodology as a frame of reference, complexity educators, unlike solidarity or criticism educators, do not base their understanding of Jewish collective identification as a litmus test of "the right Jewish approach" in response to a crisis like the fallout from October 7. Complexity educators encourage an understanding of "who we are as Jews" that emerges out of formative interactions between individuals with different points of view and life experiences. This approach values communication across differences, promoting empathy and dialogue as tools for sustaining relationships between Jews despite differences.

In the complexity approach, October 7 represents a collective trauma that triggers associations with Israel and shared historical memories of violence against Jews—memories that Jews will pay attention to and which inform the manner they interpret the intense media coverage and widespread public discussion of the unfolding events. Jews are members of the Jewish people because they perceive Israel as a country different from any other. Jews' shared memory influences an understanding of "who we are vis-à-vis one another and the wider society in which we live."

While complexity educators tend to identify as pro-Israel or as Zionists, their focus is not to advocate for support of Israel, but rather to equip learners with the skills to navigate the tensions inherent in belonging to a community or group that holds a broad spectrum of ideological beliefs. No single overarching opinion on the issue of the day should disqualify a person from participation in an educational program. The goal is placing the value of Jewish community and social cohesion as a governing principle. The following is an example from one Jewish educator:

> The monolithic/defensive approach of the organized Jewish Community that is NOT behaving in alignment with Jewish values of *pikuach nefesh*[7] and *elu v'elu*.[8] Most Reform Jews believe in *tikkun olam* but suddenly even the Reform

---

7   *Pikuach nefesh* (פיקוח נפש) is the Jewish principle that preserving human life overrides almost all other religious commandments.
8   *Elu v'elu* (אֵלוּ וְאֵלוּ) is a Talmudic phrase meaning "These and those [are the words of the living God]," expressing the idea that multiple interpretations of Jewish law or tradition can be valid and divinely inspired.

> movement has become unidimensional and shaming of diversity. I am working to create spaces for healing and connection, to honor diversity, but I feel hampered by the one-sided/not Jewish responses of most people who are scared to question because even the Reform movement has become Orthodox in its response. Where is the big tent that we say we are trying to build????

Complexity educators prioritize respectful dialogue among learners with differing viewpoints, modeling how to hold multiple truths simultaneously, while expressing and forming one's opinion and response. They emphasize the importance of maintaining communal bonds even amid ideological disagreements, framing this as a critical skill for navigating Jewish belonging in today's polarized world. Educational activities described by complexity educators in the survey include structured debates, reflective journaling, and collaborative projects that require learners to grapple with their relationship to one another and big issues of the moment. Below are two examples:

> Our goal is to teach love for Israel without shying away from its challenges. We talk openly about the difficulties but also emphasize the values and commitments that bind us as a people.

> While I agree we should teach a love for Israel we should also help our students understand that it's okay to disagree. Mainly how important it is to have meaningful conversations and listen to others.

Though the educators who adopted a complexity approach are a minority, among academics and other thought leaders who focus on "Israel education," the complexity approach is dominant. In their review of approaches to Israel education, Davis and Alexander (2023) argue that there is near broad consensus among all approaches to Israel education that educators should engage learners "with Israel in all its multiple complexities, voices, and narratives" (p. 21).[9]

---

9   Within the field of Jewish education, intellectual discussions of Jewish collectivity are most robust within the field of Israel education that has developed in recent decades. A broader discourse with a focus on education for collective Jewish identity is relatively limited and

Drawback. The complexity approach offers a strategy for enabling engagement with diversity for the sake of education, and community building in the context of crisis. Complexity educators treat their personal ideological stance on a particular issue as secondary, and view tensions between people in disagreement as opportunities for positive growth. Engaging with diversity and complexity in an intentional manner strengthens learners' connection to one another, their community, and the Jewish people. However, complexity cannot stand as a goal unto itself. Alongside communication across differences and learning about complex issues, there is a need to inculcate the "sacred," shared knowledge, beliefs, and practices that enable Jews in the first place to view Jewish communal life as specifically Jewish and personally meaningful (Davis and Alexander, 2023, pp. 22–25). How does education that embraces complexity provide an answer to the question, "What do Jews as a collective share as sacred?"

Criticism Approach

Theoretical Foundation. This approach aligns with the sociological tradition often labeled as "conflict theory," which views the ties between members of social groups as emerging not from "solidarity," but rather the ability of individuals to manage their disagreements. Conflict is inherent to group life, down to the most intimate settings of human interaction, such as the diverse interests and desires that lead to tension between parents and between them and their children. Members of a social group negotiate behavioral norms and moral frameworks, and they create and shape institutions to enable sustainable relationships despite their differences.

Conflict theory includes two distinct traditions, rooted in the works of Georg Simmel (1955) and Karl Marx (2015). The interpretation of conflict theory draws selectively on both traditions. Simmel's approach emphasizes the productive nature of conflict in shaping group dynamics and social structures, viewing conflict as generative for the continual shaping of relationships within and between groups. Marx's conflict theory provides a moral critique of inequality, with class conflict as the driving force to achieve desired social change. In this chapter I consider both the generative nature of conflict as well as the role of moral critique in the post-October 7 context.

---

requires a separate discussion. In this area, the works of Horowitz (2008); Kress (2012); and Chazan et al. (2013) are notable contributions as discussed in Kopelowitz (2021) and Kopelowitz and Pitkowsky (2024).

Expression after October 7. Drawing on the survey responses, what can be seen is that in the post-October 7 context, some criticism educators consider themselves "pro-Israel" or "Zionist," and others think of themselves as "antizionist." The common denominator is that all view the fallout from October 7 as an opportunity to challenge learners to think critically about what it means to support Israel while upholding human and Jewish values in a time of crisis. Conflict results from the educators' challenge to normative "establishment" assumptions. The educators desire a generative outcome, for the good of their learners and their relationship to the Jewish people and for desired change in the broader Jewish community. Criticism is viewed as an essential educational tool for forming deep and essential commitments to higher human and Jewish ethical standards.

Recognizing that many learners were grappling with questions about justice, ethics, and the morality of Israel's actions, criticism educators sought to validate and/or encourage those inquiries rather than dismiss them. Their written responses to the survey questions explore topics like the moral implications of the Israeli government's wartime decisions (including the treatment of Palestinians) and a rebuttal of the labelling of campus protestors and other critics of Israel as antisemites. As seen in the following two quotes, critical educators seek to expand knowledge and understanding of the multiple Jewish and Palestinian narratives about the political and historical context of the Israeli Palestinian conflict and they encourage communication across differences.

> I am a strong Zionist but am furious that there's been no disavowal of Kahanism[10] from major American Jewish institutions, despite Kahanism's role in so much of the current horror show. Meanwhile I am watching my students who engage with Olami get pulled to a rightwing constituency that dehumanizes Muslims. I make sure to maintain good relationships with all students and don't ostracize them when I struggle with the political beliefs they're acquiring because, if our organization ostracizes them, it will make them even more steely. (Zionist critical educator)

---

10 Kahanism refers to the extremist Jewish nationalist ideology founded by Rabbi Meir Kahane, advocating for Jewish supremacy, the expulsion of Arabs from Israel and the Palestinian territories, and the establishment of a theocratic state. It is widely considered racist and has been banned in Israel as a form of incitement to violence and terrorism.

As an antizionist Jew in a senior leadership position in a congregation, I am filled with anxiety as horrors in Gaza are ignored and as a result feel disconnected from Judaism—which has been my life force for my whole life. I led a dual narrative session for fifth to seventh grade using the young readers version of *The Lemon Tree*. We used an inquiry-based model and studied side by side narratives of Israeli and Palestinian history of key events that provide context for the book (British Mandate, 1948, 1967). (Antizionist critical educator)

Drawback. These two quotes illustrate both the strength and weakness of the criticism approach. The focus is on the learners' engagement with the social and moral fiber of collective Jewish life, encouraging critical thinking. The result is an understanding of collective belonging that views conflict with a moral purpose as generative but also tends to pay relatively little attention to the knowledge, values, practices, and institutions that Jews as a group regard as "sacred." What is the responsibility of the Jewish educator to nurturing the emotional bonds between Jews that enable their learners to identify as part of a diverse Jewish people? How does the answer to this question play out when one is confronted by someone who does not hold the "the right" response to a particular moral or political challenge?

Peoplehood Approach

The solidarity approach fosters Jewish unity and pride but often sidesteps difficult conversations, limiting critical engagement and potentially alienating those with diverse perspectives. The complexity approach encourages dialogue and multiple perspectives, yet it lacks a clear moral or emotional anchor, leaving learners without a strong sense of collective identity. The critical approach emphasizes moral reflection and challenges communal norms but can weaken emotional bonds to Jewish peoplehood, making it harder to cultivate a sense of belonging. Each approach provides valuable insights but, on its own, falls short of offering a holistic educational response to the challenges after October 7.

Peoplehood education is an approach to collective Jewish belonging that builds on the strengths of each of the solidarity, critical and complexity approaches. It addresses their drawbacks in order to provide Jewish educators with a holistic framework for responding to challenges faced by the Jewish people, such as the fallout from October 7. The educator's goal is to ensure that learners develop both an emotional bond with the Jewish people and the ability to grapple with complexity and moral challenges. Unlike the other approaches, peoplehood education prioritizes Jewish collective narratives as a foundation while allowing for diverse interpretations.

Theoretical Foundation. The peoplehood approach to Jewish education integrates several theoretical frameworks that together address the limitations identified in the solidarity, complexity, and critical strategies outlined earlier in this chapter. It emphasizes shared narratives, moral frameworks, and transcendent experiences as the building blocks of Jewish collective belonging—especially important in the context of upheaval following October 7.

As Rogers Brubaker (2004) argues, collective belonging is not a fixed or static attribute, but rather a dynamic process shaped by shared narratives. This understanding counters the potential rigidity of solidarity-oriented education, which sometimes treats Jewish Peoplehood as uniform or immutable. By recognizing belonging as fluid yet emotionally resonant, Peoplehood education offers a more nuanced and inclusive framework. Particularly in the post-October 7 landscape, it becomes essential to affirm shared trauma and memory while making space for the diversity of Jewish responses.

Shared Jewish narratives serve a deeper function than simply linking individuals through a common past; they form the moral architecture within which individuals locate themselves and their obligations to others. Rogers Smith (2003, 2015) refers to these as "constitutive stories," which not only define the group but offer ethical guidance. This perspective bridges the solidarity and critical approaches. While critical educators challenge communal norms by applying external or "universal" ethical standards, Peoplehood educators recognize that the group's own stories already contain moral resources. Rather than breaking emotional bonds through critique, this approach encourages learners to reflect critically within the narrative frameworks that anchors their connection to the Jewish people.

Peoplehood education also addresses a gap found in the complexity approach: while complexity educators cultivate learners' ability to appreciate multiple perspectives, they often lack a framework for anchoring belonging within that diversity. Shlomi Ravid's (2021) concept of "peoplehood consciousness" fills this gap. It integrates emotional, cognitive, and communal aspects of Jewish affiliation, affirming diversity while nurturing a unifying sense of connection. In times of crisis, such as the aftermath of October 7, this consciousness enables learners to hold tensions without retreating into disconnection or ideological silos.

Transcendent experiences offer another dimension, one often underdeveloped in critical educational strategies. Drawing on Kopelowitz (2014), these experiences—such as commemorations, shared rituals, and engagement with sacred texts—forge emotional connections that transcend ideological divides and geographic distances. In the current moment, marked by intense political and moral disagreement, these experiences become critical to sustaining a sense of peoplehood. They create opportunities for learners to feel a bond with the broader Jewish community even when struggling with its actions or narratives.

Taken together, these foundations establish a peoplehood approach that addresses key limitations of the other three strategies. It provides the emotional grounding missing in complexity education, the openness to interpretation lacking in solidarity models, and the communal coherence often absent in critical pedagogy. It recognizes collective Jewish belonging as both grounded in sacred stories and open to ongoing reinterpretation (Brubaker, 2004; Smith, 2003, 2015). It affirms diversity as a core feature of Jewish life (Ravid, 2021), while upholding the role of transcendent moments in binding Jews together across difference (Kopelowitz, 2014).

In moments of crisis, this integrated framework neither collapses complexity into consensus nor allows ideological divisions to sever communal bonds. Instead, it calls on educators to help learners sustain connection through critical reflection, shared memory, and active participation in shaping Jewish collective life. It prepares them not only to belong, but to contribute meaningfully to an evolving peoplehood—an essential capacity in times that test both the emotional and moral fabric of Jewish community.

Expression after October 7. The peoplehood approach avoids narrow ideological stances on how constitutive Jewish stories should be interpreted and it explicitly recognizes Jewish diversity. It prioritizes diversity as a core value. For example, from a peoplehood perspective, "Israel"—from biblical times to today—is integral to the shared Jewish narrative. The "Land of Israel" is not merely a geographical location, nor is the modern State of Israel just another country; both hold deep symbolic significance. However, the implications of Israel within Jewish collective consciousness vary based on ideological interpretations of this shared story.

In the aftermath of October 7, both Zionist and antizionist Jews acknowledge Israel as integral to the shared Jewish story but differ on its implications. These disagreements span issues such as Israel's conduct in the war, the Jewish state's contribution to the Jewish People, or the fundamental need for a Jewish state. The peoplehood educational approach aims to strengthen collective

Jewish consciousness while emphasizing the principle that diverse ideological interpretations of the Jewish connection to Israel shape our actions.

The following response from a congregational rabbi captures the essence of the peoplehood educational approach. It acknowledges Israel's centrality in their synagogue community, even amid differing political perspectives. The congregants' passion reflects Israel's integral role in their sense of Jewish belonging. After October 7, the rabbi has avoided taking an ideological stance, instead emphasizing the hope that engaging with Israel through formative Jewish learning experiences—rooted in Jewish diversity—will deepen emotional bonds within the community and strengthen congregants' connections to their Jewish community.

> [My challenge is] holding together a completely diverse group of community members in how they are in relationship with Israel. Leaning in, not shying away. Holding a lot of pastoral conversations when it comes to Israel. Understanding that people are passionate, and it's because they care. Reading as a community *Can We Talk about Israel?* by Daniel Sokatch.

Bonding with the historical and global Jewish people while learning new knowledge invites learners to ask, "Who am I?" and "Where do I stand?" For example, a day school history teacher recalibrated their approach to teaching the history of the Zionist movement after October 7. The focus shifted to making history relevant to current events, encouraging learners to grapple with ethical and moral questions surrounding Zionism, both past and present.

> Helping the students put the conflict and the anger at Israel and American Jews in historical context. Students don't have enough background. I teach a lot of history through primary sources. I've gone back to the early Zionist writing of the late nineteenth and early twentieth centuries to show how intense the antisemitism was then without a Jewish state as a refuge.

In the following quote, a congregational rabbi explores the complexity of being both "Americans" and "Jews." By teaching historical knowledge and Jewish religious texts, the rabbi fosters emotional bonding among congregants and with the Jewish people, while encouraging introspection and thoughtful responses to the complexities of current events.

We discussed a Hillel teaching in our first open sanctuary after 10/7. We reminded ourselves of where we were as Americans on the evening of 9/11, and then looked at the text. It was much easier now for most to prioritize, as we did in 2001, the need to be for ourselves, yet not completely having to question who we are by not abandoning completely our concern for others. The greatest discussion focused on our realization that both of these events moved our understanding from an imperative for timely action to a rueful prayer that, when the time became right again, we could recalibrate back towards the ideal of these words.

Conclusion: Weaving the Strands of Education for Collective Jewish Identification

Although rooted in the post-October 7 context, which framed the survey responses from Jewish educators, I contend that the solidarity, critical, and complexity approaches are relevant to any situation where Jews grapple with responding to crises or major challenges. Should we turn inward, do we circle the wagons and to support one another as Jews? Strive for an overarching ethical principle? Or ensure inclusion of diverse opinions within our communities and institutions?

Most survey respondents leaned toward one strategy, with the majority favoring the solidarity approach. Peoplehood education provides a framework that integrates solidarity, criticism, and complexity, fostering collective Jewish identification while addressing the limitations of each approach and amplifying their strengths.

Solidarity

Like the solidarity approach, peoplehood education underscores the importance of fostering strong emotional bonds between the learner and the Jewish people. Jewish bonding is central, as it anchors individuals within the collective and cultivates a sense of pride and belonging. Unlike solidarity-focused education, which often relies on idealized monolithic portrayals of Jewish life and Israel, Peoplehood education assumes diversity, conflict, and complexity. It encourages learners to reflect on their personal positions within collective Jewish life, understand both their similarities to and differences from other Jews, and formulate thoughtful responses to challenges.

Critical

From the critical approach, peoplehood education adopts a commitment to ethical reflection and moral accountability. Learners are encouraged to sharpen the understanding of Jewish ethics and values that guide their understanding of the world, and to grapple with the resulting ethical dilemmas. Yet, while the criticism approach promotes a particular set of ethical or moral imperatives upon which good and evil are distinguished, peoplehood education only assumes Jewish diversity in responding to crisis and challenge as the starting point for nurturing the relationship between the learner, their Jewish community, and the Jewish people. Peoplehood educators recognize conflict as integral to Jewish life but prioritize an effort at communication across differences for constructive engagement that strengthens the relationship between Jews, rather than divisiveness.

Complexity

Like the complexity approach, peoplehood education values nuance and the capacity to hold multiple perspectives, while forming one's personal opinion. Peoplehood educators also seek to equip learners to recognize and navigate their differences, while fostering respectful dialogue and empathy and recognizing that the meaning of membership in the Jewish people is ever evolving. However, the complexity approach does not make explicit the shared basis of Jewish collective life. For this reason, peoplehood education emphasizes the unifying power and sacred status of constitutive Jewish stories that are ever evolving. Peoplehood educators recognize the generative role of Jewish diversity, while seeking to deepen knowledge of constitutive Jewish stories. The goal is to address the learners' sense of emotional bond with the other Jews and the historical and global Jewish people.

Peoplehood

In conclusion, the responses of Jewish educators to the fallout from October 7 tend to emphasize solidarity, critical, or complexity approaches to nurturing collective Jewish belonging. This article suggests that peoplehood education combines the best of these approaches. The examples culled from the survey responses and quoted above show a peoplehood educational approach that recognizes shared Jewish memory in which antisemitism, past and present, ancient and contemporary Israel are part of an ever-evolving constitutive story. The educator approaches learning as an opportunity to consider ethical dilemmas, while navigating the tensions inherent in diverse Jewish perspectives. Rooted both in the constitutive stories and evolving dynamics of Jewish life, peoplehood educators pay attention to emotional as well as cognitive bonds between their learners and the Jewish people. In times of crisis, such as experienced after October 7, this integrative framework provides a pathway for educators to respond in a manner that builds and fortifies connections between Jews, without ignoring the differences between them.

Although shifting educators' default approaches to teaching Israel in moments of crisis may be challenging, peoplehood education shows a way forward by calling attention to a goal that most Jewish educators regard as important—nurturing collective Jewish belonging. Peoplehood education does not negate the desire of an educator to teach for solidarity, complexity or criticism, but rather prioritizes active engagement with Jewish collective belonging as an evolving process. Solidarity, complexity, and criticism are entry points for learners to explore their own relationship to Jewish community and the Jewish people. By fostering both intellectual inquiry and emotional connection, peoplehood education empowers learners to interpret, question, and shape the stories that define the Jewish people. Ultimately, this approach instills the understanding that Jewish belonging is not passively inherited but actively constructed, with each learner contributing to the ever-evolving collective narratives of the Jewish people—narratives in which both ancient and modern Israel play an integral role.

Exhibits

Exhibit 12.1 *We Are in a Critical Historical Moment for the Jewish People*

Statement	Percentage
Very strongly agree	73%
Strongly agree	19%
Agree	6%
Neither agree nor disagree	1%
Disagree to very strongly disagree	0%
Total	100%
Number of respondents	1375

Note. The survey item read as follows: "In thinking about the events unfolding since October 7, do you agree or disagree that 'we are in a critical historical moment for the Jewish people'?"

Exhibit 12.2 *I Have an Important Role to Play in Helping My Learners Grapple with This Historical Moment*

Statement	Percentage
Very strongly agree	44%
Strongly agree	31%
Agree	19%
Neither agree nor disagree	5%
Disagree to very strongly disagree	1%
Total	100%
Number of respondents	1213

Note. The survey item read as follows: "In thinking about the events unfolding since October 7, do you agree or disagree that 'I have an important role to play in helping my learners grapple with this historical moment'?"

Exhibit 12.3 *Dominant Educational Approaches*

Type of Question	Solidarity Items	59% are Solidarity Educators	25% are Complexity Educators	16% are Critical Educators
Attributed learners' emotions	Identification with Israel	71%	19%	27%
Attributed learners' questions	How can I best support Israel at this time?	60%	8%	11%
Attributed learners' questions	Why do people hate us?	59%	25%	12%
Educator's goal	To nurture a sense of connection to Israel	42%	4%	6%
Attributed learners' questions	How can I explain to others Israel's moral high ground in executing this war?	29%	5%	5%

(Continued)

Exhibit 12.3 *Dominant Educational Approaches* **(Continued)**

Educator's goal	To support advocacy for Israel	20%	0%	2%
	Complexity Items	**Solidarity**	**Complexity**	**Critical**
Attributed learners' emotions	Confusion	56%	80%	68%
Attributed learners' questions	How can I maintain relationships with Jews who think differently than I do about Israel?	23%	57%	52%
Educator's goal	To facilitate respectful conversation and allow for expression of opposing viewpoints	20%	56%	49%
Educator's goal	To encourage complex thinking	22%	50%	42%
Attributed learners' questions	Are Israel's actions in Gaza morally defensible?	17%	46%	49%
Attributed learners' questions	How do I stand for my own people while not closing my heart to the Palestinians?	14%	36%	22%

(Continued)

Exhibit 12.3 *Dominant Educational Approaches* **(Continued)**

	Critical Items	Solidarity	Complexity	Critical
Attributed learners' questions	How can we hold Israeli and Palestinians lives as equally valuable?	6%	18%	66%
Attributed learners' emotions	Antipathy towards Israel	4%	10%	62%
Attributed learners' questions	How can I identify with the Jewish people when Israel is inflicting pain on the Palestinians?	2%	8%	53%
Attributed learners' questions	How can I protest Israel's actions in Gaza?	1%	1%	38%
Educator's goal	To convey empathy for Palestinians' suffering	1%	4%	35%
Educator's goal	To support protest of Israeli policy	0%	0%	15%

Note. The table shows the respondents who are categorized as solidarity, complexity, and criticism educators, with a focus on the percentage of each group that selected a given educational goal, learners' emotions and questions. Respondents were assigned to one of the three strategies if they scored positively on at least two of the six items shown for each. 10% qualified for none of the three groups. 13% qualified on more than one. If so, they were assigned to one of the types based on the following priority order: Critical, Solidarity, Complexity.

Appendices

Appendix 1: Respondents to the Survey

Sector

Synagogue / congregation / minyan / religious organization	43%
Jewish day school / yeshiva	23%
Jewish supplementary school (e.g., Hebrew school, Sunday school, after-school program)	22%
College campus Jewish organization (e.g., Hillel, Chabad on Campus)	14%
Jewish youth group / movement	11%
Engagement	11%
Jewish preschool or early childhood center	7%
Something else	7%
Jewish summer camp	6%
Social justice / service learning	6%
Self-employed / independent contractor / "gig" worker	6%
Jewish Federation / foundation	5%
Israel education / advocacy organization	4%
JCC	4%
Innovation	4%

Note. The survey item read as follows: "Which of the following best describe the sector of the Jewish community in which you work? Select all that apply"

Population of Learners

Early childhood	18%
Elementary school age	42%
Teens (middle and high school)	55%
College Age	23%
Young Adult learners (20s and 30s)	23%
Adults (40+)	35%
Families	28%
Seniors	19%
Other	4%

Note. The survey item read as follows: "With which populations of learners do you work most intensively? Select all that apply"

Institution Denomination

Haredi	1%
Chabad	0%
Orthodox (other than Haredi or Chabad)	11%
Conservative	15%
Reform	28%
Reconstructionist	2%
Other	6%
More than one	13%
None—it is non-denominational	25%
Total	100%

Note. The survey item read as follows: "Thinking of the institution(s) where you work, with which denomination, if any, is it (or are they) most identified?"

Age

18 to 24	5%
25 to 29	8%
30 to 34	9%
35 to 39	11%
40 to 49	27%
50 to 50	20%
60 or older	20%
Total	100%

Note. The survey item read as follows: "How old are you?"

Work as Jewish Educator

Less than 5	12%
5–9	13%
10–14	15%
15–19	15%
20 or more	46%
Total	100%

Note. The survey item read as follows: "For how many years have you worked as a Jewish educator, in any way, either full time or part time?"

Appendix 2: Interviews Conducted

1. Jamie Simon, chief program officer, Foundation for Jewish Camp, New York, NY
2. Dr. Jonathan Golden, founder, HeartStance Education Consulting, Boston, MA
3. Liron Lipsky, director of education, BBYO, remote
4. Sharon Tash, director of education, Temple Micah, Washington, D.C.
5. Dr. Joy Getnick, executive director, University of Rochester Hillel, Rochester, NY

6. Rabbi Rick Kellner, rabbi, Congregation Beit Tikvah, Columbus, OH
7. Senior congregational educator (requested anonymity)
8. Jay Leberman, head of school, Mandel Jewish Day School, Cleveland, OH
9. Rabbi Shira Koch Epstein, executive director, Atra: Center for Rabbinical Innovation, remote
10. Chaya Silver, education director, Agudas Achim, NFTY—The Reform Jewish Youth Movement, Alexandria, VA

References

Brubaker, R. (2004). *Ethnicity without groups*. Harvard University Press.

Chazan, B. (2016). *A Philosophy of Israel education: A relational approach*. Palgrave Macmillan.

Chazan, B., Chazan, R., and Jacobs, B. M. (2013). *Cultures and contexts of Jewish education*. Palgrave Macmillan.

Davis, B., and Alexander, H. (2023). Israel education: A philosophical analysis. *Journal of Jewish Education, 89*(1), 6–33.

Davis, B., and Alexander, H. (2024). "You never told me": The pedagogical content knowledge (PCK) of Israel education. *Contemporary Jewry, 44*(2), 369–395. https://doi.org/10.1007/s12397-024-09562-w

Durkheim, E. (1995). *The elementary forms of religious life*. Free Press. (Original work published 1912.)

Garfinkel, H. (1984). *Studies in ethnomethodology*. Polity Press. (Original work published 1967.)

Grant, L., and Kopelowitz, E. (2012). *Israel education matters: A 21st century paradigm for Jewish education*. Center for Jewish Peoplehood Education.

Horowitz, B. (2008). New frontiers: "Milieu" and the sociology of American Jewish education. *Journal of Jewish Education, 74*(1), 68–81.

Kopelowitz, E. (2014). A Sociologist's guide for building Jewish peoplehood. In E. Kopelowitz and M. Revivi (Eds.), *Jewish peoplehood: change and challenge* (pp. 45–56). Academic Studies Press.

Kopelowitz, E. (2021). A framework for evaluating success in Jewish education. *Jewish Educational Leadership 19*(2), The Lookstein Center, Bar Ilan University.

Kopelowitz, E., and Pitkowsky, A. (2024). Nurturing Jewish consciousness: Utilizing values at synagogue supplementary schools to teach Israel. In S. Zakai and M. Reingold (Eds.), *Teaching Israel: Studies of pedagogy from the field* (pp. 309–332). Brandeis University Press.

Kopelowitz, E., Franco Galor, H., and Gillis, J. (2023). *Responding to this historical moment: Jewish educators, clergy, engagement professionals and the war in Israel.* M^2: The Institute for Experiential Jewish Education and the Jim Joseph Foundation.

Kopelowitz, E., Ravid S., Posklinsky I., Golden J., and Gillis, J. (2024). *Responding to the fallout from October 7th: From crisis to opportunity.* Research report commissioned by the Jim Joseph Foundation. Center for Jewish Peoplehood Education.

Marx, K., and Engels F. (2015). *The communist manifesto.* Penguin Books. (Original work published 1848.)

Novak Winer, L. (2024). "Teaching who they are: Understanding teachers' connections with Israel and how those enter into the classroom." In S. Zakai and M. Reingold (Eds.), *Teaching Israel: Studies of pedagogy from the field* (pp. 283–308). Brandeis University Press.

Pomson, A., Deitcher H., and Muszkat-Barkan, M. (2009). *Israel education in North American day schools: A systems analysis and some strategies for change.* Melton Center for Jewish Education, The Hebrew University of Jerusalem.

Ravid, S. (2021). "Building Jewish peoplehood: A work in progress." *Peoplehood Papers,* 30(August), 95–102.

Simmel, G. (1955). *The Web of group affiliations.* Free Press. (Original work published 1922.)

Smith, R. (2003). *Stories of peoplehood: The politics and morals of political membership.* Cambridge University Press.

Smith, R. (2015). *Political peoplehood: The roles of values, interests, and identities.* University of Chicago Press.

Sudnow, D. (1972). *Studies in social interaction.* Free Press.

Beyond Tinkering: Adjustments to Israel Education in the Aftermath of October 7

Alex Pomson and Samantha Vinokor-Meinrath

Background

To what extent have the events of October 7 and the subsequent war influenced the practices of those engaged in the work of Israel education? And, more broadly, how have these events contributed to adjustments in the organization of Israel education, and specifically in the relationships between Israel education and Jewish education in North American institutions?

We have had a chance to explore these questions in the course of evaluating the outcomes produced by a professional development initiative that has brought hundreds of North American Jewish educators to Israel since October 7. First and foremost, the target of our evaluation was to uncover what prompted educators to participate in this initiative, what experiences in Israel they found to be especially instructive, what educators learned from these experiences, and, finally, if and how educators have translated those learnings into their work. Additionally, the design of our evaluation has also provided an opportunity to document the ways in which the goals and practices of Israel education have shifted during the months since October 7, and how organizations are today positioning Israel education within their efforts overall. These additional data will be the focus of this chapter. They allow us to reflect on the questions stated above, while noting ways the program in Israel contributed to what we observed.

To put it differently, this chapter is not a program evaluation.[1] Drawing on an opportunity sample of educators, it describes how practices of Israel education have changed since October 7; it finds them to have become more personalized, less compartmentalized, less abstract, and less idealized. It also depicts a centripetal process in which, at the organizational level, Israel education and Jewish education have become more closely intertwined, if not thrust together.

The Intervention

The initiative being studied was a partnership between the Jewish Education Project and the iCenter, aided by M^2 and the Jewish Agency for Israel, made possible by support from the Jim Joseph Foundation and additional partners. Between February and June 2024, the initiative brought 324 educators on short trips to Israel as part of thirteen different groups. The participants came from a wide variety of sectors of Jewish education, with the largest subpopulations working in Jewish supplementary schools and synagogues (29%), summer camps (24%), and day schools (19%). Most of the participants had supervisory or management responsibility; more than half (59%) reported combining these responsibilities with front-line work with learners, and nearly a quarter reported that they only worked as supervisors or managers. Just 13% described themselves as educators without management responsibilities. These trips aimed, then, to help educators and educational leaders connect with Israelis, see for themselves the ways in which Israel has changed since October 7, 2023, and engage in joint reflection on what these changes might mean for their work and for their responsibilities as Jewish educators.

In total, thirteen groups spent time in Israel as part of the initiative. The programs were led by six different providers: the Association of Reform

---

1 See the following reports for extensive accounts of the participants' experiences in Israel, and of the immediate- and slightly longer-term outcomes created by the program. Of special note is the extent to which participants reflected on learning most while in Israel through the personal accounts of those with whom they met and wanted to recreate this experience for their own learners in their workplaces: see Rosov Consulting (2024a, 2024b).

Jewish Educators / Hebrew Union College (ARJE/HUC), Foundation for Jewish Camp, the iCenter, the Jewish Education Project (TJEP), RootOne, and Prizmah. Ten groups came to Israel during February or March 2024, and the remaining groups between April and June of that year. Most of the groups spent four days in Israel, but three were there for seven or eight days.

The program itineraries were broadly similar. They involved meetings with survivors of the events of October 7, with family members of those who were killed on that day or during the ongoing war, family members of hostages still being held in Gaza, individuals displaced from their homes as a result of the war, and individuals at the forefront of the civic response to these events. Most groups, but not all, visited communities most hard hit on October 7, and all visited Hostages Square in Tel Aviv. Those who came for longer engaged in volunteer work. Many met with artists, musicians, and intellectual leaders who have been grappling with the events of this period, and many met with Israeli educators to explore educational responses with them. The time in Israel included opportunities to process what they were seeing and hearing, and to begin considering how they would translate what they were learning into their work back home.

Data Collection

The evaluation was based on two rounds of data collection, both conducted *after* participants had returned from Israel. First, all participants were asked to complete a survey approximately three weeks after their return. The survey explored educational challenges participants faced prior to the trip, what had been their goals in taking part, what they experienced during their time in Israel, what they gained from the trip, and their preparedness to draw on their learning in their roles as educators and educator leaders.[2] 279 individuals responded to the survey, constituting a response rate of 86%. In addition, the research team conducted thirty-minute interviews with a subsample of three participants per program provider (eighteen in total across six providers) to

---

2   There is a risk that, when asking participants *after* the end of the program to reconstruct what had been their experience and motivations beforehand, they may have engaged in revisionism or may have exaggerated the program's impact. Countering this concern, the outcomes reported by these educators are generally consistent with those found in studies conducted by the same research team with similar educator groups from outside North America over the same period using a pre/post survey design.

probe more deeply into the themes explored by the survey and to be sure the voices of individual participants were captured. These interviews took place during the month after interviewees had completed the survey, typically within two months of their return from Israel, and were then submitted to thematic analysis with the aid of AI software.

A second round of data collection took place between August and October 2024 with the aim of exploring longer-term outcomes created by the program and to probe more deeply into the extent to which the Israel education practices of the participants and their organizations had changed during the past year (the focus of this chapter). In August, the 324 participants received a short survey to which 224 individuals responded (a response rate of 69%). As was the case at the time of the first round of data collection, the research team also interviewed a subsample of three participants per program provider (eighteen in total) to probe more deeply into the themes explored by the survey. These interviews took place between four and six months after participants returned from Israel.

The Context

Much has been written about the disruptive effects of the events of October 7 and its aftermath on Jewish life globally. There have been widespread reports of both younger and older people who expressed an appetite to be more closely connected to Jewish communal life, or displayed heightened interest in Jewish learning and Israeli culture, after being shocked by the lack of empathy among non-Jewish peers or among allies in social causes, or after being disturbed by rising expressions of antisemitism (Gurvis, 2024; Zuckerman, 2024). These themes were most notably expressed by JFNA's "surge" study (Kravetz, Eisenman, and Manchester, 2024), and by journalistic or first-person accounts of "October 8 Jews"—individuals whose Jewish interest was rekindled by the shocking events in Israel and the aftershock around the world (Stephens, 2024). Echoes of these trends have been seen in studies by Hersh (2024), Hillel International (2023), and Reingold and Reznik (2024) of college students during this period. A study released by Boundless noted an intensification of engagement and interest among eighteen- to forty-year-olds but also called attention to a countervailing trend in which forty percent of the young adults who had not been connected to Israel now feel less connected (Benenson Strategy Group, 2024).

Less has been written about the experiences of Jewish educators and Israel educators during this time, both in terms of how they personally have responded to these events and how they and their institutions have tried to meet the questions and inquiries from new and existing audiences and how they have responded to the pressures of this moment. The one exception is a two-phased study led by Ezra Kopelowitz in partnership first with M² and then the Jewish Education Project. Based on a survey fielded over November–December 2023, Kopelowitz and his colleagues found that "professionals were seeking clarity, facts, safety, and hope while grappling with fundamental questions about the unfolding events and their implications" (Kopelowitz et al., 2023, p. 2). A follow up survey, accompanied by interviews, offered a nuanced picture of Jewish educators employing three approaches to Israel (solidarity, criticism, and complexity) and of educators experiencing "considerable emotional strain, with many expressing anxiety and despair as they navigate teaching in the post-October 7 environment" (Kopelowitz, 2024, p. 4).

This chapter explores similar terrain to the studies by Kopelowitz and his colleagues. It constitutes an additional effort to understand the experiences and efforts of Jewish and Israel educators, and widens the lens further to consider how their organizations are structuring Israel education in relation to the work of Jewish education more broadly.

Findings

Changed Practices of Israel Education

In a foundational piece, philosopher William Carr characterized educational practice as "a species of 'doing action' governed by complex and sometimes competing ethical ends which may themselves be modified in the light of practical circumstances and particular conditions" (Carr, 1987, p. 173). In other words, educational practices are not merely sets of technical skills or procedures—they are complex, context-dependent activities that are intertwined with broader social, cultural, and ethical considerations. To put it crudely, they are the activities in which educators engage, towards some purposeful end, within specific contexts.

The educators who participated in the programs we studied made clear that their educational practices have indeed changed since October 7, reflecting, as

Carr would argue, shifts in both their goals *and* in the social-political contexts in which they work. Responding to a question in the August 2024 survey, "To what extent is your practice of Israel education today different from how it was twelve months ago?," 12% selected "very much," 42% "a lot," 33% "somewhat," 11% "little," and 2% "not at all." The 89% of respondents who selected one of the top three options also indicated that their participation on the trip to Israel contributed to this change (12% said "very much," 47% "a lot," 32% "somewhat"), 91% in total.

Open-ended survey responses solicited as a follow-up from those who indicated that their practices had changed at least "somewhat" during the last twelve months help shed light on the various ways in which educators' practices have adapted to the new reality. These qualitative responses point to three quite widespread changes, discussed below.

Connecting to the Personal

Educators have increasingly prioritized personal stories and testimonies from individuals in Israel, especially those affected by the events of October 7; this was in fact a move they had hoped to implement when interviewed about a month after their return from Israel. This approach has not only aimed to create a more relatable learning experience, emphasizing the human aspect of the Israeli narrative. It is perceived as more authentic, elevating Israelis as primary sources from whom learners could directly derive meaning. A survey respondent (a community educator) described such changes, and how the trip to Israel intensified them, as follows:

> I am a history junky and have oftentimes approached Israel education through a historical lens. The trip helped contribute to my change in practice because I have been putting a stronger emphasis on education through personal stories. I am attempting to educate through the lens of individual or group stories to make education more relatable to students.

Embracing Greater Nuance

When they first returned from Israel, interviewees made clear they had little patience for nuance; they had born witness to such stark events, they had limited appetite for complexity. Over time, as debate in Israel has intensified over how best to bring the hostages home and over what is a reasonable outcome for the war, educators, it seems, have been more willing to incorporate critical thinking and discussions that reflect the diverse realities of Israeli society, moving beyond, for example, traditional political frameworks of right and left (much as has happened in Israel). A synagogue-based educator offered an example of this shift:

> I have tailored information about Israel to individual students' interests and learning styles, creating a more engaging and effective learning experience. I have presented information from various sources, including Israeli, Palestinian, and international perspectives, fostering a more nuanced understanding of the region.

Introducing More Contemporary Content

Educators have become very interested in integrating current events into their teaching. The present moment in Israel and North America feels so significant in historical terms, whether it be the continuing trauma of the hostages, what it means to be a country at war for over a year, and the turmoil on college campuses, the educators have felt obliged to ensure that their learners are informed appropriately. A day school educator offered an example of what this move looks like:

> We have focused more on the current events of the past year and how to respond to them. For example, in our Senior class, each unit started with a meme or slogan prevalent on social media or in the news or protests and unpacked that slogan using Israel's history and current events ("From the river to the sea," "Genocide," etc.).

Differences by Education Sector

Further analysis of these changes, by means of segmenting the responses of participants from the three largest sectors represented among trip participants (supplementary school/synagogue, day school, and camp), surface differences that reflect these distinctive contexts and the goals of educators who work in them. Again, it is evident, as noted above, that educational practices take shape in the interplay between goals and contexts; the specific education sector in which people work makes a difference to their practice. Thus, camp educators have emphasized experiential learning and emotional connection; day school educators have prioritized systematic, structured curriculum development; and synagogue educators have focused on communal identity, resilience, and responding to current events. We offer two examples of how educators have described these differences playing out in their practices.

Hearing and Connecting to the Personal

Camp Educators: Camp educators reported an increased focus on storytelling, personal narratives, and real-life accounts from events in Israel to deepen campers' emotional engagement with Israel. Camp settings readily lend themselves to experiential learning, and these educators described actively working to help campers "feel connected" to Israel and incorporate hands-on activities, such as workshops and rubrics, for nuanced discussions.

Day School Educators: While they also emphasized personal narratives, day school educators highlighted integrating these into a structured, academic curriculum. They mentioned "holding two truths" and addressing the complexities of Israeli society but focused on how to teach this through established curricular changes rather than immersive experiences alone.

Synagogue Educators: Synagogue educators also mentioned integrating personal stories and emotional narratives, but they tended to focus more on fostering resilience, by means of these stories, especially in response to local antisemitism and global events. Given their community-centered role, they emphasized connecting Israel education to broader Jewish identity and peoplehood themes.

Introducing More Contemporary Content

Camp Educators: Camp educators have trodden carefully around sensitive topics, adjusting their approaches to be age appropriate and balanced between supporting Israel and acknowledging complex issues. They described rethinking the language they use, and sometimes avoiding certain topics entirely.

Day School Educators: Day school educators have generally been more direct in tackling current events and controversial issues. They described unpacking slogans like "From the river to the sea" and introducing diverse narratives, including Palestinian perspectives, which indicates a structured, intellectual approach to addressing contentious topics.

Synagogue Educators: Synagogue educators reported a growing emphasis on resilience and heroism narratives related to October 7, linking Israel's challenges to communal and personal values. This approach resonates well with synagogue settings, where many community members have sought to understand Israel through a moral and emotional lens. Additionally, these educators described making connections between Israel education and rising antisemitism, which may be a more pressing concern in a community setting than in schools or camps.

Organizational Rearrangement

While educational practices can be quite dynamic, as we have seen, evolving in response to changing contexts and demands, the organizational arrangement of education is notoriously difficult to shift. Tyack and Cuban's much-cited insight into the ways in which the "grammar of schooling" (the organizational and pedagogical forms of schooling that have persisted over the years) resist even the most concerted attempts at educational change applies to other educational settings too (Tyack and Cuban, 1995). As Krasner (2012) has noted, Jewish summer camps can be quite conservative when faced by attempts to shift how they have always done things; supplementary/congregational education has been notoriously resistant to reinvention (Aron, 2011); and, while Jewish day schools may have been unusually nimble in recent years especially in response to the COVID-19 pandemic, typically, there is often a gap between those schools that are early adopters of new ways of doing things and most other schools which evolve much more slowly.

Against this backdrop, it was quite unexpected to find that program participants reported quite extensive instances of organizational change, to which their trips to Israel had contributed (see the percentages above). Given the slow pace of organizational change in education, reported shifts of this order suggest that the respondents have overstated the significance of what they observe in their organizations; these may be instances of what Tyack and Cubin would call "tinkering" rather than anything more profound. Alternatively, it is also possible that the eruptions following October 7 were indeed so severe, and so acutely felt (irrespective of whether the respondent had participated in professional development programs in Israel), they truly resulted in a rearrangement of how organizations have been approaching the work of Israel education. In the words of a survey respondent (a camp educator): "It feels like October 7 changed everything, we've had to think very differently about all areas of Israel engagement and programming." Analysis of the open-ended responses (solicited as a follow-up from the seventy-three percent of participants who indicated that their organization's approach had changed at least "somewhat") suggest that their organizations have changed most in four ways.

Expanded Scope. There has been a noticeable shift towards incorporating weighty Israel education content into the experiences of younger learners and throughout all grades, "going deeper," as one respondent put it. In school settings, this has included adding lessons on significant texts like the Prayer for the State and IDF, and promoting a continuous connection to Israel. A day school educator explained: "We are dedicating more time to Israel education—especially in middle school but are also enhancing and revising our lower school Israel curriculum."

Greater Curriculum Integration. Organizations have become more intentional about integrating Israel education across various subjects and/or activities, rather than treating it as a standalone topic (about more of which below). Many organizations have revised their programs to include contemporary issues, historical context, and the social-political landscape of Israel. This has involved not only enhancing educational materials, but also integrating discussions on current events and their implications for Israel and the Jewish community. The following response from a camp educator was echoed by many others: "Instead of a program here or there, we incorporated Israel education into the camp experience. We also added a staff education component that we will include going forward."

Increased Collaboration. Organizations are now prioritizing partnerships with Israeli institutions and engaging more Israeli speakers and guests in their programs. This collaborative approach aims to enrich the educational experience and provide deeper insights into Israeli culture, society, and ongoing challenges. This is how an educator in an advocacy organization described the change:

> We have become much more collaborative in our programming, reaching out to others doing similar work to see how we

can partner together and resource one another, and we have been more intentional about reaching out to the Israelis in our community (*shlichim, shinshinim,* etc.) for guidance on how to navigate conversations and frame programs.

Focusing on Safe Spaces and Open Dialogue. There is a growing recognition of the need for safe spaces where individuals can discuss Israel-related topics openly. Organizations are striving to create environments where questions can be raised without fear of judgment, promoting learning and understanding across a spectrum of beliefs and experiences related to Israel. This is the account of an agency professional:

> [We have been working on] the idea of nuance and multiple narratives—it doesn't have to be supporting Israel and not considering the situation of those living in Gaza. We have been working a lot on our non-Jewish staff feeling comfortable asking questions and there being no judgement. We are all coming from a place of learning and understanding.

Again, segmented analysis of these responses reveals some striking differences across different sectors of Jewish education, reflecting the different structures, cultures, and priorities of these settings. We offer two examples of these differences.

Expanded Scope and Integration of Curriculum

Camps: Camps have been moving towards weaving Israel education into the daily camp experience rather than situated within isolated programs. The focus is on experiential learning, making Israel a part of the broader camp environment through activities, discussions, and integration with general camp programming.

Day Schools: Day school educators reported a structured, curriculum-based approach to Israel education, often tied to specific grade levels or courses. Many day schools have been formalizing Israel education with new scope and sequence documents, dedicated Israel classes, and expanded curriculum. There has been a clear emphasis on integrating Israel education across various subjects and creating a long-term framework for learning.

Synagogues: While synagogues have also expanded their curricula, they appear to have focused more on flexible, community-based education. Changes have included adding sessions or classes, and also congregation-wide initiatives like sermons, Tisha B'Av gatherings, and other communal events. These approaches have been less about formal school curriculum and more about incorporating Israel education into congregational life as a whole.

Approach to Dialogue and Controversial Topics

Camps: Camps have focused on equipping staff and campers to handle diverse viewpoints but often without delving into highly political debates. The goal has been to foster understanding and confidence in discussing Israel-related topics without destabilizing camp communities.

Day Schools: While some day schools have become more willing to incorporate multiple perspectives, they have been more cautious when framing these discussions for younger students. They have sought to balance education about Israeli culture and society with careful messaging around political content, aiming to prepare students with foundational knowledge before then engaging in more controversial topics.

Synagogues: Synagogue educators reported a striking openness to diverse perspectives, often embracing dual narratives and creating spaces for difficult conversations that include both Israeli and Palestinian viewpoints. This stance reflects a setting where adults and families engage in complex discussions, addressing varied opinions within the community.

The Deep Structure of Israel Education

If these responses suggest a field in the midst of change, responses to a couple of additional survey questions make clear that such changes—those that occur on an organizational scale—are ultimately constrained by deep-seated ideas about the relationship between Jewish education and Israel education. If organizations have adjusted their approaches, then that has happened within a deeply anchored set of scaffolding, what might be called the deep structure of Israel education.

Survey respondents were presented with the following series of images and were asked to indicate which best "describes the current relationship between Jewish education and Israel education in their workplace." The proportion of those who selected each option is displayed in Figure 13.1.

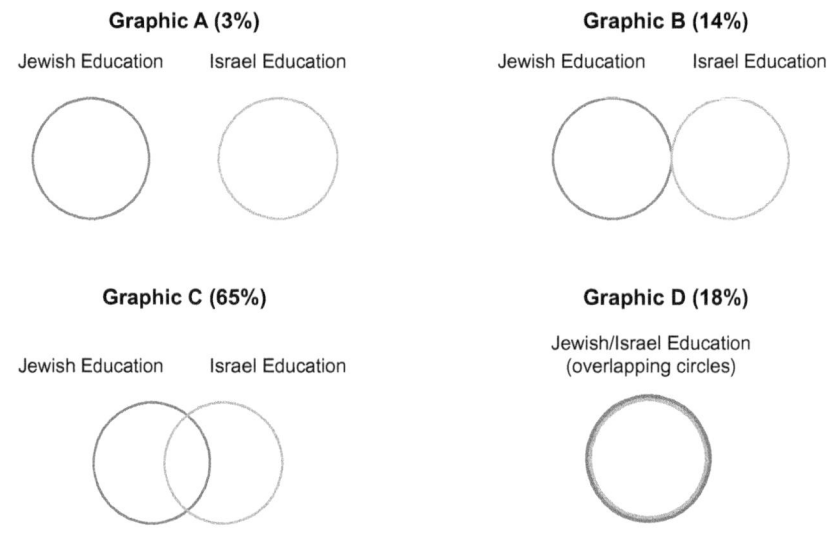

The relationship between Israel education and Jewish education

These responses indicate that in almost all of the organizations from which program participants came (a self-selecting population, for sure), Israel education is understood to be a part of or closely related to the work of Jewish education. This organizational conception is consistent with a long tradition of thought in the field of Israel education from the early twentieth century until the present day (Chazan, 2015; Zakai, 2014), even though there have always been dissenting diasporist or post-Zionist voices from Judah Magnes to the Boyarin brothers (Barak-Gorodetsky, 2021, Boyarin and Boyarin, 1993).

When explaining their selections, respondents made clear that, overall, the events of October 7 and their aftermath have set in motion a centripetal process in which Israel education and Jewish education have become more closely intertwined, if not thrust together. As an educator based in a central agency explained, "Graphic A better explains the connection between Israel and Jewish education provided by my organization. Since October 7, bringing each aspect closer together has become even more urgent." And yet, as the responses below indicate, providing explanations for the organizational arrangement selected, these arrangements are not circumstantial, they are often grounded in strong ideological orientations which are unlikely to shift, at least not in the short term (caps in the originals).

Graphic A. In the words of an arts educator, "Israel's right-wing government pretends to be the government for all Jews around the world. And the American political left projects that onto their sense that all American Jews are supportive of Israel's right-wing government. It's a toxic situation. The fact is, the Israeli government is a government for Israelis, not for Jews. And American Jews are not a monolith. So, our educational approach has intentionally moved AWAY from seeing Israel and Jewish education as intertwined, but intentionally separating the two."—arts educator.

Graphic B. According to a Jewish engagement educator, "There is some overlap, but not all things ISRAEL are JEWISH and not all things JEWISH are ISRAEL."—Jewish engagement educator.

Graphic C. "We have always believed that having a meaningful relationship with Israel is a core component of Jewish identity. As a Zionist summer camp, this is part of our values. While there is a lot of overlap in our Jewish and Zionist programming, we still do have elements of our program that focus more on one over the other which is why I chose the partially overlapping circles and not the fully overlapping ones."—camp educator.

Graphic D. "We have always been proud Jews and proud Zionists but now more than ever those two identities are bonded together."—day school educator.

If educating about Israel has become more central to the work of organizations engaged in Jewish education, that move plays out within set of arrangements formed by strong gravitational forces which demarcate how Israel's place in Jewish life is understood.

Reflections

The events of October 7 and their aftermath have been profoundly unsettling for both Israeli Jews and for Jews globally. Jewish life in Israel and pretty much everywhere else looks less secure today than it did on October 6, 2023. The more than seventy-year-old post-Holocaust concept of Israel as a safe refuge has been deeply shaken, and the already outdated concept of Israel as *shlilat hagola*—the negation of the diaspora—has surely been bankrupted once and for all. At the same time, foundational concepts of global Jewish peoplehood, and of shared Jewish fate have been newly energized. Not only do Israeli and non-Israeli Jews possess a shared fragile condition, their well-being seems to depend quite heavily on one another. These seismic shifts are surely no less profound than those that followed the Six Day War, if not the founding of the first Jewish State in almost two thousand years.

It is no wonder then that these sharp interruptions to the arc of contemporary Jewish history should see reverberations in how educators think about and go about the work of Israel education. Jewish educators have not been able to go back to business as usual; they have needed instead to formulate new master stories about Israel and find sensitive ways to explicate the difficult realities of the present moment, not least the resurgence of antisemitism.

The educators who participated in this study have been fortunate to draw on the resources they gained during their programs in Israel: they have witnessed for themselves the ways in which Israel has changed since October 7; they have interacted with Israelis whose stories and expressions have been both an inspiration and a proof text; and, as participants in a structured professional development experience, they have participated in facilitated conversations that helped incubate new ways of thinking about their work. They have had, therefore, special advantages in developing ways to address the tasks that all Jewish educators are confronting at this time; what they have created in their various sectors may yet serve as a model for others. The practices of Israel education with which they have started to engage are more personalized, less compartmentalized, less abstract, and less idealized. Today, it seems, Israel education is freighted with greater personal significance for educators and for many learners than was the case in the recent past. The stakes are higher today given the extent and intensity of efforts to delegitimize Israel in public spaces where such attacks were previously unimaginable.

Fifteen years ago, a study of Israel education in day schools found that this field was "fragmented, lacking in scope and sequence, and heavily reliant on experiential education," even while it was advanced by a powerful set of vehicles (Pomson et al., 2009). Studies of Israel education in camp settings and synagogues have been less extensive, but those that were conducted found a similar lack of coherence and focus (Grant, 2007; Aharon and Pomson, 2018). In more recent years, the situation probably improved at least in some settings thanks, for example, to the efforts of the iCenter, the Center for Israel Education at Emory University, and to sustained investment in the preparation of educational leaders who have know-how to design and implement more effective experiences of Israel education. Nevertheless, participants in this study convey a sense that, since October 7, their organizations have seen a renewed impetus to address these long-documented chronic weaknesses in the field. They are making efforts to knit Israel education more fully and more systematically into the fabric of their organizations while also grounding their work within a richer set of direct relationships with individuals and organizations in Israel. If these efforts gain traction, it will represent a major step forward for the field.

And yet, these changes will only go so far without renewed and far-reaching consideration of the relationships between Jewish education and Israel education. In settings animated by a concept of Israel education that sees it, at most, as adjacent to the work of Jewish education, or as partly overlapping with it, a reworking of the practices and arrangements of Israel education will be challenging. Such efforts will not go beyond tinkering. Without being more fully integrated into the larger purposes of Jewish education, Israel education will remain, for many, a reactive endeavor—driven by the need to respond to the latest events in Israel—or it will be a thin, sentimentalist expression of Jewish peoplehood. A renewed Israel education for our time surely needs a bolder vision.

References

Aharon, N., and Pomson, A. (2018). What's happening at the flag pole? Studying camps as institutions for Israel education. *Journal of Jewish Education, 84*(4), 337–358.

Aron, I. (2011). Congregational schools. In H. Miller, L. Grant, and A. Pomson (Eds.), *International handbook of Jewish education* (pp. 691–712). Springer.

Barak-Gorodetsky, D. (2021). *Judah Magnes: The prophetic politics of a religious binationalist.* University of Nebraska Press.

Benenson Strategy Group (2024). *Views on Israel and Jewish identity.* Boundless.

Boyarin, D., and Boyarin, J. (1993). Diaspora: Generation and the ground of Jewish identity. *Critical inquiry, 19*(4), 693–725.

Carr, W. (1987). What is an educational practice? *Journal of Philosophy of Education, 21*(2), 163–175.

Chazan, B. (2015). A linguistic analysis of the role of Israel in American Jewish schooling. *Journal of Jewish Education, 81*(1), 85–92.

Grant, L. (2007). Israel education in Reform congregational schools. *CCAR Journal: A Reform Jewish Quarterly,* Summer, 3–22.

Gurvis, J, (2024) 'I just felt this urgency': For some, Oct. 7 fueled a renewed dedication to becoming Jewish. JTA. January 10, 2024.

Hersh, E. (2024). *A year of campus conflict and growth: An over-time study of the impact of the Israel-Hamas War on U.S. college students.* Jim Joseph Foundation.

Hillel International (2023). More than one-third of Jewish college students are forced to hide their Jewish identity, new Hillel poll finds. November 20. https://www.hillel.org/more-than-one-third-of-jewish-college-students-are-hiding-their-jewish-identity-on-campus-new-hillel-international-poll-finds/.

Kopelowitz, E., Franco Galor, H., and Gillis, J (2023). *Responding to this historical moment: Jewish educators, clergy, engagement professionals and the war in Israel.* M²: The Institute for Experiential Jewish Education and the Jim Joseph Foundation.

Kopelowitz, E., Ravid, S., Posklinsky, I., Golden, J., and Gillis, J. (2024). *Responding to the fallout from October 7th: From crisis to opportunity. A survey of Jewish educators and engagement professionals.* The Jewish Education Project.

Krasner, J. B. (2012). *The Benderly boys and American Jewish education.* University Press of New England.

Kravetz, M., Eisenman, S., and Manchester, D. (2024). 'The surge,' 'The core' and more: What you need to know about the explosion of interest in Jewish life. *eJewishPhilanthropy*, May 9. https://ejewishphilanthropy.com/what-you-need-to-know-about-the-surge-of-interest-in-jewish-life/

Pomson, A., Deitcher, H., and Muszkat-Barkan, M. (2009). *Israel education in North American day schools: A systems analysis and some strategies for change.* Avi Chai.

Pomson, A., and Wertheimer, J. (2022). *Inside Jewish day schools: Leadership, learning, and community.* Brandeis University Press.

Reingold, M., Reznik, S. (2024). Navigating crisis together: Canadian Jews, Israel, and October 7. *Contemporary Jewry*, 44, 885–902. https://doi.org/10.1007/s12397-024-09572-8

Rosov Consulting (2024a). *Jewish educators coming to Israel: Gaining clarity, confidence, and enhanced connection.* The Jewish Education Project.

Rosov Consulting (2024b). *Jewish educators returning from Israel. Reconceiving Israel Education in the Midst of Seismic Events.* The Jewish Education Project.

Stephens, B. (2024). The year American Jews woke up. *New York Times*, October 4.

Tyack, D., and Cuban, L. (1995). *Tinkering toward utopia: A century of public-school reform*. Harvard University Press.

Zakai, S. (2014). "My heart is in the east and I am in the west": Enduring questions of Israel education in North America. *Journal of Jewish Education*, *80*(3), 287–318.

Zuckerman, G. (2024). Jolted by Oct 7 attacks, more U.S. Jews feel drawn to their faith. *Wall Street Journal*, October 15.

Conclusion[1]

Matt Reingold

The chapters in this volume testify to the power of Jewish education to serve as a life raft amidst turbulence. Faced with a traumatic moment that was then followed by an extended war, Jewish educational institutions adapted in response to two emerging crises: the one abroad in Israel and the one at home in the diaspora where antisemitism and anti-Israel rhetoric were so prevalent. Schools and camps, and the educators they employ, provided learners of all ages with rich content and meaningful socio-emotional learning experiences designed to help contextualize the conflicts, construe meaning from them, and prepare responses to them. These sites became incubators—protective barriers and preparers for reentry—that allowed Jewish children to navigate the conflicts.[1]

In the first part of this conclusion, I want to highlight the ways that the chapters in this volume speak to each other and offer a coherent narrative about education after October 7. From there, I will offer a research-informed educational proposal for Jewish educational spaces as they transition from a post-October 7 reactive mode to a post-October 7 proactive mode. Rather

---

1   I am grateful to the input of Amy Goldsweig, Chani Greenwald, Marc Wolf, and the anonymous reviewers whose observations and insights have helped shape this chapter.

than responding to the external stimuli in Israel and in the Jewish diaspora, an educational shift is needed where learning in a post-October 7 world is habituated.

Though they have a shared interest in exploring educational responses to October 7, the chapters included in this volume are set in different types of educational spaces, are concerned with the experiences and perspectives of different stakeholders, and they offer different conclusions about how October 7 changed Jewish education in the diaspora. Despite these differences, I believe that a series of inflection or tension points that cut across multiple articles exists and that these reveal seminal considerations facing Jewish and Israel education after October 7.

First is that a tension exists for educators between wanting their learners to engage with the sometimes traumatic realities of contemporary Israeli society while also promoting alternative educational and psycho-social-emotional goals that avoid addressing the conflict. This tension exists even though, as Sivan Zakai and Lauren Applebaum point out, that learners in fourth and fifth grade are already deeply aware of the conflict and are already forming clear opinions about the nature of the conflict. This tension is woven throughout a number of the chapters in this volume. In the case of the Orthodox schools that Rona Novick and Jenny Isaacs studied, the tension revolved around a desire to increase students' associations with Israel by directly engaging with October 7 and a belief that doing so would exacerbate students' anxieties about Israel. A similar tension was observed by Tal Vaizman at the two camps where he conducted ethnographic research. On one hand, there was a desire to create a space for Israeli staff to lead programs about October 7, but this competed with a concern that doing so may lead campers to feel discomfort. At the overnight camps that I studied, senior staff grappled with wanting to afford Israelis the space to publicly share their experiences on October 7 because doing so would deepen their campers' understanding of Israeli experiences alongside a desire to ensure that camp remained a place primarily associated with fun. At the early childhood center that Meir Muller, Lyndall Miller, and Alana Rifkin Gelnick studied, they observed a tension between educators' desires to preserve their students' innocence by shielding them from the war alongside a concurrent desire to build resilience by providing learners with the opportunity to discuss the conflict in the classroom. Lastly, the German Jews that Maor Shani, Jana Gerber, and Marie Herb interviewed were also interested in shielding their children, but, in their case, they wanted to protect the children from increased antisemitism by having them hide

Jewish symbols. Their concern with doing so was that it would limit their children's abilities to express pride in being Jewish. When considered in light of each other, the articles offer a powerful statement about the tensions between teaching from the head and teaching from the heart, between teaching from an intellectual vantage point or an emotional vantage point. The articles reveal that there are moments for each, that no simple solution exists, and that there is tremendous value in finding a way to bring these two perspectives into concert with each other.

A second point of tension evident in the chapters revolves around how educators navigated between their hired roles and unanticipated personal and professional considerations that emerged after the terror attack. The educators Benji Davis studied struggled to teach about Palestinian experiences after October 7, even though they had previously supported teaching this history. Intellectually these educators believed that it was important to teach Palestinian history, but emotionally they felt unable to do so. Other teachers, as in the case of the ones interviewed by Vardit Ringvald and Sharon Schoenfeld, felt torn between wanting to embrace the professional role of being an Israel educator that was thrust upon them and an awareness that they lacked the professional training to be an Israel educator. A third example of teacher tensions can be found in Michal Shapira Junger's article. The educators on whom their chapter focused experienced the very real tensions of living simultaneously in two spaces—physically in the diaspora, spiritually and emotionally in Israel—and the need to balance their administrations' curricular expectations and their personal desire to teach in response to October 7. Though each of the chapters reveals different variables for why the educators struggled, the common link between them is that these people's equilibrium was disrupted and needed to be recalibrated in light of the changing circumstances in their personal and professional lives.

The single-greatest tragedy in Israeli history also led some educators to reexamine the pedagogical and philosophical underpinnings of Jewish and Israel education. Ezra Kopelowitz's portraits of teacher types raises fundamental questions about best practices and ideologies in the teaching of Israel and what is most needed to meet the moment. In Alex Pomson and Samantha Vinokor-Meinrath's study, they observe how, since October 7, Jewish education and Israel education have become increasingly intertwined, and they wonder about the implications of this development. Lastly, tension is readily apparent in Jon A. Levisohn's proposal for the future of Jewish education. In his model, Jewish education should simultaneously prepare students to be capable of responding to the realities of being Jewish in the present and capable of envisioning and working towards an alternative North American Jewish future. In charting distinct visions for the future of Jewish education, these three chapters emerge from an initial orientation which believes that the Jewish educational landscape has been fundamentally altered and that new models are needed.

There is no question that many of these points of tension existed well-before October 7, but the terror attack and subsequent outbreak of war has thrust them to the forefront of the practical, philosophical, and ideological considerations of Jewish and Israel education today. In the paragraphs that follow, I recommend three practical interventions that are designed to respond to the tensions. I preface these interventions with an understanding that, to be most effective, they require cultures that are receptive to change. I conclude by modeling what it might look like to put these three recommendations into practice.

1. Israel Education Mission Statement

In many chapters in this volume, the absence of an Israel education mission statement or philosophy of Israel education (or at least one that was understood by the educators) was all too apparent. Teachers grappled with competing values and, at times, made choices that prioritized one option over the other despite not knowing their institution's official policy. The enormity of October 7 can provide educational institutions an opportunity to reset their Israel education philosophies by identifying their core values, desired outcomes, and expectations of staff. The drafting of this type of document should not be the end in and of itself but the means to an end. The end should be an Israel education experience wherein the institution's Israel education philosophy is aligned and woven into the contours of its educational programming thereby creating opportunities to maximize learner experiences.

Mission statements or statements of philosophy like this do have positive influence on organizational behavior because, provided they are adhered to, they unite stakeholders around a common vision and goal (Davis et al., 2007). In order to be effective, the mission statement must be aligned with the organizations' values and it must contain a clear set of "values and self-concept, (desired) public image, and concern for internal and external stakeholders" (Braun et al., 2012., 440). The types of documents that I am envisioning must move beyond vague and token statements of being "pro-Israel" and "Zionist" and instead must clearly and explicitly identify what the institution stands for and against. In order to secure support from educators and other employees, Jewish institutions must engage their stakeholders in the design and review phases as these are predictors for increased use of mission statements (Braun et al., 2012). Securing this support will contribute to educators' increased willingness to use an Israel education framework that can guide the creation of their programs and lessons and ensure that their professional work is mission aligned.

2. New Approaches to Professional Development

Educational institutions must invest in additional models of professional development for their Israel and Israel-adjacent staff. Educators cannot be expected to intuitively know how to ensure that their content is mission aligned. Therefore, professional development that provides practical training and application of the mission statement is needed. Effective professional development is practical in nature, engaging educators in their primary roles as teachers and making explicit how the training can be integrated into their professional practice (Borko, Jacobs, and Koellner, 2010). It should also be an ongoing experience, woven into a school's culture (Borko, Jacobs, and Koellner, 2010). The types of professional development that I am proposing must be conducted within individual institutions and not conducted in tandem with other institutions. This is to ensure that the training that is offered provides mission-aligned professional development.

Mission-aligned professional development is not the only type of training that is needed. Chapters throughout this volume revealed the ways that educators assumed (or were asked to assume) new roles in the aftermath of October 7. This included Hebrew-language teachers becoming Israel educators, Israel emissaries becoming community educators, and early childhood educators creating space for war in their learning centers. Whether these new roles were initiated at the behest of institutions or by the teachers themselves, concomitant with a willingness to perform these new roles was a feeling of unpreparedness for doing so. It is therefore essential that educational institutions help train their educators for these new roles. What was professionally demanded of Jewish and Israel educators after October 7 is not unlike the expectations placed on experienced educators to change their pedagogical approach in light of education reforms. A predictor for successful implementation of new professional expectations is having the educators assume the role of students and experience firsthand what they are expected to do in their own learning sites before participating in reflective exercises about their experiences as learners (Borke, Jacobs, and Koellner, 2010). To that end, in addition to providing educators with practical examples of what they can do in their classes, affording them the opportunity to experience being a student in a class taught by a practitioner who has mastered the new approach will allow them to see what it looks like in practice so that they better understand what is expected of them.

3. Professional Learning Communities

In order to successfully implement professional development initiatives and create mission alignment in their Israel education, educators must be given space to learn and grow from their colleagues, ideally in an ongoing capacity because doing so has been proven to maximize effectiveness (Hsiao and Lin, 2022). Professional learning communities (PLCs) afford educators opportunities to "focus on a shared mission of collective capacity building" (Sai and Siraj, 2015, p. 45) and collaborative work culture in order to reflect on what is happening in their personal professional practice, with the ultimate goal being to improve student learning (Vescio, Ross, and Adams, 2007). In the case of Jewish educational spaces after October 7, educators need opportunities to reflect on new best practices for teaching Israel and for approaching their students' needs. Furthermore, by embracing a fail-forward orientation to learning and growing, PLCs can provide educators a space where professional problems can be workshopped together.

PLCs provide more than just an opportunity to engage in professional development alongside colleagues. One of the common refrains from teachers cited in this volume were feelings of loneliness as they tried to regulate their own emotions about October 7 alongside teaching about it. As community spaces where professional development happens, PLCs provide educators with social and emotional benefits that directly impact on their professional practice. The conjoining of community with professional learning creates a space for "mutually supportive relationships" (Stoll et al., 2006, p. 225), which also mitigate against the loneliness and isolation that teachers report feeling (Hsiao and Lin, 2022). Though research suggests that the primary motivator for joining a PLC is not being a member of a community but rather gaining professional development, community-formation ultimately determines whether members choose to remain a part of the PLC over time (Hsiao and Lin, 2022). The implications of these findings for Jewish educational spaces in the wake of October 7 are significant. Provided that the initial attraction of the PLC is its professional relevance and offering useful content about teaching after October 7, joining a PLC that is framed around education in the post-October 7 world has the potential to reduce the emotional toll affecting Jewish educators during this prolonged crisis.

The recommended measures will only go as far as the educators on the ground are willing to adapt their practice to implement new approaches to teaching. Securing buy-in is essential, and PLCs have been shown to have a direct and measurable impact on shifting institutional culture. This is because, at their core, they foster an environment that is open to change (Stoll et al., 2016). Interestingly, crucial to PLCs' success is the extent to which participating in collaborative communities is embedded within the culture of the organization (Admiraal et al., 2019). Therefore, with institutional culture playing a role in determining the level of tolerance for establishing PLCs, before cultural changes related to post-October 7 education can be implemented, educational spaces must first foster a receptive culture towards PLCs.

Concert and Complexity

Each of these three interventions can be implemented independently, but I believe they work best when operating in concert with each other. Absent a robust vision of Israel education, professional development runs the risk of being undertaken piecemeal and not in a comprehensive or integrated way. Aligning professional development to pre-established values and desired outcomes will help ensure that meaningful learning occurs. But meaningful learning only sticks when it becomes habituated through practice, reflection, and opportunity to share amongst a community of similarly invested people. Professional learning communities are therefore essential in serving as spaces where the vision and the professional development can be refined and honed in order to meaningfully impact Jewish education.

If I were to be asked what the guiding principle of an Israel education philosophy should be, I would encourage institutions to emphasize creating a space that welcomes a culture of complex Israel education. In the years leading up to October 7, scholars of Israel education have been regularly arguing for the inclusion of some form of complexity in how Israel is taught (for example, Alexander, 2015; Reingold, 2017, 2022; Sinclair, Solmsen, and Goldwater, 2013). Based on Ezra Kopelowitz's article in this volume, it seems that this type of complex Israel education is not happening in most Israel education spaces after October 7. With the majority of teachers teaching Israel through a pedagogical framework of solidarity, there is a disconnect between educator goals and learners who need and want to learn fuller portraits of Israel (Reingold, 2017, 2024). Rather than retreating in on ourselves following October 7 and teaching Israel solely to build solidarity by substantiating claims in favor of Israel, the moment must be met with a willingness to either return to a model of complex Israel education or embrace a process of designing Israel education anew.

It is understandable why teachers may want to emphasize a love of Israel or a pedagogy of solidarity at this moment. In the wake of October 7 and the rise in anti-Israel discourse and behavior in the public sphere, ensuring that learners have spaces where Israel is taught from a place of compassion is essential to their Jewish well-being. I contend, however, that teaching complexity does not mean teaching students 'bad sides' to Israel. It is an orientation to content that shows a fuller and more complete picture of Israel. It introduces nuance and perspectives from diverse vantage points, allowing students to see the rich tapestry that is Israeli civic discourse and to then find their place within it.

My own approach to complexity is expansive and not only recognizes that learners' ages must inform the parameters of complexity, but suggests that institutional cultures must also play an important role. What is appropriate complexity in one space may not be appropriate in another, and sensitivity to community norms and institutional expectations is important. This is a crucial component of engaging relevant stakeholders in dialogue about the parameters and borderlines of complex discourse. I would urge institutions to solicit input from stakeholders who hold differing identity markers—gender, ethnicity, politics, religion—in order to ensure that the complexity that exists in our own spaces is reflected in making decisions about complexity in Israeli spaces.

Educators need to be taught pedagogical strategies and provided with access to texts (print, creative, and media) that reveal complex ideas and a range of perspectives. This is no small feat, and institutions must foster a culture where teachers are receptive to new approaches to teaching and open to teaching materials whose contents do not reflect their own thinking about Israel. PLCs framed around techniques for teaching this type of complexity and offering educators curated content of a range of perspectives on Israel may provide an initial impetus to join. From there, communities must be cultivated and grown, with attention spent on validating the challenges experienced by the educators, where deeply committed Israel educators can openly diverge in their beliefs while still working in concert with each other.

What I am suggesting is not simple; it is something I also struggle with. In my own teaching, I have made use of post-October 7 political cartoons by Israeli artists whose positions on the hostage exchange not only run counter to my own thinking but are, in my opinion, offensive. Despite my personal discomfort with some of these texts, I have continued to employ them by placing them in dialogue with cartoons that offer different readings of current events. I have made this choice because doing so validates the political identities of all the learners in the room. My experience shows that, if learners do not see themselves represented in the selection of texts, they may infer that their ideas are invalid, and they will be less willing to engage with the texts and the perspectives of others. More importantly, it is necessary to show multiple sides to an issue because I am interested in exposing my learners to the diversity of Israeli society. Whether or not I like a particular Israeli ideology is irrelevant when it comes to my selection of texts; what matters is that *Israelis themselves* have validated the ideology at the ballot box and in the streets, and only if I teach it can my learners come closer to understanding the diversity of Israeli society.

Finding ways to introduce nuance and complexity into Israel education is difficult, but it is essential. When educators only select texts that reflect their approach to Israel or texts that affirm a particular position, nuance and complexity are sacrificed, and it is students who lose out as a result. This is because they are deprived of the opportunity to encounter Israel's diversity, the right to make their own informed decisions about Israel, and the ability to find themselves in Israeli society. As Jewish educational spaces recalibrate after October 7, leaning into the complexity of it all—Israel, the diaspora, the diaspora-Israel relationship—is the key to unlocking the next chapter in Jewish and Israel education and to ensuring that our learners are best prepared to meaningfully encounter Israel and the wider world.

References

Admiraal, W., Schenke, W., De Jong, L., Emmelot, Y., and Sligte, H. (2019). Schools as professional learning communities: what can schools do to support professional development of their teachers? *Professional Development in Education, 47*(4), 684–698. https://doi.org/10.1080/19415257.2019.1665573

Alexander, H. (2015). Mature Zionism: Education and the scholarly study of Israel. *Journal of Jewish Education, 81*(2), 136–161. https://doi.org/10.1080/15244113.2015.1035979

Borko, H., Jacobs, J., and Koellner, K. (2010). Contemporary approaches to teacher professional development. In P. Peterson, E. Baker, and B. McGaw (Eds.), *International encyclopedia of education*, vol. 7 (pp. 548–556). Oxford University Press.

Braun, S., Wesche, J. S., Frey, D., Weisweiler, S., and Peus, C. (2012). Effectiveness of mission statements in organizations—A review. *Journal of Management and Organization, 18*(4), 430–444. https://doi.org/10.5172/jmo.2012.18.4.430.

Davis, J. H., Ruhe, J. A., Lee, M., and Rajadhyaksha, U. (2007). Mission possible: Do school mission statements work? *Journal of Business Ethics, 70*(1), 99–110. http://www.jstor.org/stable/25075273

Hsiao, J.-C., and Lin, S. S. J. (2022). How energy maintains social sustainability of teachers' learning communities: New insights from a blended professional learning network. *Sustainability, 14*(6), 3636. https://doi.org/10.3390/su14063636

Reingold, M. (2017). Not the Israel of my elementary school: An exploration of Jewish-Canadian secondary students' attempts to process morally complex Israeli narratives. *The Social Studies, 108*(3), 87–98. https://doi.org/10.1080/00377996.2017.1324392

Reingold, M. (2022). Secondary students' evolving relationships and connections with Israel. *The Social Studies, 113*(2), 53–57. https://doi.org/10.1080/00377996.2021.1954866

Reingold, M. (2024). Arts-based learning in Israel education: A qualitative inquiry into using political cartoons to study current events in Israeli society. *Journal of Jewish Education, 90*(2), 150–174. https://doi.org/10.1080/15244113.2023.2296135

Sai, X., and Siraj, S. (2015). Professional learning community in education: Literature review. *The Online Journal of Quality in Higher Education, 2*(2), 65–78. https://www.tojsat.net/journals/tojqih/articles/v02i02/v02i02-07.pdf

Sinclair, A., Solmsen, B., and Goldwater, C. (2013). *The Israel educator: An inquiry into the preparation and capacities of effective Israel educators*. Israel Education Research Briefs. Consortium for Applied Studies in Jewish Education (CASJE).

Stoll, L., Bolam, R., McMahon, A., Wallace, M., and Thomas, S. (2006). Professional learning communities: A review of the literature. *Journal of Educational Change*, 7, 221–258. https://doi.org/10.1007/s10833-006-0001-8

Vescio, V., Ross, D., and Adams, A. (2008). A review of research on the impact of professional learning communities on teaching practice and student learning. *Teaching and Teacher Education*, 24(1), 80–91. https://doi.org/10.1016/j.tate.2007.01.004

Contributors

Matt Reingold is Senior Project Lead at Rosov Consulting. An experienced researcher with over sixteen years teaching in Jewish day schools, Matt is also the author of four books about Jewish and Israeli comics and graphic novels. This includes *The Comics of Asaf Hanuka* (Academic Studies Press, 2024). He is also the co-editor of *Teaching Israel* (with Sivan Zakai, Brandeis University Press, 2024). Matt also regularly posts about Israeli cartoons on Instagram @CartooningIsrael.

Lauren Applebaum Lauren Applebaum is the Interim Director of the School of Educatoin and Director of DeLeT Programs at the Hebrew Union College and an affiliated scholar at the Jack, Joseph and Morton Mandel Center for Studies in Jewish Education at Brandeis University. Along with Sivan Zakai, she directs the Learning and Teaching about What Matters Project.

Benji Davis is an educator and scholar specializing in the philosophy and pedagogy of Israel education. He is an Assistant Professor at Yeshiva University's Azrieli Graduate School of Jewish Education and Administration and the founding director of IMPACT Israel Education.

Alana Rifkin Gelnick is the founder and CEO of Dreamearly, dedicated to empowering educators and leaders with innovative strategies in early childhood education. Prior to founding Dreamearly, Alana served as the associate principal of SAR Academy in Riverdale, New York, for a decade.

Jana Gerber is pursuing psychology at Osnabrück University, with a research focus on trauma processes and adaptive coping mechanisms, particularly in the context of discriminatory experiences and antisemitism.

Marie Herb is pursuing her bachelor's degree in psychology at the University of Osnabrück, where she investigates the psychosocial implications of collective trauma among Jewish communities in Germany.

Jenny Isaacs is the chair and an associate professor in the Department of Psychology at Yeshiva College in Yeshiva University. She is a child clinical psychologist who teaches, does research primarily on social and emotional development, and works as a methodological and statistical consultant.

Ezra Kopelowitz is a sociologist whose expertise is in Jewish education, community, and issues of collective Jewish identity. He is the CEO of Research Success Technologies, co-director of The Center for Jewish Peoplehood Education, and a faculty member in Spertus Institute's (Chicago) MA program for Jewish professional studies.

Jon A. Levisohn is the Jack, Joseph and Morton Mandel associate professor of Jewish educational thought at Brandeis University, where he also directs the Jack, Joseph and Morton Mandel Center for Studies in Jewish Education. He is the author, most recently, of *Teaching Historical Narratives: A Philosophical Inquiry into the Virtues of Historical Interpretation* (Bloomsbury, 2024).

Lyndall Miller is a researcher and consultant in Jewish early childhood education, with a focus on inquiry and leadership development, currently working with the Masor School for Jewish Education and Leadership at American Jewish University. She was previously the developer and director of the Jewish Early Childhood Education Leadership Institute (JECELI).

Meir Muller is the Associate Dean of Community Empowerment at the University of South Carolina, specializing in early childhood education and promoting justice through a lens informed by Jewish tradition.

Rona Milch Novick is the dean emerita of the Azrieli Graduate School of Jewish Education and Administration at Yeshiva University. A clinical psychologist, she publishes, teaches, mentors, speaks, and consults widely on the intersection of psychology and Jewish education.

Alex Pomson is the principal and managing director at Rosov Consulting. His latest book, co-authored with Helena Miller, is *Jewish Lives and Jewish Education in the UK: School, Family and Society* (Springer, 2024).

Vardit Ringvald is the director of the Brandeis University Consortium for the Teaching of Hebrew Language and Culture and a research professor at the Mandel Center for Studies in Jewish Education. Her current work includes a focus on the intersection of Hebrew language and culture in pedagogy and practice.

Maor Shani is a social psychologist and researcher at the Department of Developmental Psychology, Osnabrück University in Germany, and at Ariel University in Israel. He is also a Fellow at the London Centre for the Study of Contemporary Antisemitism and serves as Director of Research and Evaluation at the Institute for Experiential Jewish Education. His academic work focuses on intergroup relations, political socialization, antisemitism, and coping with racism, stigma, and discrimination.

Michal Shapira Junger is a Jewish education researcher and educational entrepreneur. She is a postdoctoral fellow at the Jack, Joseph and Morton Mandel Center for Studies in Jewish Education at Brandeis University. Her research focuses on teachers' personal and professional identity and teaching practices at multicultural intersections, such as teaching emissaries in the Jewish diaspora, binational schools in Israel, and Hebrew language instruction.

Sharon Schoenfeld holds a master's degree in teaching Hebrew as a second language. She is currently the director of Kayitz Kef / Hebrew at Camp at the Brandeis Consortium for the Teaching of Hebrew Language and Culture. Her work focuses on experiential Hebrew immersion initiatives and the mentoring and training of program leaders.

Tal Vaizman is a researcher and educator, currently serving as a fellow in Israel Studies at George Mason University. His scholarly interests include Israeli culture and music, streaming-era identity, socialization, youth culture, and music education. As a fellow with the Collaborative for Applied Studies in Jewish Education (CASJE) at George Washington University, he explored youth culture and Jewish education in Jewish summer camps, along with the implications of October 7th and the war in Israel and Gaza.

Samantha Vinokor-Meinrath serves as the senior director of knowledge, ideas, and learning at The Jewish Education Project. Her latest book is *#Antisemitism: Coming of Age During the Resurgence of Hate* (Bloomsbury, 2022).

Sivan Zakai is the Sara S. Lee professor of Jewish education at the Hebrew Union College-Jewish Institute of Religion and an affiliated scholar at the Jack, Joseph and Morton Mandel Center for Studies in Jewish Education at Brandeis University. Along with Lauren Applebaum, she directs the Learning and Teaching about What Matters Project.

www.ingramcontent.com/pod-product-compliance
Ingram Content Group UK Ltd.
Pitfield, Milton Keynes, MK11 3LW, UK
UKHW021840120126
466804UK00006B/18